BUDDHA

BUDDHA

A Story of Enlightenment

Deepak Chopra

HarperCollins *Publishers* India

First published in India in hardback by
HarperCollins *Publishers* in 2007

HarperCollins Publishers India, Cyber City, Building 10-A, Gurugram,
Haryana-122002, India
www.harpercollins.co.in

First published in paperback in 2010

This edition published in India in 2018 by HarperCollins *Publishers*

ISBN: 978-93-5029-003-3

9th impression 2018

Designed by
Joseph Rutt

Printed and bound at
MicroPrints India, New Delhi

MIX
Paper
FSC
FSC™ C218906

This product is made of FSC®-certified and other controlled material.

HarperCollins Publishers, Macken House, 39/40 Mayor Street
Upper, Dublin 1, D01 C9W8, Ireland

Author's Note

Whoever sees me sees the teaching.
—BUDDHA

In writing this book, I took a deep breath and created new characters and incidents in the life of one of the most famous people who ever lived. Famous, but still very obscure. I wanted to bring Buddha out of the mists of time, to fill him out in flesh and blood while still preserving his mystery. Fact blended into fantasy centuries ago in the story of the prince who became a living god. Or is "god" the very thing he didn't want to be? Was his deepest wish to disappear from the material world, remembered only as an inspiration of perfection?

The Buddha story, as it gathered momentum for two millennia, became chock-full of miracles and gods that got stuck onto its surface. Speaking about himself, Buddha never mentioned miracles or gods. He held a doubtful view of both. He showed no interest in being revered as a personality; none of his many sermons mentions his family life or gives much personal information at all. Unlike Christ in the New Testament, he certainly didn't see himself as divine.

Instead, he saw himself as "someone who is awake," which is what the word *Buddha* means. That's the person I've tried to capture in this book. Here in all his mystery is the principal human being who ever gained enlightenment, who spent his long life trying to wake up the rest of us. Everything he knew, he knew from arduous, sometimes bitter experience. He went through extreme suffering—almost to the death—and emerged with something incredibly precious. Buddha literally became the truth. "Whoever sees me sees the teaching," he said, "and whoever sees the teaching sees me."

I wrote this book as a sacred journey, fictionalized in many of its externals but psychologically true, I hope, to what the seeker's path feels like. In all three phases of his life—Siddhartha the prince, Gautama the monk, and Buddha the Compassionate One—he was as mortal as you and I, yet he attained enlightenment and was raised to the rank of an immortal. The miracle is that he got there following a heart as human as yours and mine, and just as vulnerable.

Deepak Chopra

PART ONE

SIDDHARTHA THE PRINCE

1

The Kingdom of Sakya, 563 BCE

One crisp spring day King Suddhodana turned in his saddle to survey the battlefield. He needed a weakness to exploit, and he was confident the enemy had left one for him. They always did. His senses were closed to everything else. Screams of the wounded and dying were heightened by the hoarse commands of his officers bellowing orders and calling on the gods for help. Torn by hooves and elephants' feet, cut by iron-rimmed chariot wheels, the land oozed blood as if the earth itself were mortally wounded.

"More soldiers! I want more soldiers now!"

Suddhodana didn't wait for anyone to obey. "If any man within the sound of my voice runs away, I will kill him personally!"

Charioteers and infantry moved toward the king, battered figures so filthy with fighting they could have been demiurges fashioned from the mud of the field.

Suddhodana was a warrior king, and the first thing to know about him is this: he mistook himself for a god. Along with his army, the king would kneel in the temple and pray before he went to war, but he put no trust in divine help. Leaving the gates of the capital behind, Suddhodana turned his head for one last look at home. But as the miles lengthened from Kapilavastu, his mood changed. By the time he came to the battlefield, its roiling activity and the smells that assaulted his nostrils—straw and blood, soldiers' sweat and dying horses—carried Suddhodana into another world. It smothered him completely in the belief that he could never lose.

The present campaign wasn't of his doing. Ravi Santhanam, a northern warlord along the Nepalese border, had taken one of Suddhodana's trade caravans in a surprise attack. Suddhodana's retaliation came almost immediately. Even though the warlord's men had the advantage of the high ground and home terrain, Suddhodana's forces steadily chewed into their holdings. Horses and elephants trampled over the fallen, dead or still alive but too weak to escape. Suddhodana guided his mount next to the belly of a rearing bull elephant, narrowly avoiding the massive feet as they plunged downward. Half a dozen arrows had pierced it, driving the beast into a frenzy.

"I want a new line of chariots, close file!" He had seen where the enemy front was exhausted and ready to buckle. A dozen more chariots pulled up in advance of the infantry. Their metal-bound wheels clattered across the hard ground. The charioteers had archers standing behind them who unleashed arrows into the warlord's army.

"Make a moving wall," Suddhodana shouted. "I want to crush their line."

His charioteers were experienced veterans; they were hard-faced, merciless men. Suddhodana rode slowly before them, ignoring the strife only a short distance away. He spoke quietly. "The gods command that there can be only one king. But I swear that I am no better than a common soldier today, and you are as good as kings. Each man here is part of me. So what's left for the king to say? Only two words, but they are the two that your hearts want to hear. *Victory*. And *home!*" Then his command cracked like a whip.

"All together—move!"

Both armies rushed screaming into the breach like opposing oceans. Violence brought contentment to Suddhodana. His sword whirled as he split a man's head with a single blow. His wall was advancing, and if the gods willed it, as they had to will it, the enemy forces would open, one corpse at a time, until Suddhodana's infantry moved in, a tight wedge gliding forward on enemy blood. The king would have scoffed at anyone who denied that he was at the very center of the world.

AT THAT HOUR Suddhodana's queen was being carried in a litter through the depths of the forest. She was ten months pregnant, a sign, the astrologers said, that the baby would be extraordinary. But in Queen Maya's mind nothing was extraordinary except the anxiety that surrounded her. She had decided, much too impetuously, to travel back to her mother's home to have her baby.

Suddhodana hadn't wanted to let her go. It was the custom for new mothers to go home to deliver, but he and Maya were inseparable. He was tempted to refuse, until in her guileless way Maya asked his permission in front of the assembled court. The king couldn't refuse his queen publicly, despite the dangers involved.

"Who will accompany you?" he asked with an edge of harshness, hoping to frighten her away from this foolhardy plan.

"My women."

"Women?"

He raised his hand in grudging assent. "You'll have some men, whoever can be spared." Maya smiled and withdrew. Suddhodana didn't want to argue, because in truth his wife mystified him. Making her afraid of danger was futile. The physical world was like a thin membrane she glided over, as a midge glides over the surface of a pond without breaking the water's skin. Therefore, the world could touch Maya, move her, hurt her, but never change her.

The queen departed from Kapilavastu a day before the army. Kumbira, the eldest court lady, rode at the head of the procession as it moved through the forest. It was a meager company, consisting of six soldiers too old to serve in the war astride six nags too weak to charge the enemy. After them came four litter bearers, who had taken off their shoes to negotiate the stony path, shouldering the tasseled and beaded palanquin bearing the young queen. Maya made no sound hidden behind the swaying silk drapes, except for a stifled moan whenever a bearer stumbled and the litter took a sharp jolt. Three young ladies-in-waiting, who grumbled in low voices about having to walk, brought up the rear.

Gray-haired Kumbira kept her gaze moving, aware of the dangers that lurked on both sides. This road, which was just a narrow cut in the granite slope, had begun as a smuggler's trail when poached deer hides, spices, and other contraband were trafficked to Nepal; it was still favored by bandits. Tigers were known to snatch their prey from terrified bands of travelers in this area, even in the brightest hour of the day. To ward them off, the bearers wore masks facing backward on their heads, believing that a tiger will only leap from the rear, never directly at a person who is looking at it.

Kumbira rode up the trail until she was abreast of Balgangadhar, the head guard. The warrior regarded her stoically, wincing a little when the queen cried out again.

"She can't hold out much longer," Kumbira said.

"And I can't make the road any shorter," Balgangadhar grumbled.

"What you can do is hurry," she snapped. Kumbira knew he was ashamed at not being with the king in battle, but Suddhodana wanted one elite guard to honor his wife.

With the slightest bow from the shoulders that etiquette permitted, the guard said, "I'll scout up ahead for camp. The locals say there's a woodcutter's clearing with some huts in it."

"No, we move together," Kumbira protested.

"There are other men here to protect you while I'm gone."

"Really?" Kumbira cast a critical eye over her shoulder at the ragged band. "And who will protect them, do you suppose?"

• • •

THEY WILL TELL YOU that Maya Devi—the goddess Maya, as she became known—arrived by moonlight in Lumbini Grove, one of the most sacred sites in the kingdom. They will tell you that she did not give birth in the forest by accident. Destiny guided her there. She expressly wanted to visit the sacred grove because a huge tree stood there like a pillar to the mother goddess. Maya's premonition had told her that this birth would be sacred.

In reality she was a frightened, fragile young woman who barely escaped being lost in the wilderness. And the sacred tree? Maya clung to the trunk of a large sal tree because it was the closest and most common tree in the clearing. Balgangadhar had found a sheltered place beside the trail, and the royal palanquin arrived there only moments before Maya went into the final stages of labor. The court ladies formed a close circle around her. She held on tight, and deep in the night she was delivered of the son her husband the king so desperately wanted.

Kumbira died long before the legends grew, so she is not pictured in them, barking commands to the scurrying women, shooing away the men, nearly scalding herself to bring a kettle of water on the run from the bonfire. It was she who first held the baby. Tenderly she scrubbed the blood from his tiny body, making the squalling newborn ready to show to Maya. The queen lay quietly on the ground, almost listless. The first nursing, an important ritual in the native custom, would come in the morning. Despite the baby's apparent good health, Kumbira was worried, made anxious by every nocturnal sound but most of all by Maya's labor, which had been too long and painful.

"Now my husband can die happy," Maya whispered in a tired, weak voice. "And I will not be cursed when I am gone." Kumbira started. How could Maya think about death at that moment? Kumbira's eyes searched the darkness surrounding their stranded camp. The younger court ladies were full of praise for the brave new mother, relieved that the ordeal had come to an end, buoyant at the prospect of returning home to their soft beds and paramours. Their happiness increased when the full moon, an auspicious omen, rose over the treetops.

"Here, Your Highness," said Utpatti, one of the handmaidens, leaning close. "There is something you must do."

Before anyone could stop her, Utpatti opened Maya's robe and exposed her breasts. Embarrassed and confused, Maya quickly pulled her robe together again with one hand.

"What are you doing?" she demanded.

Utpatti drew back. "It will help with the milk, Your Highness," she whispered, looking unsure of herself. She gave sidelong glances at the other women. "Having moonlight on your breasts. Country women all know that."

"Are you from the country?" Maya asked.

The others tittered. Making a show of not being bothered by them, Utpatti said, "Once."

Maya leaned back again and exposed her full breasts to the moon. They were heavy with milk already.

"I feel something," she murmured. Her mood had changed; a note of ecstasy was in her voice, clearing away the pain. If she wasn't a goddess herself, she exulted in being touched by a goddess, the moon. She took her infant and held him up.

"See how quiet he is now? He feels it too." At that moment Maya believed in her heart that her wishes had been fulfilled. There is a name in Sanskrit that expresses this idea. She lifted the baby higher.

"Siddhartha," she said. *He who has attained all desires.* Recognizing the solemnity of the moment, the court ladies bowed their heads, even the ever-wary Kumbira.

2

The gray rain blanketed Suddhodana and his men as the towers of home loomed over them. The sentry shouted from his post, and the great wooden gates of the capital opened. "Look sharp!" sergeants shouted down the line. Few citizens had turned out to greet them. Suddhodana knew that the huddled clumps of women lining the street were there to search the army with anxious faces, praying that their husbands and sons were still among the living.

That morning the queen had awakened at dawn in case her husband returned early, but then the rains set in, slowing everything. The trip down from the mountains had passed in a kind of blurred ecstasy, which grew stronger even as Maya's body began to fail. There was much whispering at court because she had refused the services of a wet nurse. "It cannot be that loving my child will kill me," she said.

Her mind returned to a dream that had visited her ten months ago. It began with Maya waking up in her private bedchamber. She shaded her eyes against a light that had appeared in the room. Out of the light emerged three angelic beings in the form of smiling young maidens. Sitting up, Maya immediately recognized her visitors for what they were—*devas,* or celestial beings.

The three devas gestured for her to join them. In wonder that they had chosen her, Maya climbed from her warm bed to follow.

With a glance over their shoulders, they walked through the walls of her bedroom as though through smoke. Maya never felt the wall as she too passed through it. On the other side she was pulled faster, until the palace grounds and the world beyond blurred in passing. A brighter light loomed ahead, and in a moment Maya saw that it was the sun reflected off snow. Daylight dazzled across the crystalline surface of a high mountain lake circled by sentinel peaks.

The Himalayas (for she knew with certainty that the devas had brought her there) had been distant, imposing presences all her life. Maya never imagined being among them, and now the three maidens led her to a pebble shore on the opposite side of the lake. Its surface was calm and mirror-bright.

The devas began disrobing her. Maya wasn't disconcerted; she grew relaxed. Almost as quickly as they took her clothes away, they fit her with the finest garments she had ever seen. With silent smiles they reached out to touch Maya's belly. The contact was warm and exciting. She stepped into the water of the lake, deeper and deeper. Then she awoke, finding herself sitting up in bed as if she'd never left it. Except that her bedchamber was filled by a creature whose eye captured her gaze. Expanding from the eye was a whiteness that took the shape, as Maya's mind cleared from sleep, of an enormous elephant as pale as snow. The creature looked at her with warm, confident intelligence. Then it lifted its trunk in a kind of salute. Unexpectedly, a burning hunger filled Maya. Then she woke again, sitting up in bed but alone. The unaccustomed desire was still within her and wouldn't be denied.

Quickly, almost shaking, she quit her bed, throwing on her robe, and ran to her husband's bedchamber. In the dim candlelight, Suddhodana lay twisted in the sheets. After their years of barren hopes for a son, he often slept alone now. Another king might have taken a lover who could provide him with a son. Another king might have simply had his wife murdered or locked away as a madwoman to dissolve the marriage contract. But

Suddhodana hadn't done those things. He had remained as fierce and loyal in love as in war.

Tonight will be different, Maya told herself. *I have been blessed.* Cautiously, not wanting to awake Suddhodana too suddenly, she lay beside him on the bed. Gently she stroked his face, drawing him up from sleep. His hands turned to fists at first, then his eyes opened and looked into hers. He started to speak, but she laid a finger over his lips.

She was not wild with desire, not its prisoner or slave. With her husband's legs entwined with hers, she didn't want pleasure as much as union. She encouraged him with words she never imagined saying. "Don't make love to me like a king. Make love like a god."

The effect was dramatic. Urgently, he reached for her, and she saw the wonder in his eyes. For so long their coupling had been perfunctory, neither of them believing that anything would come of it. But tonight he felt some of the strong belief that had awakened within her.

When she was ready, she rolled her hips and took him inside her. Her breath caught in her throat. The strange need within her reached a crescendo. For a few moments she entered that darkness of bliss that imitates immortality. Gradually she returned from it with a sigh, to find that the king was holding her in a tight embrace. He pulled her to him as if trying to meld his flesh completely with hers. They kissed and caressed; only her exhaustion in delight kept Maya from speaking what she knew with certainty: they had created a child.

The dream had sustained her in the terrifying trip through the forest and the pain of her labor. Now it was returning in more ghostly form every day. Her head sank into the pillow. *It was still a lovely dream,* she thought, and an escape from her great weariness. She even thought it would be better to live in her dream forever, if only she could.

• • •

IN THE ROYAL NURSERY Suddhodana gazed down at his son with awe and love. The baby had been presented to him in crimson silk swaddling clothes. He was certain the infant recognized him; it even grew in his mind that Siddhartha had kept his eyes shut until that moment, a fantasy no one dared to correct.

"Should he be sleeping this much? Why is his nose running? If he's left alone for a moment, I will have someone whipped." Suddhodana's demands were incessant and maddening. As was the custom, Maya would be quarantined for a month after the delivery, subject to cleansing and religious rituals. Suddhodana chafed at this, but he could do nothing about it except sneak in by candlelight after the queen was asleep to gaze at her for a few moments. He wondered if new mothers always looked so wan and weak. Suddhodana pushed his troubling thoughts aside.

"Let him always be clothed in silk, and when they get soiled, throw them away. If you run out of silk, tear apart the court ladies' saris if you have to." Suddhodana wanted nothing with a hint of uncleanliness to touch his son's skin. But silk was also a symbol, since Suddhodana was on the Silk Road returning home when a messenger sent by Kumbira reached him with the news that he had a son and a wife who were both alive.

Every morning the king strode forward through the ring of women that stood fanning the young prince with their shawls. Reaching down into the cradle, he withdrew his son and held him aloft. He stripped off the diaper.

"Look at him." Suddhodana displayed his son in all his naked glory. "Well made." All of the ladies knew what he was referring to. Kakoli, the royal nurse, started to mumble something agreeable.

"Impressively made," Suddhodana said. "Not that I have your experience, Kakoli." Suddhodana laughed and thought again how easy it was with his son in his arms. "Don't blush, you old hypocrite. If he was twenty years older and we could take forty years off you, you'd fall off your feet running after it."

Kakoli shook her head and said nothing. The handmaidens tittered and blushed. Suddhodana was certain they were more entertained than scandalized by his bluntness.

ASITA AWOKE in the forest thinking about demons. He hadn't for many years. He could remember glimpsing one or two in the past, on the fringes of a famine or a battle, wherever bodies were being harvested. He knew the misery they caused, but misery was no longer Asita's concern. He had been a forest hermit for fifty years. The affairs of the world had been kept far away, and he passed whole days in a hidden cave when he retreated even from the affairs of animals, much less those of men.

Now Asita knelt by a stream and considered. He distinctly saw demons in his mind's eye. They had first appeared in the dappled sunlight that fell on his eyelids at dawn. Asita slept on boughs strewn over the bare ground, and he liked the play of light and shadow across his eyes in the early morning. His imagination freely saw shapes that reminded him of the market village where he grew up. He could see hawking merchants, women balancing water jugs on their heads, camels and caravans—anything, really—on the screen of his closed eyes.

But never demons, not before this morning. Asita walked into the nearly freezing mountain stream, his body naked except for a loincloth. As an ascetic, he did not wear clothes, not even the robes of a monastic order. Lately he had felt an impulse to travel very high, nearly in sight of the snowcapped peaks on the northern border of the Sakya kingdom. Which put him close to other *lokas,* worlds apart from Earth. Every mortal is confined to the Earth plane, but like the dense air of the jungle tapering gradually into the thin atmosphere of the mountains, the material world tapered off into subtler and subtler worlds. Devas had their own lokas, as did the gods and demons. Ancestors dwelt in a loka set apart for spirits in transition from one lifetime to the next.

Asita had been raised on this knowledge. He knew also that all these planes merged into each other like wet dyed cloths hung too close on the line, the blue bleeding into the red, the red into the saffron yellow. Lokas were apart and together at the same time. Demons could move among humans, and often did. The reverse, a mortal visiting the demon loka, was much rarer.

He plunged his head under the water, then flung it back, sending long streams dripping from his uncut beard and hair. On days when he needed food, Asita carried his begging bowl down into one of the villages. Not even the youngest child was frightened to see a naked old man on the street with hair and beard down to his waist. Ascetics were a normal sight, and it was a sacred duty, if a wandering hermit showed up at one's door near sunset, to offer food and hospitality.

Asita wasn't hungry this day, however. There were other ways to keep the *prana,* or life current, going. If he did visit the demon loka, it would take enormous prana to sustain his body. There would be no air for his lungs to breathe among the demons.

He allowed the brilliant Himalayan sun to dry his body as he walked above the tree line. Demons do not literally live on mountaintops, but Asita had learned special powers that allowed him to penetrate the subtle world. He had to get as far away as possible from human beings to exercise these abilities. The atmosphere was dense around population. In Asita's eyes a quiet village was a seething cauldron of emotions; every person—except only small infants—was immersed in a fog of confusion, a dense blanket of fears, wishes, memories, fantasy, and longing. This fog was so thick that the mind could barely pierce it.

But in the mountains Asita could find a bedrock of silence. Sitting in that enveloping emptiness, he could direct his mind, as clean as the flight of an arrow, to any object or place. It was really the mind that went to the demon loka, but Asita had such one-pointed clarity that he could travel with it.

And so it came about that the demon king Mara found himself staring at a most unwelcome intruder. He glared at the naked old man sitting in lotus position before his throne. Nothing like it had happened in a long while.

"Go away," Mara growled. "Just because you got here doesn't mean you can't be destroyed." The old man didn't move. His yogic concentration must have been strong, because his lean brown body, as tough as the sinew showing under its skin, grew sharper in outline. Mara would have commanded some lesser demons to torment the intruder, but these hermits weren't so easily dismissed, so Mara bided his time.

After a moment the old man's eyes opened. "You do not welcome me?" His voice was mild, but Mara read irony in it.

"No! There's nothing for you here." The dead and departed passed through Mara's hands, but it displeased him to meet mortals under any other circumstances.

"I didn't come for myself. I came for you," the old man said. He rose and looked around. The demon loka is a world as varied as the material world, and it has its regions of greater and lesser pain. Since torment did not threaten Asita, he beheld only a dense, noxious fog surrounding him. "I bring you news."

"I doubt it." Mara moved restlessly in his seat. As temple paintings often depict him, his throne was made of skulls. His body was red with flames spitting around it, and instead of one horrible face he possessed four, which turned like a weathervane, presenting fear, temptation, disease, and death.

"Someone is coming to meet you. Soon, very soon," Asita said.

"Millions have met me," Mara shrugged. "Who are you?"

"I am Asita." The old hermit stood up and faced Mara directly. "Buddha is coming." This caused a slight tremor, nothing more, to run through Mara's body. Asita noticed it. "I knew you would be intrigued."

"I doubt you know anything." Mara wasn't simply being arrogant. To him, Asita was a blank. There was nothing to hold on to, no ground for temptation or fear to stand on. "Who picked you as messenger? You're deluded."

Asita ignored this and repeated the word that had made Mara tremble. "Buddha is coming. I hope you're prepared."

"Silence!"

Until that moment Mara had paid as much attention to Asita as to a small seasonal famine or an insignificant plague. Now he leaped from his throne and shrank to human size, keeping only one of his four demonic faces, death. "What if he comes? He'll abandon the world, just as you did. Nothing more."

"If you believe that, then you have forgotten what Buddha can do," Asita said calmly.

"Really? Look!" Mara opened his mouth, which was solid blackness behind his fangs. The blackness expanded, and Asita could see the mass of suffering that Mara embodied. He saw a web of souls caught in turmoil, a tangle of war and disease and every version of pain that the demons could devise.

When he felt that the spectacle had had its effect, Mara slowly closed his mouth again, and the darkness receded back inside him. "Buddha?" he said contemptuously. "I'll make them think that he's the demon." The prospect brought a smile.

"Then let me speak as a friend, and I will tell you your fatal weakness," Asita said. He sat down in lotus position, folding his legs over each other, making the *mudra* of peace with his thumb and forefinger. "Being the monarch of fear, you've forgotten how to be afraid yourself."

Enraged by this insult, Mara roared and swelled to monstrous size as the hermit suddenly faded away. He could feel the possibility of Buddha like the faintest light before dawn. Still, Mara was blind. He believed humans would ignore yet another pure soul. This was a mistake. The child on the horizon would be noticed because what he stood for was destiny.

3

The silk curtains to Maya's chamber parted, and Kumbira rushed out. The only thing she could be grateful for was that no one else knew yet. Her slippers padded quickly, quietly down the corridor. Night had fallen. The seventh day of the full moon was rising after the baby prince's birth, casting bars of ghostly light onto the polished teak floors of the palace. Kumbira paid no attention.

After dinner Suddhodana had retired to the nursery to be alone with his son. When Kumbira ran in, breathless and speechless, her face wore an expression he had seen only once before, when his father, the old king—

"No!"

The cry sprang from him involuntarily. Horror chased the gladness from his heart and clamped tight bands around his chest.

Sorrowfully, Kumbira drew her sari over her head to mask her face. Tears dripped from her tired eyes.

"What have you monsters done to her?" Suddhodana demanded. He swept past Kumbira, knocking her to the ground with a glancing blow. At the canopied bed, the king tore the drawn sheets away to reveal his wife. Maya looked as if she only slept, but the stillness that claimed her was complete. Suddhodana dropped to his knees and took her hands, whose coolness seemed temporary, the kind he could rub away whenever she felt a chill. Involuntarily he started to rub them now.

Kumbira allowed an hour to pass before she crept into the room with a retinue of court ladies. They were there to console but also to bring dignity. Grief, like everything else surrounding a king, was a matter of ritual. The moment Suddhodana consented to leave, attendants were prepared with ointments, winding sheets, and ceremonial marigolds to adorn the body. The wailing women were on call, and of course a dozen Brahmins with prayers and censers.

"Highness." With a word, Kumbira brought all this to the king's attention. Suddhodana looked up blankly. Kumbira waited a moment to see if she would have to repeat herself. As he gently placed Maya's arm across her chest, Suddhodana shuddered. It wasn't just that his wife had often slept that way, one arm folded across herself, the other across him. It was also that the king felt a slight stiffness creeping into Maya's limbs. Touch being the sense most cherished by lovers, he knew that he could never touch her again. He nodded curtly, and the wailing in the corridors began.

Grief is to demons what music is to mortals. Unseen and unheard, Mara walked through the palace. The formality of death is strict. Yama, the lord of death, is aware of every last breath, and he gives permission for the *jiva,* or individual soul, to pass into the other world. The lords of karma await to assign the next lifetime, sitting in judgment over the person's good and bad actions. Cosmic justice is meted out by the devas, the celestial beings who lavish the soul with rewards for good actions, and the *asuras,* or demons, who rain down punishment for wrongdoing. Demons do not have a free hand, however. The law of karma is precise and exacts only the punishment that is deserved, not an ounce more.

This made Mara's presence unnecessary, since Maya was already in the care of the three devas who had come to her in her dream and who met her again as she took her last breath. To die in one world brings birth in another. But Maya lingered in her body as long as she could. She willed her last spark of life energy to flow through her hand to Suddhodana as he knelt by the bed clutching it.

None of this concerned Mara, however. He walked past her bedchamber and directed his steps farther, to the nursery, which was now empty of nurses, guards, and priests. The new baby was completely unprotected. Mara crossed to the cradle and peered down at the wide-eyed child. The young prince lay on his back with his throat bared to the first predator that walked by.

But even the king of demons cannot cause physical harm directly. Demons' work is to amplify the mind's suffering. Mara would try to do that with this child, since no baby is born without the seeds of pain in its mind. Gazing down at the cradle, Mara let his face slide through a number of nightmarish masks. *You'll never see your mother again*, Mara thought. *She's gone away, and they are hurting her.* Siddhartha kept his gaze fixed, yet Mara was sure that the baby had heard. In fact, Siddhartha recognized him. Mara was sure of it.

"Good," the demon said. "You showed up."

He leaned closer to whisper in the baby's ear. "Tell me what you want. I'm listening." This was always the key, to play upon your opponent's desire. "Can you hear me in there?" The baby kicked his feet.

"So many souls need you," Mara said wistfully, resting his arms on the cradle. "But here's the joke." He paused to lean in closer. "When you fail, they'll wind up with *me!* I'm letting you in on the secret so you won't say I was unfair. Become a saint. It will only make you a better instrument of destruction. Won't that be delicious?" As if in answer to his question, the wailing over the dead queen grew louder. The baby looked away and fell quickly asleep.

FUNEREAL SMOKE, oily and thick, twisted through the air and tainted the sky as Maya's body burned atop the huge pile of sandalwood logs that had been chopped from the forest. The *ghatraj*, king of the funeral site, was a huge, sweaty man. His face reddened as he shouted orders for more wood, a higher flame, more melted ghee to pour over the body. The ghee had been churned from the milk of sacred cows. Priests walked slowly around the pyre chanting while the wailing women tossed thousands of marigolds into the fire. Behind them hired mourners whipped themselves in their grief and endlessly circled the body.

The spectacle made Suddhodana sick. He had defied the Brahmins by not taking Maya down to the ghats by the river. On his orders the funeral pyre had been built in the royal gardens. Maya had remembered playing there as a child, when noble girls from the region were brought to court on the chance that any might please young Suddhodana. It was fitting that her last resting place would be somewhere she loved. Secretly Suddhodana knew that this was a gesture born of guilt as much as of love. He was the one who still had a future.

Canki, the highest Brahmin, finished the rites by lifting an ax in the air. The most sacred moment had arrived, when he would pray for the release of Maya's soul while Suddhodana smashed the remains of her skull to release the spirit inside. The king approached the pyre, his expression stony. He glanced down at a necklace in his fist crafted of rubies and gold. He'd given it to Maya on their wedding night, and now he gently placed it next to the skull.

When Suddhodana turned away without raising the ax, Canki didn't hesitate to put his hand on the king's arm—for the moment, he was ruler here.

"You must."

Suddhodana held no deep contempt for the priesthood, and he knew that he had broken a sacred custom when his role was to uphold it. But at that moment the priest's touch revolted him. He turned his back and walked steadily toward the palace.

A woman was blocking his path. "You must look on him, Your Majesty. Please."

In the moment it took for him to hear these words, Suddhodana realized that Kakoli the nurse was blocking his way. She carried Siddhartha in her arms and hesitantly pushed him forward. Tears glittered in her eyes. "He's precious. He's a gift." Since his wife's death, the king had had nothing to do with his son. He couldn't help feeling that if the boy had never been born, his wife would yet live.

"I should look at him? Let him look at this."

Suddhodana glared at the nurse as he snatched the infant from her. The baby started to cry as his father lifted him above the heads of the mourners, giving him a good look at the smoldering corpse.

"Sire!" Kakoli tried to grab the child back, but Suddhodana fended her off. Everyone turned around to stare. Suddhodana defied them with a look.

"His mother died!" he shouted. "I have nothing left." He wheeled on Kakoli. "Is that part of the gift?" The old nurse covered her mouth with one shaking hand. Her weakness only enraged Suddhodana further. He took a step toward her and was glad to see her shrink back from his threat. "Stop sniveling. Let Siddhartha behold what this filthy world is really like."

He handed the baby back and strode toward the palace. He entered the great hall, his eyes looking for a new target that would promise more fight than women and priests. Suddhodana needed a battle right now, something he could throw himself at with abandon.

He stopped short at what he saw. An old charwoman was kneeling on the floor, scraping ashes out of the fireplace with her gnarled hands. Gray, unkempt hair hung down in her rheumy eyes. When she looked at him, she smiled, revealing a toothless maw. Suddhodana trembled. His own personal demon was here. He stood frozen in place, wondering bleakly what harm she meant him.

The old crone shook her head as if in sympathy. Slowly she took a fistful of ash from the cold embers and held it over her head, letting the ash trickle down into her hair. She was mocking the mourners outside and him at the same time.

Your poor, beautiful wife. We have her now. And we love her as much as you did.

The char rubbed ash in her face, making dark streaks and smudges until only her wrinkled mouth and piercing eyes were left untouched. She had him trapped. If he broke down, releasing all his pent-up grief and horror, it would open a breach that the demons could exploit. Every time he thought of Maya his mind would be invaded by hideous images. But if he resisted her, clamping down his grief with steel bands, there would never be a release, and the demons would hover around him.

The crone knew all this and waited for his reaction. Suddhodana's eyes lost their anxiety and became hard as flint. In his mind's eye he conjured up Maya's face, then he took an ax and smashed her memory, once and for all. The air around him stank of funeral smoke drifting in from the garden. He had made the warrior's choice.

A HUNDRED OIL LAMPS flickered in the reception hall, each one held high as courtiers craned for a better look. At first the spectacle had been fairly calm, but when the animal sacrifices began, the cries of baby goats and the gleaming of knives changed the atmosphere. Restless now, the courtiers began to mill around, raising a clamor over the chanting Brahmins.

In the middle of the melee stood Suddhodana, growing impatient. It was the official naming ceremony for his new son, and also the time when the baby's birth chart would be read aloud by the court astrologers, the *jyotishis*. Siddhartha's destiny would be pronounced and his whole life affected from this moment on. But pronounce was the one thing they weren't doing. Instead, the four old men bent over the cradle, stroking their beards, mouthing ambiguous commonplaces. "Venus is beneficly placed. The tenth house shows promise, but the full moon is aligned with Saturn; his mind will take time to develop."

"How many of you are still alive?" Suddhodana grumbled. "Four? I thought there used to be five."

The implied threat was empty. Astrologers were strange but revered creatures, and the king knew it was dangerous to cross them. They belonged to the Brahmin caste, and although the king could hire them, he was only of the Kshatriya caste, which meant that in the eyes of God they were his superiors. After Maya's funeral Suddhodana had spent days alone, refusing to unbolt his bedroom door. But there was a kingdom to look after, a line of succession to hold up to the world and his lurking enemies. It would be a sign of weakness for Suddhodana's entire lineage if the astrologers had anything dark to say.

"Is he safe, or is he going to die? Tell me now," Suddhodana demanded.

The eldest jyotishi shook his head. "It was the mother's karma to die, but the son is safe." These words were potent; everyone in the room heard and believed them. They would deter a potential assassin, in case someone had been hired to clandestinely murder the prince. Now the stars predicted the failure of any such attempt.

"Go on," the king demanded. The nearby clamor subsided in anticipation.

"The chart belongs to one who will become a great king," the eldest jyotishi intoned, making sure that these words too were heard by as many people as possible.

"Why didn't you say so to begin with? Get on with it. Let's have it all." Suddhodana was barking impatiently, but inside he felt tremendous relief.

The astrologers glanced nervously at one another. "There are ... complications."

"Meaning what, exactly?" Suddhodana glared, daring them to take back a word of their prediction. The eldest jyotishi cleared his throat. Canki, the high Brahmin, moved in closer, sensing that he might have to intervene.

"Do you trust us, Your Highness?" the eldest jyotishi asked.

"Of course. I've only executed one astrologer, maybe two. What do you mean to say?"

"The chart foresees that your son will not rule Sakya." Dramatic pause as the king cursed under his breath. "He will hold dominion over the four corners of the earth."

At this, general consternation broke out. Courtiers gasped, a few applauded, most were stunned. The jyotishi's words had their intended effect. But Suddhodana stiffened.

"How much am I paying you? Too much. You expect me to believe such a thing?" He forced a bemused tone. He wanted to test the old man's resolve.

Before the jyotishi could find a reply, however, there was a stirring in the crowd. The oil lamps, which had moved back and forth in the air like wandering stars, became still. Courtiers parted and bowed, making way for someone who had just entered the room—an eminence.

Asita, Asita.

Suddhodana didn't have to hear the whispered name as it was passed along. He knew Asita on sight; they had met long ago. When Suddhodana was seven, he had been woken up by guards in the middle of the night. A pony was waiting for him beside his father, who rode a black charger. The old king said nothing, only nodding for the retinue to move forward. Suddhodana felt nervous, as his father often made him feel. They rode in a pack of guardsmen toward the mountains, and just when the boy thought he would fall asleep in the saddle, the old king stopped. He had the boy placed in his arms, and they went alone up a scree slope toward a cave above their heads. The mouth of the cave was hidden behind brush and fallen boulders, but his father seemed to know where to go.

He stood in the dawn light and called, "Asita!" After a moment a naked hermit came out, neither obedient nor defiant. "You have blessed my family for generations. Now bless my son," the king said. The boy stared at the naked man, who appeared by his beard, which was not yet completely gray, to be no more than fifty. How could he have blessed anyone for generations? Then the old king set him on his feet; Suddhodana ran forward and knelt before the hermit.

Asita leaned over. "Do you really want a blessing?" The boy felt confused. "Tell me truthfully."

Suddhodana had received many blessings in his short lifetime; the Brahmins were summoned if the heir apparent had so much as a runny nose. "Yes, I want your blessing," he said automatically.

Asita gazed at him. "No, you want to kill. And conquer." The boy tried to protest, but Asita cut him short. "I am only telling you what I see. You don't need a blessing to destroy." As he said these words, the hermit held his hand over the boy's head, as if administering what had been asked for. He nodded toward the old king, who stood some distance away out of earshot.

"Take death's blessing," Asita said. "It's the one you deserve, and it will serve you well in the future. Go."

Bewildered but not offended, the boy got to his feet and ran back to his father, who seemed satisfied. But as time unfolded, the boy came to see that his father was a weak king, vassal to rulers around him who dominated with stronger will and greater armies. He came to be ashamed of this fact, and although he never quite knew what Asita meant by death's blessing, Suddhodana did not object when his own nature turned out to be fierce and ambitious.

"You honor us." Suddhodana dropped to his knees as Asita approached. The hermit looked older now, but not three decades older, the time since they had last met. Asita ignored the king and walked directly to the cradle. He glanced down, then he turned to face the jyotishis.

"The chart." Asita waited until the scroll of sheepskin was passed to him. He gazed at it for a moment.

"A great king. A great king." Asita repeated the words in a flat, emotionless voice. "He will never be."

Tense silence.

Asita replied, "What do I care about thrones?" He might have been indifferent to the king, but Asita could not take his eyes away from the baby.

"Without a doubt there is a great ruler in his chart," the eldest jyotishi insisted.

"Do you not see that?" Suddhodana asked anxiously.

But the hermit acted strangely. Without replying, he knelt before the baby with his head bowed. Siddhartha, who had been quiet up to now, took an interest in this new person; he kicked his feet, and one of them brushed the top of Asita's head. Suddenly tears began to roll down Asita's cheeks. Suddhodana bent down to lift him to his feet. The revered ascetic allowed this gesture, which under normal circumstances would have been a serious affront to a holy man.

"What did you ask?" he said, seeming like a withered old man at that moment.

"My son—why will he not rule? If he's fated to die, tell me."

Asita looked at the king as if noticing him for the first time. "Yes, he will die—to you." The court stirred restlessly, but Suddhodana, who should have asked all this in private, was beyond caring who overheard. "Explain yourself," he said.

Asita paused, seeing confusion and dismay in the king's face. "The boy has two destinies. Your jyotishis were right about only one."

Although he was speaking to the father, Asita's gaze never moved from the infant. "Your will is to make him a king. He may grow up to choose the other way. His second destiny."

Suddhodana looked totally bewildered. "What is this second destiny?"

"To rule his own soul." A relieved smile crossed the king's face. "You think that's so easy?" said Asita.

"I think only a fool would exchange the world for such a destiny, and I will make damn sure my son isn't a fool."

"Once he dies to you, you will be sure of nothing." The king's smile vanished. "You're making a mistake. Ruling the world is child's play. To truly rule your soul is like ruling creation. It is above even the gods."

The old hermit wasn't finished. "You too are in his chart. It says you will either suffer over your son as no father ever has or you will bow down before him."

Suddhodana's disbelief was a roar. "You're wrong, old monk. I can turn him into what *I* want." Suddhodana's face was mottled with rage. "Now get out! All of you!"

Even for gossip-hungry courtiers, the drama had been too much. Half the oil lamps had already sputtered out. In the dim light their retreating figures looked like insubstantial shadows bowing their way out of the king's presence. The jyotishis led the way with profuse apologies and anxious blessings. Canki wanted to be last in the room, but he found it politic to go when the king glared daggers at him. After a moment only Asita was left.

With the audience gone, Suddhodana could speak freely. "Is all that you said true? Is there nothing I can do?"

"No matter what I say, you will do it anyway." Without reproof, Asita began to leave, only to be held back once more.

"Tell me just one thing. Why did you weep tears when you saw my son?" asked Suddhodana.

"Because I will not live long enough to hear the immortal truth that Buddha will speak," Asita said.

4

The next morning Suddhodana rode his warhorse up the hillside toward the imposing Shiva temple his father had built on the crest. The king's melancholy had changed overnight, replaced by determination. A score of bullock carts were gathered outside the temple gates, the great patient beasts searching lazily for grass sprouting from the earth packed hard by the sandals of devotees.

Suddhodana dismounted and let his horse graze with the bullocks. He strode into the main temple courtyard, which was filled with milling worshippers and sellers of sandalwood and ghee for ritual offerings. Awed eyes followed his progress, but Suddhodana had no time for ceremony. He had ridden without an entourage because he had a secret purpose in mind; he didn't summon Canki to the palace because he was too impatient to wait for him.

Now he burst into the inner sanctum, where the air was a heavy, sweet-smelling pall. A lone priest was performing the ritual Rudravishek. Slowly he poured ladles of milk over a tall polished stone, the Shiva lingam. The liquid left a faint blue veil on the ancient river rock. In the darkness Suddhodana's eyes narrowed; they stung from the residue of pitch and incense hanging in the air.

"Canki!"

The priest stopped the oblation and turned toward the bellowing voice. The king's eyesight had adjusted, and he recognized the high Brahmin himself at the altar. Some rich devotee, probably marrying a third or fourth wife, had paid handsomely for the ceremony.

After a glance Canki turned back to his task. "I'm not finished yet," he said.

The king came up and seized the ladle from his hands. "You are now."

Canki bowed, then led the king away, padding silently over the stone floor on bare feet. He was quite capable of defying royalty, protected by his Brahmin privilege. Canki was solid and imposing, despite the rolls of fat exposed as he went, bare-chested, across the cobbled courtyard toward the cloister where the monks lived. The Brahmin lowered his heavy body onto a leather stool inside his cell, pointedly not waiting for the king to take a seat first. Suddhodana let the insult pass. "If you talk to God, you already know why I'm here," he said.

"I know that God wishes to please you in every way, Your Highness." Canki gave a fawning smile meant to win over an angry king.

"I want my son to rule the world." Suddhodana said the words without hesitation. "Is this possible?"

"Every father would want—"

Suddhodana stepped closer, magnifying the threat he posed. "No! Either this is God's will or it's not. You are to tell me. Much rests on this. More than your life, in fact."

The balance between castes was delicate. If the rulers had a political reason to support religion, they did; if the priests needed to bring the people under their sway, they exerted influence over the rulers by promises of divine favor. Canki knew the system very well, and he also knew, despite his high caste, whose hand rested on the sword.

He said, "You face many obstacles in this endeavor, Your Highness. But it can be done."

"How?"

"Seek to control the infant prince's mind. He must be taught to think like you. To believe like you. And to lust as you lust."

This last was a barb, but Suddhodana waited patiently, hearing truth in the Brahmin's words. If anyone knew how to control others' minds, Canki did.

"Train him well, as a complete warrior. Place his whole sense of worth on fighting, and on you." Canki paused. "Am I helping?"

Suddhodana realized at that moment why the jyotishis had been so nervous. They had consulted the high Brahmin as soon as they cast Siddhartha's chart. No doubt they could foretell the king's displeasure.

"Is that all I have to do?" Suddhodana's tone was cutting; they both knew his suspicion toward priests.

"No. The most difficult part comes last." Canki went to the window and pointed outside at a large stone statue of Shiva. "I am reminded of Lord Shiva's story. You know it, of course." This was another barb; the Brahmin continued without waiting for a reply.

"Venerable sages had gathered in the forest to meditate, and Lord Shiva desired to learn from them. But he was mischievous, and he brought a woman with him to their retreat. This was a test, for the woman was actually Lord Vishnu in disguise. But the sages were too blinded with rage to see this. They vowed to kill this sacrilegious intruder, so from the sacred fire they engendered a monstrous tiger. The beast leaped upon Shiva, but with one fingernail he stripped the tiger of his skin and wrapped it around his shoulders. Then he thanked the sages for their courtesy in supplying him with a meditation cloak.

"The sages' fury redoubled after this impudence. The sacred fire absorbed their rage, and a second monster sprang out, this time an enormous serpent. But Shiva choked it with his hands and wrapped the carcass around his neck. He thanked the sages for providing him with a necklace. At that point they grew so furious that a third monster sprang from the fire—"

"Stop!" Suddhodana's patience had reached its limit. "If you think what I must do is too difficult, spare me your parables. Just tell me outright."

"Make your son a total prisoner."

The starkness of these words hit Suddhodana in his chest like a rock. Canki read his dismay and hurried on.

"This is a soul whose spiritual tendencies will be almost uncontrollable, and your only chance is when the boy is young. To make Siddhartha into a great king, never let him leave these walls," the high Brahmin said. "He must believe this is a paradise. If he once sees suffering, your son will never obey you again. You'll lose him forever."

Suddhodana was stunned. "For how long must I do this?"

"Thirty-two years."

"And there's no other way?" The king had become extremely deliberate, as if weighing a death sentence. It revolted him to think that he had acquired a conspirator. Someone who had power over him from this day on. He felt smothered by the rage and helplessness whirling inside him.

Involuntarily his sword arm moved, and the next instant he had the Brahmin pinned to the floor with the edge of his blade. "You think you've achieved something today? Then remember the rest of Shiva's story. Out of the sacred fire leaped a third monster, a hideous dwarf. Shiva pounced upon it and held its throat under his heels, crushing it. Who was that dwarf?"

"Ignorance." Canki choked out the word.

"Don't prey upon my ignorance, then. I know more than you suppose." The king released the priest from underfoot. Suddhodana's nature couldn't be held in check. It was only tempered by this gnawing desire, only a day old but gripping at his spleen, to father the ruler of the world.

He departed with one last word for Canki. "Just be sure that you live long enough to see what I'll do with you if this plan fails."

Within the hour the king issued orders, dispersing his own people and banishing them from his city. His son would never be allowed to see suffering in any form—sickness, aging, or dying. Standing on the ramparts of the castle, he could see long trains of wagons leaving Kapilavastu. The rains had already come in torrents that washed away crops and flooded houses. Those least likely to survive were the old and sick. Lepers were hunched against the rain wrapped in dirty rags to cover their faces. Cripples who could not walk the roads were tossed wholesale into supply wagons from the army, with soldiers ordered to drive them far away and dump them in remote villages. The oldest were sole survivors, and these were thrown into separate army wagons. They were told that homes awaited them in a better place, a cruel way of hinting at the reality—they would be abandoned in the forest a day away.

Only the nobles were exempted, and those under strict conditions. Venerable figures like the astrologers were sworn never to be seen by Siddhartha at any time, under pain of banishment. Others not yet old could remain at home, but if they grew ill or aged, they would be confined under house arrest. All funerals would take place at night, without public ceremony. The burning ghats were moved two miles downriver. Suddhodana knew how to organize a battle campaign, and the first rule is that victory is more important than the costs it entails. This campaign would be no different.

Ruler of the four corners of the earth. He had memorized the words in the chart. How would that feel? he wondered. After three days the great wooden gates of Kapilavastu closed; the bitter cries of those who had to leave and those who had to let them go were silenced. The job was complete.

THREE WOMEN CHASED a small boy across the park. They ran over lawns kept immaculate by slaves on their knees with clippers, through gardens filled with flowering jasmine whose fallen blossoms were swept from the path every morning. It wasn't a serious chase, but the boy, Siddhartha, pretended it was. When he sped up or took a sudden zigzag, his pursuers did too. But you didn't have to be seven years old to notice that they never caught him.

Not only that, but the three women always ran in the same order. First came Prajapati in her gold-embroidered sari the color of peacock blue, although on other days it could be vermilion or emerald. Prajapati was the prince's aunt, sister to his dead mother. Suddhodana had formally given her the status of a wife, but the two had no conjugal relations. The king was paying honor to her and acknowledging her role as stepmother to the prince.

The heavy gold bangles in her ears tinkled softly as Prajapati ran. Behind her came two peasant girls, considerably younger and slimmer than Siddhartha's aunt. They wore coarse cotton saris with no embroidery, their ears had small silver bangles in them, and they slowed down enough so that Prajapati was always first.

"Channa, Channa!" The boy called out his friend's name.

On days like today, when the sun was out and the morning air was cool, the world his father had built for him was big enough, and he didn't wonder what lay beyond the high walls surrounding the palace grounds.

"Prince, stop!" cried one of the aunties.

"Oh, Prince, do come back!" another begged.

Siddhartha veered toward the stables. He wasn't running away from the women for recreation. He had made a discovery that he wanted to show Channa. As long as he was supervised, the king allowed him this freedom. The stables were much better for a boy than a palace, anyway, and once he crossed the threshold, Siddhartha's aunties always stopped short. Prajapati had never set foot in a stable, and although the peasant girls certainly had, their newfound station as royal servants prevented them from entering a precinct where only males belonged.

Hearing his name, Channa appeared at the stable door. He jumped and waved his fists, encouraging Siddhartha on. If it had been him racing the prince, he would have won easily, being taller and stronger despite the fact that they were born the same week.

Siddhartha dashed inside. "Hide!" he cried.

There was no need for him to be hidden from anybody. The rules of the chase were well known to all, but Channa grabbed Siddhartha by the arm and pulled him inside, as if hauling a fellow soldier to safety inside an armed fortress. The two boys raced past the stalls where warhorses were kept when in heat or giving birth to spring foals. Their heels kicked up clouds of dried dung that the sun turned into glowing auras around them.

"Here!" Channa led the way to a feed bin. It smelled of fresh hay with a sour undertone of rotted hay beneath. This was a favorite retreat since they could burrow as deep into the hay as they wanted to escape detection. Siddhartha perched on top of a nearby bale and reached into his pants. He pulled out a tiny creature.

Channa's face fell. "It's just an ant," he said, disappointed.

"No, it isn't. Look closer."

The feed bin was dim, but now Channa saw that the insect, a large black soldier ant common around the stables, was still clutching its prey, a dead termite, in its jaws. The termite, which wore stiff papery wings, was newly hatched and twice as large as the ant.

"Where did you find it?" asked Channa, still unimpressed. But he saw that Siddhartha was excited.

"By the water fort." This referred to one of the floating pavilions on the shore of a lotus pond in the park. "I saw the whole battle."

The event had taken place that morning when Prajapati found Siddhartha wandering away from the palace. He was sitting on the ground beside the pavilion staring intently at the dirt. A string of black soldier ants was clashing with sentry termites at the entrance of a small colony.

Prajapati stopped a few feet away. "Who's winning?" she asked.

"That doesn't matter. It's something else."

Siddhartha was staring at a particular soldier ant carrying a dead termite in its jaws. The ant had reached an obstacle in its path, a large pebble. The pebble was five times the ant's size, and it was already carrying a load twice its weight. For half a second the ant paused, then it started to climb up the pebble. The way was too steep and it fell back, but this was no deterrent. The ant climbed up again, fell back again, climbed up a third time.

"How foolish! It should just go around," Prajapati said.

Siddhartha shook his head. "The mighty don't go around."

"Is an ant so mighty?"

The boy ignored her amused tone. "*He* thinks he is. That's what counts."

"I could step on him. Then how mighty would he be?"

At that moment the boy said something quite surprising. "God could step on my father, but he still thinks he's mighty."

Prajapati was nonplussed. "It's not the same thing."

"Why not?"

Siddhartha glanced at her with his wide brown eyes, eyes that had seemed twice the normal size when he was an infant. But before his aunt could reply, he returned to the ant, scooping it up in his hand. His whole attention was focused on it. "If you think you're mighty, that's all that counts. No one is really mighty."

What a strange child you are, Prajapati thought, but she hid this from Siddhartha, saying, "I never thought of it that way."

"What do you think?" he now asked Channa, having told him everything.

Without a word his friend shot his hand forward and pinched the black ant in half between two fingers. "I think we need to find a better game. That one's no good."

He shoved Siddhartha into the hay, and when the prince came up sputtering stalks of long grass, he shoved back. The boys' tussle was interrupted. "Channa!" The boys looked up as if on command from the god of the stables.

Bikram appeared at the gate of the feed bin, his bulk almost filling it. He wore a thick leather apron and metal-fitted leggings, as he always did in mating season when a stallion could unexpectedly lash out with its hooves.

Stooping, Bikram picked up a clod of horse manure and flung it at the two peasant girls lingering at the stable door. Prajapati had left them to wait until Siddhartha emerged again. The girls squealed as the clod barely missed them; they had already started backing away. Siddhartha and Channa crowed in triumph.

Bikram wasn't smiling. "I need you, boy."

Channa ran after his father, who was the king's stablemaster when there was no battle to fight. Not that there had been many since the birth of the prince. The kingdoms of Kosala and Magadha to the east had made peace with Suddhodana, and he had relinquished his need for raiding frontier villages to add to his domain.

Although he was less than half the size of his broad, beefy father, Channa's frame promised that same height and bulk one day. He could hear commotion from a far stall that was different from horses in heat. Bikram noticed that Siddhartha was trailing behind them. "Not you, young prince," he said. "Just the boy."

Siddhartha stopped short, confused. "Why not?"

"Because your father would have my hide. This isn't for your eyes. Stay put until me and the boy come back for you." Bikram wasn't stern with the seven-year-old, who was never addressed as "boy." He just made clear what was needed. Siddhartha obeyed automatically.

He hung back as Channa and his father rounded the corner and entered an open stall. The gate shut behind them. Siddhartha squatted in the straw-covered dirt. His eyes roamed over the array of saddles and bridles hanging on the wall; he caught the clinking of hammers on the smithy's forge out back. Listening intently, he thought he heard Bikram's muttered voice, then Channa's.

The boy was uneasy being left alone. He had a secret. Not the kind he was ashamed to reveal so much as one he couldn't fathom.

To escape thinking about it, he gazed up at the stable roof. It was old, and the timbers had warped over the winter, letting in the rain and beams of bright sunlight when the weather was clear.

His eyes caught a sunbeam now, and he watched motes of dust dance in it.

Look closer.

Siddhartha shivered and tried not to listen. The words in his head didn't feel like his own. They came unlike ordinary thoughts. The voice had begun about a week earlier—this was his secret—and almost always said the same thing. *Look closer.*

The sunbeam fell warmly across his eyelids, and he felt dreamy. The dust motes seemed to seize his attention and grow bigger.

What if we are made of dust? All things that come from the earth are only dust.

Siddhartha looked down at his arm and brushed away the film of dried dung that had settled on it. More dust flew up into the sunlight.

I am just dust, he thought.

He jumped to his feet and began to run.

Only dust.

The voice had turned on him, was suddenly harsh and mocking. Siddhartha didn't want to hear it anymore, and it was all the boy could do not to cry. He raced toward the stall where Channa had gone. He paused at the gate, not wanting to be seen this way, weak and shaken. Above him, in the shadowy rafters, an unseen figure sat. Eyes watched the boy trying to calm down, and a calculating mind considered its next move.

Siddhartha pushed at the gate, but it was locked from the inside.

On the other side Bikram's voice was sharp. "Hold her down, I said."

Siddhartha heard a horse whinnying in pain and hooves clomping against the ground. He peered through a crack in the gate. A sick old mare was lying on her side, heaving and quivering. At one end crouched Channa, trying his best to hold the mare's head still. At the other end Bikram was tying her hind legs together with rope; he had already tied the front legs, and they clomped helplessly against the ground. Bikram stood up. Siddhartha saw the grimness in his face and the fear in Channa's.

"It's going to be all right," the boy whispered into the mare's ear, which twitched as if hearing a nearby predator. Eyes rolling wide and white with terror, the horse sensed what was coming.

"I need you to be strong," said Bikram. "You know why the prince couldn't be here for this?"

"No."

His father shrugged. "No need. Just remember, he can't be here, understand?" Channa nodded. "Once everyone's asleep tonight, we'll take her outside the gates and bury her. He doesn't ever need to know she's dead." Channa nodded again.

Above Siddhartha, an unseen figure—Mara himself—peered down, considering his next move. He had waited a long time to rejoin the boy and draw him closer. Close enough to become a voice in his head. The demon clapped his hands, wondering if the boy might look up, but Siddhartha's eyes were fixed on the scene in the stall. Bikram picked up a heavy ax and turned the blunt side of the blade outward, like a club. He walked slowly to the mare's head.

"Look away, boy."

Channa did as he was told; his father raised the ax high in the air, brawny knots standing out from his bare arm. Out of the corner of his eye Channa saw him bring the ax down; there was a loud thud and the crunch of bone, but in the instant before, as if sensing its fate supernaturally, the old mare screamed.

Siddhartha heard it as he ran, a piercing pitiful cry that made the other horses shiver in their stalls. He was terrified, but he hadn't witnessed the blow. Something pulled the boy away at the last second—weakness, or a better impulse?—saving him from the grisly sight. Panicked, he ran outside, putting as much distance between himself and the stables as he could. Prajapati's two young servants saw him and gave chase.

Mara knew the moment was ripe. He was suddenly beside Siddhartha, arms and knees pumping as he matched him stride for stride.

"Yah!" the demon shrilled. "Giddyap! Let's see you run!"

Siddhartha turned his head, and his eyes widened. It was only a quick, panicky glance, but Mara was certain he'd been seen. It was the first time, a milestone.

Turning his gaze from the horrible sight, Siddhartha focused on the palace ahead of him. The building was huge and ornate, a thing of beauty according to every visitor the young prince had held audience with. He ran through an arched doorway, not slowing at all. Soon he reached the closed door of his father's bedroom. No one had followed him, and gradually his breath stopped burning in his chest. Cautiously, hearing the murmur of voices from within, Siddhartha tried the lock. It was open. Moving with the natural stealth of a child, he pulled the door open and peered inside.

His father's private chambers were vast and ornate. The best silks and the finest gold made up the bedding and decorated the furniture. Polished floors gleamed with candlelight, and a small group of men huddled around his father's bed.

Suddhodana sat propped up by pillows. The men around him were court physicians, who poked and prodded, examining their royal charge gingerly.

"Get on with it," he grumbled. "If you're here to get me closer to dying, don't bother. Time is taking care of that."

Siddhartha drew back. He had never known his father to be sick, barely recognized these men as doctors. They had rarely appeared in his short life, and only before dawn. The king didn't want his son to be awake when he needed tending. But Siddhartha could vaguely remember, as if seeing through a fevered haze, the same poking and prodding he now observed.

One of the physicians gestured to another, who held a large wooden bucket with a lid. Removing it, the second physician reached inside and withdrew a large, fat leech.

"Lie back, Your Majesty. This will be the last time, I promise." The lead physician was a thick man with gentle hands. He was called Gandhik, Siddhartha remembered. Taking the leech, Gandhik applied it directly over his father's heart. It was all Siddhartha could do to remain silent when he saw the six leeches already feeding on his chest. Swollen and dark, they looked like they were trying to crawl inside him.

"Disgusting," the king snapped. "You and your so-called arts." He heaved a sigh of resignation. "Disgusting."

"Hold still, Your Majesty," Gandhik directed in a quiet, patient tone.

"I want to be strong again," Suddhodana said. Then he shook his head. "Who am I fooling? I want to be *young* again."

Lying there on the pillows, his graying hair feathered out around him, the king permitted the indignities of medicine as a distraction—they kept him from dealing with the passage of time. Every day seemed to be a weight around his neck, depriving him of another ounce of strength.

"You will be strong after this," Gandhik promised, holding another writhing leech pinched between his forefinger and thumb. Something in his reassurance sounded false, even to himself.

"Idiots!" the king exploded. "Flatterers! I might as well suck my own blood." He glared at the leech and struggled with giving up on the whole damned business of medicine, only to lean back, his eyes closed, no longer willing to look. "Get on with it." Cautiously, Gandhik applied the final leech to the king's chest.

Siddhartha's eyes focused on this, but his mind was fixed on something he couldn't comprehend: his father showing fear. This sent tremors through him, as if he had been standing on a mountainside that suddenly began to slide out from under his feet. Siddhartha backed away and closed the door without a sound.

When he turned around, he nearly ran over another boy in the hallway.

"What are you, a spy?" the stranger said. He had a taunting voice and disdainful eyes, which looked down on Siddhartha almost six inches above his own eyes.

At the word *spy*, Siddhartha jumped. "I'm not," he stammered.

The older boy's eyes narrowed suspiciously. Siddhartha blushed with shame, and suddenly he knew without being told that someone important had just entered his life.

5

It took a moment before Siddhartha had enough presence of mind to ask, "Who are you? Why did you sneak up on me like that?"

The other boy stared without reply. He wore heavy embroidered clothes that marked him as the favored of some king's court. Under them, his body was already developing muscles on a lean frame. He must have been at least twelve.

"I didn't sneak up. You're just too blind to see."

"Sorry."

Siddhartha's meekness made the other boy draw himself up to his full height and cross his arms. "I came looking for you. Didn't they tell you?" Siddhartha shook his head, which earned him a pitying look. "You don't talk much. Do you spend the day under a rock? You look pale enough."

Each taunt was having less and less effect. Siddhartha knew he wasn't pale, and though cowed at first, he wasn't afraid of the stranger. He said, "You must be my cousin. They said you were coming."

"See? Even you can make sense if you try."

Siddhartha said nothing. The arrival of this aggressive visitor added one more unwelcome shock to the day. His father limited the number of people who saw his son and limited even further the number who actually had a conversation with him.

"Do you think you can remember a name? Mine's Devadatta, and I'm just as good as you are. Try and remember that too."

Siddhartha would have bowed in greeting and was tempted to even after this barrage. He recalled what his father had told him: "You're getting lonely. We have to do something about that." The next day an order was sent to summon a suitable companion, and Suddhodana congratulated himself on his choice. Devadatta was born to a branch of the Sakyan royal line and was old enough to travel on a saddle up the steep trails from his home kingdom, where he held the rank of prince.

Devadatta was tired of bantering, so he grabbed the cap Siddhartha was wearing and dangled it out of reach, watching the smaller boy try to jump up and snatch it back.

"We need to have an understanding, just you and me," he said. "They made me leave home against my will. I'm not old enough to get my way. Not all the time, I mean." Devadatta smiled, his mouth a narrow, tight line. "I didn't want to come to this godforsaken place. Or to meet you." He jammed the cap on Siddhartha's head again.

Siddhartha took a step backward so he could bolt down the hallway if he had to.

"You're really scared of the leeches, aren't you?" Devadatta taunted.

"No." Siddhartha said, ashamed that he'd been seen but not wanting anyone to think he was afraid.

Devadatta lifted his shirt to expose a dozen fresh scars all over his chest. They were bright pink half-moons against his dark skin.

"I had a fever last month; they leeched me so I wouldn't die. That's why they're in there with your papa. He'll probably die too." Devadatta stared the smaller boy down. "I wasn't a baby about it. Not like you. Go ahead, touch them, if you're really not scared."

Unwilling to endure any more, Siddhartha turned and fled

down the long hallway. He wanted to get away from everything: his cousin, the physicians with their bucket of bloodsuckers, and most of all the helpless feeling that he was trapped in a nightmare. Deriding laughter burned in his ears as he ran.

SOON SUDDHODANA WAS EXULTING in Devadatta's presence. "This is a prince of the blood. Treat him like my second son," he announced in open court. In private he set the usual spies on the newcomer, who was probably acting as a spy himself. In the king's mind he had accomplished two goals at once. His son, who showed signs of a dangerous passivity, would have a model to follow, someone close to his own age but tougher. In addition, a neighboring kingdom, intimidated by Suddhodana's wrath if it refused, had given up its heir apparent to his control. Having caught Devadatta in a trap, Suddhodana lavished smiles on the boy and catered to his whims, which promised to be precocious and plentiful.

That year, at the arrival of spring, the king threw a feast to celebrate. Siddhartha was awake before dawn, brightening up at the prospect of what lay ahead. He knew that people lived outside the palace walls, but he could only imagine what that must be like. The most mundane thing—walking along a dusty road through a market town—must be amazing (although he'd never seen a town and only knew about roads to faraway places from books). All he had to do was ask people about themselves, and Siddhartha was certain they would recount wondrous stories.

When the festivities began, however, the rush of new sensations was beyond anything he had imagined. Colorful banners emblazoned with pictures of the gods, bright lanterns, and gold-embossed decorations transformed the palace grounds into a mythical place. He ran through flocks of jugglers and acrobats; he listened open-mouthed to wandering storytellers in garish masks who had spent years learning how to keep villagers in suspense as they described Hanuman, king of the monkeys, flying with a mountain in his hands because a rare herb that grew there was needed to heal the battle-wounded Lakshman, brother of the divine Lord Rama. The monkey god couldn't find the herb, so he ripped up the entire mountain in order to return in time. Would he? The audience gasped, ignoring the fact that they had all heard the tale a hundred times.

But nothing was better than the manic hour when the celebrants ran around the grounds hurling fistfuls of dyed powder at each other. Clouds of red, green, and yellow filled the air. Shrieking ladies ran away from panting pursuers, coyly allowing themselves to be caught, then breaking into peals of laughter as they threw dye in their paramours' faces. Within minutes everyone was covered in a patchwork of hues.

Two older girls a little ways away suddenly caught his eye. Standing beside one of the tables heavily laden with food, they chattered, pretending not to look in Siddhartha's direction.

They know I'm a prince, Siddhartha thought, smiling a little. This made him braver, and he approached, concealing the pouches of scarlet powder behind his back. He worked hard to remain innocent looking. When he was within a few feet of them, he sprang his surprise. A red fog hung in the air for a moment before the wind pulled it away. The two girls squealed and laughed, enjoying his unexpected attention considerably more than the prank. When the air cleared there was an awkward pause.

"Hello," Siddhartha said. The two girls exchanged a look, as if trying to decipher this message. The braver one took a deep breath.

"Hello," she replied. No guards descended; nothing exploded. So the other one tried saying a word. "You're the prince?" Not as if she doubted it, but as if she might not have the right to ask.

Siddhartha nodded. "My father is the king."

The girls lapsed into silence. Siddhartha wasn't sure how well things were going. He wished he weren't alone.

"Hey, cousin!"

Siddhartha turned around to see Devadatta a few feet away. He had his fist poised in the air, and a second later he threw with all his might! A green cloud billowed out. Siddhartha was reaching into his own pouch, happy to join in, when he felt a sharp pain in his forehead. He staggered back, then touched the spot. His hand came away stained a warm, sticky crimson. Devadatta had put a rock in with the powder before he threw it.

A new surprise, not the pain, held Siddhartha's attention. He had yet to see his own blood. His cousin was laughing at him and looking toward the girls, expecting them to appreciate the joke. But they had run away in alarm. Devadatta shrugged and turned his attention back to Siddhartha. "Let's play again, only try to stay awake this time, okay?" He stooped down to find another sharp rock.

Siddhartha was never far from watchful eyes, and it was only a moment before Suddhodana arrived on the scene as Devadatta threw his second missile, not bothering to disguise it with dye. It hit Siddhartha in the chest and made him cry out. He doubled over with a wince. Devadatta considered this a favorable outcome and had another rock in hand already, but he spied the king and hesitated. There was a small crowd around them now. Suddhodana nodded at Devadatta, "Go on."

The boy didn't need any more encouragement. He threw again and hit Siddhartha in the shoulder, hard enough to draw blood again. None of the onlookers came to the rescue; even Prajapati, late to arrive, glanced at the king and knew that she couldn't interfere. Siddhartha looked around. His face flushed with shame, and he wanted to run, but his father's voice stopped him.

"No! Stay and fight."

The courtiers exchanged nervous glances; some of the more tenderhearted ladies clutched their hands to their breasts. Suddhodana kept his eyes on his son, watching stonily for a response. When the boy didn't move, only gazing vaguely into the distance, his father gave a small, almost indecipherable snort, which Devadatta took as a signal that he had won. He relaxed and dropped the rock in his fist, giving one last look of pity at his victim. He pushed his way through the spectators and was gone.

Suddhodana stepped forward and knelt beside his son. "Listen to me. You can't let him do that. In this family, we fight." Siddhartha hung his head, biting his lip. "You're my only son, aren't you?"

"Yes, Papa."

"From now on, there's not going to be any more 'papa,' you understand? From now on it's 'sir.'"

Siddhartha felt a rock being put into his hand, and his father's much larger hand closed it into a fist.

"Go."

The king stood up, and the courtiers parted the way, making a path in the direction Devadatta had gone. Siddhartha felt the sharp edges of the flinty stone against his palm. He gathered himself to run but had taken only a step when his father's voice stopped him.

"Here, let me clean you up first." Suddhodana bent over and wiped the blood from the boy's forehead. "You have to see him to fight him. It might get in your eyes." His father's tone still had an edge, but Siddhartha instinctively knew that in those few seconds his father had changed, had felt a twinge of remorse or tenderness. The next instant he was being given a rough shove and found himself running hard toward a pavilion beside the pond where Devadatta had disappeared.

SIDDHARTHA ROUNDED THE CORNER of the pavilion by the lotus lake beyond the sight of his father. He ducked into an archway that led inside, then he made an escape near the water's edge. He didn't care where his cousin was. He dropped the rock clutched in his fist; the flinty edges had dug red indentations in his palm. His other wounds were throbbing, but Siddhartha ignored the pain.

He threw himself down among the tall reeds by the pond. It was almost the only real hiding place he had ever found. Panic distorts time, so he had no idea how long it was before he began to feel better. But his heart eventually stopped racing, and in the aftermath of distress he began to feel drowsy and drained.

Siddhartha was his father's son, yet he wasn't. There were no words to express why this was true. The heavy expectations weighing on his shoulders mystified him. The rocks thrown at him, the humiliation that followed—all hurt. But worse was knowing that Devadatta, a cruel stranger, filled his father's expectations better than he did. Siddhartha watched a hawk circling on motionless wings overhead. Unable to see beyond the palace walls, he could still gaze above them. Then the hawk closed its wings like scissors and dropped toward earth. In less than a second it changed from an emblem of escape to a deadly missile hurtling down upon an innocent prey.

At that moment, although he scarcely suspected it, not Siddhartha but Devadatta was the prey. Devadatta had fled from his victory in high spirits, tinged with the bitterness of knowing that he was still the king's prisoner. The boy was bored with the childishness of the festival. He slowed his pace, and then noticed that a man, a stranger, had appeared from nowhere. He was tall and cloaked in the coarse hemp of a traveler. Despite the man's stealth and the difference in their sizes, Devadatta wasn't afraid; his arrogance protected him. His hand felt for the dagger at his side.

The cloaked stranger raised an admiring eyebrow as if to say, *We have a man here after all.* He drew his own dagger.

"Come on," he said. "You deserve to die."

Devadatta backed away, startled. "Why?" His voice still betrayed no fear, and he unsheathed his own weapon, ready to fight.

"Not for anything you've done, but for what I'm going to make you do." Quicker than the eye could catch, the stranger lunged forward, grabbed Devadatta's dagger by the blade, and snatched it from his grasp. Then he burst out laughing at the boy's stunned reaction. The stranger's hand held the razor-sharp blade tightly, yet not a drop of blood appeared.

"You were unkind to draw on me," the stranger said calmly, "but Mara is kind enough for two." He handed Devadatta his knife back. It was as hot as a burning coal, and the boy dropped it with a shriek of pain.

"Damn you, demon!"

Mara bowed ironically at being recognized so quickly. "Not many are brave enough to curse me. Not on first meeting. Usually they're more occupied with their terror."

Devadatta glared back defiantly. "Why are you here? I'm not going to die." He uttered these words with impressive certainty. Mara said nothing in reply. One arm lifted, bringing the edge of his cloak with it. The cloak was lined with black. Devadatta's gaze fell on it for an instant before the blackness seemed to expand. One moment the cloak was making a small billowy circle around Mara's head; the next it swelled to enclose the boy before the entire pavilion disappeared, and Devadatta found himself in total darkness, warm and suffocating.

With a shriek he plummeted into a looming void. There was no telling how long he fell, but it was certain that when he landed, it was with a bone-jarring crash. For a moment Devadatta writhed helplessly, the wind knocked out of him, before he became aware of hard, cold stone beneath his body.

"Where am I? Speak!" he shouted.

"Oh, I'll speak, never you fear."

Mara's voice was right beside him. Devadatta reached out to strike, as enraged as he was frightened. Or, to be more precise, he dealt with fear by turning it into rage. His fists struck empty air. Mara admired the boy. It was rare for someone so young to be fearless in peril, no matter how much was empty bravado. Mara needed someone with certain qualities: hotheaded, reckless, unable to judge the limits of his own danger, wily but stupid enough to fall into the lure of arrogance. This one would do.

"What do you want?" Devadatta shouted into the empty blackness. He gradually became aware, however, that this blackness wasn't total; he could see a faint glimmer in the distance. From that and the stone underneath him, he surmised that he was in a cave and, since the air was frigid, a mountain cave.

Mara could have explained everything, but he preferred to watch and wait. Arrogance and bravado have their limits, so he bided his time—an hour, then two, then six—until he heard Devadatta's teeth chattering and sensed the despair rising in his chest.

"You are here to learn," said Mara.

The broken silence made Devadatta jump. He controlled his anger this time; his mind had had time to work, and he knew that he was in a demon's power. Exactly who or why was still unclear, but he had to be careful of more traps. Two were enough.

"I'm a prince; I can bargain with you," he said, his eyes moving from side to side in case the demon showed himself. Which Mara did, appearing as he had in the pavilion, a tall stranger in a black cloak.

"You aren't listening. I said you're here to learn."

"Learn what?" Pause. "I'm listening."

Mara caught the note of defeat in the boy's voice; he couldn't pretend to himself any longer that he had the upper hand. "Learn to be king," said Mara.

"Don't be ridiculous," the boy flared. "I'm going to be king, anyway. I don't need you for that, whoever you are."

"Ridiculous! My dear fool, you gave away your chances the moment you set foot away from home. There is no throne waiting for you back there, not now or ever."

"Liar!"

This heated outburst made Mara decide to wait again, and so he delayed another few hours while Devadatta grew colder and lonelier and the weight of the demon's words had sunk in. Then, because he knew that gratitude can be as effective as fear, Mara clapped his hands, and a small campfire appeared in the cave some yards away from the boy. Devadatta rushed over to it and warmed his shivering body. "The only throne you have a hope of capturing is Siddhartha's," said Mara. The firelight made Devadatta's eyes gleam. As always, the demon had grasped an idea that was already in his victim's mind. "His father is too strong. You cannot overthrow him. But it is through him that you will depose the son."

Every added word inflamed Devadatta, who forgot the distress and danger he was in. He hadn't genuinely hated his small cousin; his feelings up to now had been a mixture of pity and jealousy. "It won't take much to get rid of him," he said.

The cloaked stranger held up his finger. "More than you think. Much more."

The boy took this as an insult to his physical strength, the one advantage he knew that he had over his cousin. "You don't think I can crush him? All it takes is a knife or an arrow when we're out hunting."

"Think again. The king would have you killed immediately. He wouldn't even care if you did it. He'd know it was you."

Devadatta paused. He and Suddhodana were enough alike that he saw the truth of this. Wouldn't he kill anyone in the vicinity of the prince if he were the father and his son died mysteriously? After a moment's deliberation Devadatta said, "If I let you teach me, what will it cost?"

Mara laughed. "You have nothing to give. A prince without a throne is also a prince without a fortune. You must be slow if you didn't consider that. Too slow to bargain, except with your life. I'm going."

"Wait, you can't leave me here!"

The boy sounded agreeably terrified. Mara clapped his hands again, and the sputtering campfire went out. He was satisfied with the opening he'd made. Let the boy rest a night in the cave. He would be afraid of freezing to death, but Mara could keep the spark of life going. He had the minutest control over death, after all.

"Wait!"

The boy called louder, but his sinking heart knew that he was alone now. There was nothing near but the settling blackness and the glimmer of light coming from the mouth of the cave. Devadatta headed for it, creeping with one hand on the stone wall to steady himself. He climbed over rubble, and he felt something—a rat?—scramble over his foot. When he reached the light, the cave opened out into a sizable mouth. Devadatta stepped from the cave onto ice-hardened snow, which extended in all directions. He was near the top of a Himalayan peak, the kind of place that the truly fearless yogis sought out for their solitude. But Devadatta felt no holy presence in this hostile landscape. There was no sign that any human being had ever been there, not the faintest trace of a trail going downslope. All Devadatta could spy was the last wink of the fading sun before it disappeared beneath the horizon. His mind searched for words and failed. Standing between himself and the fast-descending blackness was nothing.

6

It took Devadatta most of the night to figure out how to escape from the cave. While there was still a glimmer of light in the sky, he staved off despair by scouring crevices for kindling to burn and scraps of vegetation to gnaw on. Not that he could have started a fire with his bare hands. Eventually he stopped this fruitless activity and busied himself with hating Mara. He fantasized about the revenge he would wreak if he survived. The night was so thick he lost all concept of time. Finally there was nothing to do but curl up on the stone floor of the cave, shivering and defiant, and wait to die.

It took a while longer to give up hope entirely. Only when there was no possible way out did his mind stop whirling in panic, and then Devadatta considered a simple question: Could demons physically transport a person anywhere? What if the cave was just an illusion? The moment he considered this possibility, two things happened. He heard the faintest echo of Mara laughing at him, and he fell fast asleep. When he woke up, he was lying on the ground near the pavilion on the spot where the demon had shown himself. Devadatta sat up, rubbing his stiff, aching limbs. The sun was setting, and so he must have lain unconscious there for hours.

He walked onto the veranda that circled the pavilion. Torch flames were reflected on the water of the lotus pond. From the distance he heard drunken laugher. The king's revelries were continuing into the night. Devadatta headed toward the sound. For some mysterious reason his ordeal in the cave didn't drain him. He felt stronger, in fact. He craved more than ever to do exactly what he had set out to do that morning: lure one of the maids into a corner and torment Siddhartha. Both desires came to mind again, and they aroused him to the point that he began to run. Devadatta didn't care if he ran into a girl or Siddhartha first. Neither would come away forgetting the encounter.

Why can demons roam the mind in this way, taking advantage of innocent people? What made Devadatta prey to the terrors of the cave was a tiny thing: he was claustrophobic. As an infant he had almost suffocated in his thick swaddling clothes when a careless nurse left him wrapped up in the sun. Mara knew this weakness, and all he had to do was to throw his cloak over the boy. Devadatta's mind would do the rest. It would erupt with the memory of being suffocated and begin to panic. It was easy for the demon to shape mindless panic into a nightmare. The boy couldn't wake up from the nightmare; it held him in its grip for as long as Mara wanted. A moment of terror could be transformed into a week in the dreaded cave. And Mara could accomplish the same thing with anyone.

ALONE AND DISCONSOLATE, Siddhartha roamed the grounds. It had become his habit to be alone as much as he could. He felt he had no other choice. "People seem to be afraid of me. They barely look at me or they run away. Why?" he had asked Channa not long before.

"You think I'm afraid of you?" Channa shot back.

"Not you. The whole rest of the world."

This wasn't exactly true. If you are holding a fragile egg and are afraid of dropping it, you are afraid not of the egg but of the consequences. The same was true of the courtiers around Siddhartha.

So many doors were shut to Siddhartha, so many faces held low to the ground, so many eyes averted that he felt bewildered and mistook their attitude for fear. Even Bikram fell to his knees and prostrated himself when Siddhartha came into the stables. The only exception was if Channa was also present; the king had told Bikram he could stand then because a father shouldn't be humbled in front of his own son.

"They're just scared not to be perfect," said Channa when Siddhartha wouldn't let the thing go. "The king would find out."

"And then what?"

Channa pointed to the high palace walls. "He throws them out. That's what I hear." Channa thought of the horses he and his father buried beyond the walled perimeter. "Only they're not dead."

Siddhartha knew in his heart of hearts that the horses that disappeared from the stables didn't leave alive, and it made him anxious that something dark happened to a lord or lady who suddenly vanished from the morning levee when the king assembled the court for a greeting and allowed them to watch silently as he ate breakfast. None of Siddhartha's favorites had disappeared yet, thankfully.

"When I'm the king, nobody gets thrown over the wall," he said, but that was a rare remark; Channa would never recall another time when Siddhartha referred to taking the throne, not in the near future, the distant future, or ever.

Siddhartha's mind was wandering through these gloomy thoughts as he stood alone by his favorite pool, the one surrounded by tall reeds. He knelt down and paddled his hands in the cool water. The pond was shallow there, and in the shadow of a floating lotus he saw something—the nymph of a dragonfly creeping slowly over the mud. Siddhartha watched it. The miniature monster moved steadily, fearlessly, on the prowl. A tiny silver minnow swam by, and with a startling leap the nymph snatched it in its jaws. The minnow shuddered once and was still, its eyes open and shiny even as it died. Siddhartha shuddered along with it. Why did he feel the pain of such a tiny, insignificant creature?

"A very good question. Maybe it's your gift." Startled, Siddhartha stood up to see an old man in front of him, a hermit. His skin was brown and weather worn. He wore a flimsy silk shawl thrown over his torso and a rough hemp skirt. The hermit was leaning on his staff by the waterside, gazing at the boy, his eyes unreadable in their depth.

The hermit said, "You found me. And very quickly at that."

"I didn't find anyone. I was just here," Siddhartha protested.

The hermit smiled, which made papery creases at the corners of his eyes, something Siddhartha had never seen before. Everything about the stranger made him seem like an apparition. "These things don't work quite the way you suppose. I am Asita."

An older boy, or a very different one, would have wanted to know how someone else's voice got into his head. Siddhartha accepted that something inexplicable could still be real. "Why are you here? Does my father know?"

"Another good question. To which I can give a simple answer, since your other question is more complicated. Your father would be very displeased to see me here. Does that matter?" Before Siddhartha could reply, Asita said, "Of course it does. He's the one you look up to."

Siddhartha took this as a criticism. "Everyone looks up to him. He's king here."

"Let's not worry about that for the moment. Have you heard other voices in your head? Tell me the truth." Siddhartha hung his head. "I thought as much. You have a feeling nature, a very deep one. You will sense things that other people can't. Unfortunately, not all those things will be good for you. There's nothing I can do about that, do you understand?"

"I don't want to be different, but you say I have to be. No, I don't understand."

Asita took a step toward him and laid a rough hand on his shoulder. "No mother, and a father you trust completely. We have to take that into account."

Siddhartha grew more uneasy. "I can hear the guards coming. You have to go. You said you shouldn't be here." Soldiers were shouting at each other from the far side of the pond, and the voices were getting closer.

The stranger shook his head. "I can take care of them."

Whatever he meant was a mystery to Siddhartha, because Asita did nothing that he could see. Yet when three guards came combing the tall reeds, they didn't see the two of them standing there in plain sight. The boy hesitated.

"It's your choice," said Asita calmly. "Call for them, or stay and listen to me." Without a word, the boy waited until the guards were safely away. "Good," Asita said. "I am only here to show you a few things. If I keep protecting you, you won't find your own way, and you must do that."

"How have you been protecting me? Are you the one who keeps me here, inside these walls?"

"No. I have been protecting you in many ways, but not physically."

Asita bent down and looked the boy in the eye. "Your father wants to live through you. But he doesn't have that right. Believe me." Siddhartha looked away, biting his lip. "You are so young. I only wish—" Asita's voice trailed off, and he stood up again. "No one's fate was ever decided by talking. I have something to show you, and now it's time."

Overhanging the water was a large rose-apple tree in full bloom. "I told you that you have a gift, but it's not a simple one. Already you have begun to experience it, but each time you do, you are tempted to run away. Does this tree remind you of anything?" Siddhartha shook his head.

"You were barely four years old. It was time for the spring plowing, and your father held a feast like this one. It was his role to go out into the fields and plow with the common farmers, a great sight. Everyone wanted to see it, including your nurses. So they left you under a rose-apple tree, just like this one. You don't remember at all?"

Siddhartha didn't know what to say. A strange sense inside him, like a clearing mist, made him uncertain. Asita went on. "Nobody realized it, but you were watching closely, and as the plow blades turned the fresh earth over, you saw something very tiny but very disturbing. The bodies of insects and worms had been chopped into bits by the plow, along with other small newborn creatures. How did you feel?"

"I can't remember how a baby feels."

Asita's gaze didn't waver, and Siddhartha hung his head. It took a moment before he murmured, "I wanted to cry. Why should I cry over a half a worm?"

"You felt as if you had seen your own family hurt, and this frightened you, didn't it? No need to answer. We both know. The feeling was too big for you. But something else happened next—"

At that instant Siddhartha lost the sound of Asita's voice, because the clearing mist inside him revealed the scene the hermit was describing. Siddhartha saw himself in his baby's robes sitting under the tree. He saw himself look up at the overhanging blossoms, and suddenly he was back there again. But what he felt was no longer anguish at the small creatures cut to bits by the plow. Something new had washed over him. The beautiful tree, the immense blue sky, the inrush of the spirit of spring—they made him hurt again, but this time with a pang of pure joy. And yet somehow the two things were connected. The sight of violence, which hurt so much, transformed into a joy that wanted to burst out of his chest.

Siddhartha came back to himself, gazing at Asita, who seemed to be reading his thoughts. "That was your gift. You mustn't run away from it."

"Did I run away then?"

"No, you didn't have a conscience then." Asita said. "You didn't know enough to feel ashamed or different. You fell into that beautiful thing for hours, and when they found you, everyone was astonished that you hadn't moved from the same spot all day. They were so astonished they didn't even notice something much more interesting."

Siddhartha held up his hand. "Don't say it."

"Ah. So someone did notice."

Although he had sat under the rose-apple tree all day, the tree's shadow hadn't moved. It stood in the same place overhead. And so the child was shielded against the sun's fierce heat until his nurses ran back again.

"Is that what you call protecting me?" asked Siddhartha, unsure whether to look upon this as a miracle or just one more thing that made him not like other children.

"You are troubled, and you shouldn't be. Come."

Asita sat down under the tree now. Siddhartha watched as the hermit crossed his legs and straightened himself until his spine was perfectly erect. From long practice he made this look effortless.

"Now, you try," Asita said.

The boy imitated the position, which felt strangely comfortable considering that he had never seen it before.

"Hands like this." Asita held one hand on each knee and circled his thumb and forefinger. Siddhartha followed and then closed his eyes after he saw the hermit close his. They were both quiet. At first the boy was only aware of his surroundings. The air was cooler under the tree; the noon sun filtered lazily through the still canopy of leaves and flowers. Siddhartha felt drowsy, and for a moment he might have nodded off. But he was awake when the voice in his head said, *Can you be still, without thinking? Don't talk to yourself. Just breathe gently.*

These words came into his head like his own thoughts, but he knew that they must be Asita's. The two of them seemed to be connected. Siddhartha accepted this fact without questioning it. The old hermit wasn't like anyone he had ever met. Certainly not like Canki, whom the boy vaguely feared. Then Siddhartha caught himself. He wasn't supposed to think. After a moment his mind stilled. This happened naturally, like a breeze calming over a cool lake. He became aware of his breath going in and out in a soft rhythm. The whole thing was pleasant, soothing. He had the sense, almost physical, that he was sinking down into the earth or was being lowered into a well. Only his descent wasn't frightening and what waited below wasn't sheer blackness. It was more like a welcoming sleep, except that he remained awake in its arms.

Siddhartha lost track of time. Once he opened his eyes again, Asita was leaning on his staff watching him.

"They're coming for you," he said soberly. Siddhartha knew he meant the guards sent out by his father. "Can you remember what I've just showed you?"

Siddhartha nodded, although he wasn't really sure that he had been shown anything. Asita picked up his doubt.

"Here is your safety. This is going to be your special place. When you feel confused or when someone is trying to make you what you are not, come back to this tree. Sit and close your eyes. Wait for the silence. Do nothing to make it come to you. It will come of its own accord."

They could hear the return of soldiers shouting to each other by the pond. "Will I find you here?" asked Siddhartha.

Asita shook his head. "I had to think long and hard about even coming today. You are still in danger."

"From what?" Siddhartha's spirit was so settled that he was only mildly disturbed by Asita's veiled warning.

"From everyone who thinks they know what your future should be. You are not alone. They are always watching."

"I know." Siddhartha's voice was as sober as the hermit's.

"Well, let that be. I am withdrawing my protection now, as of this moment. I don't want to be like one of them."

Asita's voice had become tender and somewhat strange. Siddhartha didn't understand why the old man's gaze seemed so sad, or why he took a moment to bend over and touch Siddhartha's feet. But the moment he did, the boy found himself closing his eyes again, and once more he descended into the well of silence, deeper this time, deep enough so that he didn't hear Asita depart.

"Hey, over here!"

The shout was close by, and Siddhartha heard running footsteps approaching. He slowly opened his eyes to see a ring of guards around him. Some looked agitated, others relieved. The officer among them gave an order: "Run and tell the king." He knelt down beside Siddhartha. "Where have you been? Did someone take you away?"

Siddhartha shook his head. He wished they would all leave. It would be much better if they did, if he didn't have to return with them.

He wanted to close his eyes again, but instead he heard himself say, "I've just been here. Sitting by myself."

The officer looked doubtful. "We've circled the place half a dozen times."

If this was an implied question, Siddhartha didn't answer it. He was too aware that his body was getting to its feet, as if another person were in charge of his muscles. He himself was still inside the silence. More people were running up now, including various courtiers dressed for the feast, some wobbly from drink. What time was it? He was surprised to see the sun low on the horizon.

The soldiers led the way, and Siddhartha felt himself return to the world. Everything was back in focus. His father greeted him with open arms and not a word about whether he had fought with Devadatta. With the tension broken, the revels became twice as raucous, continuing long past midnight. Siddhartha was allowed to stay up. He spent a closely guarded hour watching the dancers and tumblers, then went to his room and threw himself into bed, exhausted but with a head full of images that kept him awake a long time.

Erasing a memory isn't a simple process like erasing scribbles off a chalkboard. The eyes have the longest memory, followed by the nose. Who doesn't remember the blinding white snows of yesterday, the swooning scent of a rose, the brilliance of an unfurled peacock's tail? But try to imitate a robin's song, something you've heard a thousand times. Few people can. Still less can we remember anything told us that was wise. Siddhartha swore to himself that he would never forget Asita's words, but the years passed and the hermit's message became more and more vague. Besides, what are a few profound sentences compared to the thousands of days that follow? In the prince's case, each day was full to bursting, and by the time he was nearing adolescence, Siddhartha had forgotten that he had ever been under Asita's protection or that it had ever been withdrawn.

The king kept his word and allowed his son's education to be completely ruled by the high Brahmin. Canki's was the first face the prince saw when he stepped out of his room in the morning and the last when he returned at night. Naturally, this constant familiarity made him trust his teacher. The heavy hulk of a man treated him well and told him many useful things. It was rather like being followed around by a learned ox. But just as naturally, Siddhartha escaped his schooling whenever he got the chance. He had worn a path to the stables by the time he was six, and it deepened every year. There he could waste endless time with Channa, whether to lie in the straw and discuss the future, saddle a horse to ride (both boys together, one to hold the reins, the other to kick with his spurs), or groom a mount that was lathered up and quivering from a hard workout. Most of the time they practiced fighting, the one thing Channa never tired of.

If Bikram happened to be watching over them, then the boys' fighting followed strict rules. "We may have to kill, but we don't butcher. We fight with style," Bikram insisted. "Style is what makes the battling human." He only half believed this motto, but it gave him a sense of dignity, and when he couldn't help but see the carnage of battles long past in his mind's eye, Bikram's only refuge was his dignity—he had killed too many enemies the dirty way.

Before being handed a sword, each boy had his chest wrapped in thick straw padding bound with burlap on the outside. Their blades, shorter and lighter than a warrior's, were dulled along the edge and the points shielded with a lead ball. These measures ensured that neither would get seriously hurt. "Don't dull 'em so much as they won't feel it," Bikram ordered the armorer. "Bruises but no blood."

As referee, he shouted, "Touch!" to make them part each time one sword made a hit. But there was only so much that could be done about Channa's fierce temper. The boy would keep whaling away even after his foe was hit, and then Bikram would jerk him back with a scolding oath and a cuff on the ear. They both knew he was secretly proud.

Often Siddhartha felt bad about besting his friend. But Channa had it coming. Each small victory he managed meant days of listening to him crow. Both of them bore colorful bruises from the blunted blades.

One day, when the boys had just turned fourteen together, it began as a typical match. Channa tirelessly lunged and slashed, which was his favored style. Siddhartha would watch and sidestep when he could, playing the sinuous panther to Channa's clumsy bull.

"Hit!" Channa cried out, but he was premature. He had only landed a glancing blow to Siddhartha's burlap tunic. The reckless thrust gave him too much momentum, and as he hurtled past, Siddhartha slapped him on the butt with the flat of his blade.

"I called a hit, didn't I?" Channa grumbled. Siddhartha just shrugged. Channa hated the grin on his friend's face, and rather than argue he risked a second lunge, which also missed. Siddhartha fisted Channa's shirt in his free hand, lifted his sword to his friend's throat, and drove him back against the stable wall. Their breath hit each other's faces as they glared at each other.

Is this what my father takes such joy in? Siddhartha asked himself. He knew by the way he talked about war and being in battle how his father felt about the struggle to survive under bloody conditions.

There was no referee this day because Bikram had been called to the smithy to help hold an unruly warhorse that was being shod. The boys took advantage by fighting harder to test each other's limits.

Setting himself, feet apart and weight balanced as he'd been instructed, Siddhartha attacked with his blade. He had already learned that he had reach and height as his advantage. He'd grown to be the leaner and taller of the two. He struck quickly, getting as much brawn behind the blow as he could. Channa lifted his sword and blocked, steel ringing against steel. The harsh noise always made a few of the horses snort and stamp nervously in their stalls.

"Just say when you want me to stop playing around," Siddhartha taunted. They were both sweating heavily after an hour's practice. The swelling of muscles in their limbs was suggesting the contours of men, not boys.

"Playing around?" Channa said. "I'm getting sore from holding back so you can stay in the match."

Although his strength was flagging and air burned his lungs as he breathed, Siddhartha pursued Channa, driving his foe before him.

"Hit!"

This time it was Channa calling out that he had been struck with the point of Siddhartha's sword in the chest. The prince smiled grimly, shaking his head. *Let's have this one out,* the smile said. Seeing Channa stumble off balance, Siddhartha tossed his sword with a quick twist of the wrist and caught the hilt overhand, using it like a dagger to plunge into Channa's heart. He felt the fierce exultancy of his dominance, and in an instant he was kneeling over Channa's body, the edge of his blade tight against his friend's throat.

He let Channa up, not looking into his eyes. If their gazes met, he knew Channa wouldn't be able to disguise a flicker of hatred, the despising look of the defeated. There was something else too. He thought he heard someone approaching all but silently. But before he could find out, Siddhartha felt his legs go out from under him. As he had turned away, Channa had stuck his boot out and tripped him. Siddhartha fell facedown on the stable floor, spitting out dung dust. The next thing he knew Channa had rolled him over and was shoving the point of his sword into Siddhartha's throat. Even shielded with lead, the tip dug painfully into his flesh.

"You forgot to finish me off," Channa said. He wore his usual gloating grin, the one reserved for when he recovered from the threat of defeat. But his eyes were dark with a feeling that left a cold spot in Siddhartha's heart

"See?" Channa said, leaning over him so their faces were only inches apart. "That's the difference between you and me, Siddharth'." He smiled confidently. "I'm not even thinking about not killing you."

"Did one of you girls talk about killing?" The two boys were startled. Without a sound Devadatta had appeared. "You'll never see the day, I promise." He drew closer, bestowing a pitying smile on them.

"Care to give it a try?" Channa blurted out impetuously. He raised his sword under Devadatta's chin.

Siddhartha stiffened. The three of them were constantly in each other's company. "Throw the three of them together," Canki had advised Suddhodana. "If we isolate the prince, he will sense that we have designs on him." It was another of the small irritants in their relationship that the Brahmin couldn't stop talking like a conspirator. "Why teach him to hate Sakya's enemies when we only have to put him in the same room with an enemy of his own?" The jealousy that Devadatta harbored toward his younger cousin was no secret.

"I don't mind the boy and his cousin. They're both royal," Suddhodana conceded. "But why Channa?"

"We will give the prince someone he can trust and confide in. The day will come when you won't be able to read his mind, and he will stop telling you what he really thinks. Then we can turn to Channa and find out everything."

Secretly the king had doubts about this plan, but he had his own reasons for agreeing to the Brahmin's suggestions. Devadatta would be able to report on the priest's lessons in case they went too far in extolling the Brahmins at the expense of warriors. And Channa might serve as an informer in Siddhartha's private life—Canki was right about that.

This arrangement at school sorely rankled Devadatta from the first. He, a Kshatriya, had never physically touched or shared food with anyone like Channa, a despised half-caste. This was the term for someone of unknown parentage, and it was true that Channa had never known his mother. Her name was never mentioned, nor did his father say why she had abandoned them. Bikram himself had been born in the stables he now managed. When Canki gathered his three pupils for lessons, Devadatta turned his back on Channa; there was never an occasion when he addressed him directly. For Channa to dare to pick a fight with him now was an outrage.

Devadatta considered what to do. The two obvious possibilities were to dismiss the taunt with cold silence or attack without warning. Inflicting a swiping cut with his dagger would do. But Devadatta was eighteen now, already a man. Men don't respond to boys' threats. The nicety of the question teased him, and he decided the one thing he couldn't do was let the insult pass.

"What sort of test did you have in mind?" he asked. He spoke slowly, and as he did, he lifted up the point of Channa's sword and unscrewed the lead ball. "We've had enough of pretending."

Channa was brave, but he was also fourteen. He stared nervously at the naked point of his sword as Devadatta pulled his own weapon from its scabbard.

"Up to you, boy," Devadatta said. He watched Channa's Adam's apple tremble. They both knew that Devadatta could run him clean through without fear of reprisal.

But there was something else that no one but Devadatta knew. The fear he inspired did not come from his own menace. Siddhartha may have forgotten Asita, but his cousin had not forgotten Mara. He wasn't allowed to. The demon fanned every ember of resentment in him until it glowed red hot. There was no mistaking the demonic element in Devadatta's character. When he picked a fight, he could intuitively read his opponent's weakness, and he gave no quarter once the clash began. Mara had also made him an extraordinary seducer. Devadatta moved in with unswerving confidence, capable of using honeyed flattery or the grossest suggestion, and he didn't give up until the prize was won. His passions had drawn him into the lowest places—alleys and taverns where the pretensions of caste were thrown aside. However, it was not this that made him extraordinary in matters of lust. It was his complete ferocity toward any rival, even a husband, who stood in his way. Devadatta didn't mind using a blade to persuade another man that his woman was free for the taking. There were rumors of clandestine murders that had resulted when the man put up too much resistance. Whether the rumors were true or not, more than a few villagers walked around with livid scars on their faces or across their chests.

"I don't want to fight you. We were just practicing," Channa mumbled.

"Not good enough. You challenged me. Now you have a choice. Apologize on your knees, or get ready to wake up dead tomorrow."

Devadatta smiled, but he wasn't pressing the issue for his own amusement. He had a point to make about crossing lines that shouldn't be crossed. If Channa had been able to see beyond Devadatta's threats, he would have realized that his enemy wasn't secure enough at court to actually kill Siddhartha's best friend.

"Stop it!" Siddhartha stepped in between the two. He had hesitated for a moment, knowing that if he intervened, the fight would be deflected toward him. Channa would hotly deny that he was about to back down; Devadatta would curse Siddhartha for snatching away his prey. But that didn't happen. Instead, both opponents shoved him aside with looks of hot rage.

"No, this has gone far enough." Siddhartha stepped in again, and this time Devadatta screamed at him with pure malevolence, "Get out of the way!" But the hand that knocked him back with a stiff, clipped punch was Channa's. The look in his friend's eyes said, *Don't you dare save me from this! I will never forgive you.*

Siddhartha was stunned. He couldn't actually see Mara working inside his cousin, but he saw that Devadatta was not an arrogant aristocrat at all. He was a slave to his violent passions. And Channa was too. At that moment there was no difference between them.

They're not even people. What's happened to them?

Siddhartha asked this question, and his vision seemed to pierce the two. Their bodies became transparent, like the filmy membrane of a fish's tail, but instead of seeing blood coursing through the membrane, Siddhartha saw lives. Each person was a package containing many lives, all crammed into the tiny space of a body. A wave of hostility surged from the darkest past of both fighters. Devadatta was only the carrier of this wave, its instrument, as infected people carry typhoid. But Channa? How could he be a carrier too?

Siddhartha did not reason any of this out. He felt it. Neither Devadatta nor Channa had looked his way. He drew his sword and leveled it between them. "Go ahead and fight," he said, staring them both down. "But you will have to fight with my sword between you, and if you touch it, you have challenged me, and that's the same as challenging the throne. Is that what you want?"

Neither knew if this was a ridiculous ploy or brilliant diplomacy. The two foes backed away, continuing their combat through hating looks. Devadatta sheathed his weapon, gave an arrogant bow, and left without a word. Channa ran away with a look of barely concealed contempt. The wind blew through the stable windows; gradually the air cleared. It was left to Siddhartha to wonder if his gift had visited him again. If it had, why should he take on the pain that others denied they even had?

I'm the one they're going to blame. I kept them from killing each other.

The deepest cut, the one that would not heal for years, was the contempt he'd seen in Channa's eyes. If he as much as Devadatta was a carrier of hatred, then there was no difference between them, and the distinction between friend and enemy was meaningless. Something between Siddhartha and Channa, the unspoken vow two boys take that nothing will ever step between them, at that moment started to die. There was no escaping it. Yet if Siddhartha could have found a way to erase just one memory, this would have been the one.

7

You just might do. In a pinch."

"Just? Thank you very much." The youth in the mirror smiled at being teased. At least Kumbira still thought of him as a child, if no one else did.

"From me, that's saying a lot," she replied.

Kumbira regarded Siddhartha with an appraising eye. His ceremonial dress fit perfectly. He stood in front of his reflection with a flutter of young ladies-in-waiting around him. On this day, when he turned eighteen, he would be acknowledged as the heir to old Suddhodana. He had begun the robing ritual bare-chested and bare-legged before all the layers of cloth, oils, and perfumes were piled on. Each of the women, Kumbira imagined, would have looked upon him with lust-filled eyes if they dared.

And why not? she asked herself. There must be taller and richer princes in the world, but not in their world. Still, she could see the boy in him. Much of Siddhartha's innocence was yet his. Kumbira cherished that about him without being able to point it out to anyone. What his father wanted to instill was the opposite of innocence.

"Let me ask you something, Kumbira. How happy should I be right now? If anyone knows, it must be you."

"Don't talk nonsense!" Kumbira's eyes narrowed, and she sniffed at him. "What am I smelling? He doesn't smell right. More sandalwood!" Immediately one of the young attendants raced away to the royal store of unguents and spices.

"It doesn't matter how I smell, Kumbira. I'm not dessert."

"Don't be so sure."

The girls tittered, and she saw his brief smile fade as he regarded himself in the glass. The approaching day had seemed to dim any joy Siddhartha once found in it. Kumbira had caught him off guard at moments when sadness darkened his eyes and held his mouth tight and narrow. It nearly broke her heart to see him so withdrawn.

She approached from behind and laid a rich silk sash across his chest. "What's the matter? Whisper in Kumbira's ear. I'll send your troubles to the gods, and they'll never dare return." Siddhartha shook his head. Kumbira sighed. "Are you determined to spoil everything? The rest of the palace and the people have been looking forward to this for a long time." He didn't answer.

"Young men, that's what it is!" Kumbira snapped her fingers at the girl sitting at the toiletry table, her momentum stopped by the prince's mood. "Rose water to sweeten the temper." The girl grabbed the proper vial and hurried over to anoint Siddhartha's flowing black hair, which curled at his neck. Kumbira tucked in a stray lock. Every detail had to be managed precisely. The king was introducing his heir to the world. As much as Kumbira feared royal wrath, she wanted this day for the prince as fervently as she would have wanted it for her own son.

Siddhartha pulled on the jewel-encrusted coat held out for him. He groaned and shifted under its weight. "Somebody must have made a mistake. This is meant for one of the elephants."

A girl giggled, and Kumbira shot her a look. Even though he had been surrounded by women for two hours, something made Siddhartha's head turn. He saw one of the youngest attendants try to cover her amusement by coughing and waving a hand in front of her face as if she were choking. Kumbira was poised to drive the girl from the room when she noticed something more unsettling than a breach of decorum: Siddhartha had evidently chosen that moment to discover how beautiful the young girl was. His eyes widened, and he unconsciously assumed a bolder stance, like a peacock preening before a hen.

Kumbira was wise in such ways. She had witnessed the behavior of men for many years, and this reaction was unmistakable. She held her tongue and waited to see what would happen. Although aging, Prajapati kept a close eye on her charge, and everyone remarked, not with complete approval, on how chaste Siddhartha remained. Now Siddhartha's eyes were still caught by the young girl who had laughed at him. Sujata was young and soft, rounded in all the right places, with flowing hair and smooth skin. Even more attractive, though, was her discomfiture: she was blushing now at the prince's interest in her. That, Kumbira knew from experience, was a challenge no warrior could resist.

But instead of confronting the girl's behavior with the arrogance that highborn men often exhibited before a potential conquest, Siddhartha blushed as well. For an uneasy moment the silence between the two young people held sway in the dressing room. Hastily Kumbira stepped forward between them, breaking the eye contact. She started to wind a red turban around Siddhartha's head.

"Here," he said, taking the cloth from her hands. "You have to leave me something to do for myself." Expertly he wound the turban, but his eyes stayed on Sujata.

Where is she from? Kumbira couldn't recall. Country girls were regularly brought to court as servants, and this one was new. Kumbira had grown accustomed to such as her. The king constantly replenished the supply of fresh faces around the prince the way one would restock a trout stream.

"You're not here to gawk, girl," Kumbira warned, raking Sujata with a disapproving stare.

The girl dropped her gaze to the floor. "I wasn't, milady."

"Don't talk back. You have a lot to learn. Perhaps you should begin somewhere else." With a flurry of hands Kumbira shooed her away. "Go, go!" Disconcerted, Sujata bowed and left the room.

"She could have stayed," Siddhartha murmured. Kumbira said nothing. She wasn't angry with the girl; she had only dismissed her to save the prince from being impulsive in front of tongues that would spread rumors throughout the palace. If he was seriously interested in Sujata, or even casually inclined, he could summon her in private.

Siddhartha sank back into a moody silence as the final touches were put on his costume, in the form of a peacock feather dashingly stuck in his turban and delicate white satin slippers on his feet. With a last frown at his reflection, he made for the door, then turned back.

"What's her name?" His voice was almost too low to catch.

"Sujata," said Kumbira. He repeated it under his breath. "So you noticed one," Kumbira said. "Finally." Despite the small feeling of apprehension that niggled at her, she couldn't help teasing him. Siddhartha frowned, but he was too unsure of himself on these grounds to put much into the effort. He reached into his robe and pressed something into Kumbira's palm, a heavy coin.

"Silence is golden," he said with a shy, serious expression.

Kumbira nodded, and Siddhartha left noiselessly on slippered feet. They shared a small secret now, yet Kumbira felt inexplicably that he was drawing away from her permanently. There was no reason why this should be so, but she squeezed the gold coin in her hand like the memento of a lost cause. If only she understood the boy.

A PROWLING TIGER crouching in wait or an eagle in its aerie may find it simple to be alone, but humans don't. We have many ways of being alone, and each has its peculiar complications. On the day that Siddhartha turned eighteen, three people felt completely alone in the palace. Siddhartha was alone because he didn't know who he was and couldn't ask anyone. The king was alone because he feared that his project was about to fail. Devadatta was alone because he had been dragged down into private torment without hope of rescue. These three experienced very different forms of loneliness, yet they had one thing in common. They fought to make sure that no one else suspected.

Suddhodana stood on the ramparts watching the long train of litters, wagons, and carts bringing his guests and their retinues to the capital. From down below some had spotted him and waved or got down from their conveyances to bow in salutation. He stood still, not acknowledging their greetings. The weather was fine, the roads to Kapilavastu clear. He had sent out a band of troops to patrol the mountain passes where bandits lurked. In his mind this day was not a coming-of-age feast but a political event. There would be baked peacocks draped in their feathered skins as if still alive, saffron rice steamed with an equal weight of sesame seeds, whole kid goats roasted in butter, betel leaves wrapped in silver foil, honey wine to drink, rose conserve whose scent almost induced a swoon, barley beer in huge casks as the night worn on, and women's flesh offered in dark private alcoves for dessert. But all this richness was actually a show of force. His guests knew it. Most of them appeared on Suddhodana's orders, not by invitation. He was presented with the delicate task of transferring their fear and respect, which had been owed to him over many bloody years, to his son. The prospect filled him with gloom.

His eye shifted to the tower where Siddhartha was waiting before his official appearance. "I don't want you mingling. Don't greet anybody, don't let anyone see you. We want them to feel awe when they first set eyes on you. This is your stage, and you have to master it completely."

"I will do all you ask," Siddhartha replied.

"Stop it, I don't want words. What good have words ever done me? This is the first day of your future. Unless you fill them with fear, these people will one day turn into your enemies, that I promise."

"Fear?" Siddhartha considered the word as if it came from a foreign tongue. "I'm not a threat. Why not keep it that way?"

"Because fear is policy. It's protection. People are either at your feet or at your throat. It's up to you which one." Suddhodana delivered these axioms with complete conviction.

"You protect me, and I'm not afraid of you," Siddhartha reminded him. This was true. The distance between father and son had wavered over the years, sometimes reaching a pole of complete misunderstanding. But Siddhartha had never been afraid of his father or of what disobedience might bring out in him. As he had grown, the prince acquired a combination of qualities that baffled the king: mildness alongside courage, patience shored up by will, trust combined with sharpness of mind. Suddhodana could never predict which one would emerge. He was reminded every day that two different people seemed to live inside one skin.

"Hasn't the Brahmin taught you anything?" the king burst out impatiently. "What I'm telling you is real, it's true. Without creating fear, you can't get respect. Without respect, you can't have peace among potential enemies. Once it comes to bloodshed, nobody is afraid enough. Passion makes men fight to the death, and fear in battle is forgotten or despised. It's useless once the swords are drawn. But fear will keep men from getting to bloodshed, if you manage it right."

This wasn't a studied speech, but it was no impulsive outburst, either. Suddhodana had planned to confront his son with the realities of a king's existence. The time had to be ripe; the boy had to be old enough to accept the lesson but not so old that he would imagine himself wiser than his father. Suddhodana could only pray that his timing was right. He studied Siddhartha's face for a reaction.

"How is fear managed?" asked Siddhartha. His hesitant tone wasn't encouraging, but at least he had asked the right question.

"Fear should be applied like medicine," his father replied. "Use just enough as a remedy but not so much that it becomes a poison. Medicine isn't pleasant. But the pain it causes cures a greater pain." Suddhodana had practiced this analogy until he thought it was easy to understand and forceful enough to be remembered.

"Fate has dealt us a fortunate hand," Suddhodana went on. "We have the mountains to the north and west guarding our backs. I've fought on that front occasionally, but my eye keeps looking east. To the east you have strong kings, in Magadha and Kosala. Together they could overwhelm us by sheer numbers. They are almost strong enough to do it without allying. But they don't attack because I inflicted pain on them first. I bit their throats like a small dog that can drive back a bigger one because it's more fierce. The big dog will remember the bite and forget that its enemy is actually smaller."

"You cast a spell," Siddhartha said. It was a peculiar remark, and it stopped his father cold.

"More than a spell. I killed real men. One day you will too."

There, I've said it. He had put before his son an inevitability, not simply a possibility. "A king has never existed who didn't fight and kill," he said with emphasis.

"So I'll have to decide," Siddhartha said. His thoughtful tone angered the king.

"No, there is nothing to decide. If you can't get that into your head—" Suddhodana stopped himself. He remembered that he had the gods on his side. However confused the prince might be, he was still young, and his birth chart explicitly promised what lay ahead. There was no need to intimidate or goad him. Suddhodana changed tack. "I shouldn't have said that. What I meant was, if you can't do this for me, you are not the son I know you to be."

Siddhartha had accepted this milder rebuke calmly. He parted respectfully from his father, each of them satisfied that he had been successful in disguising how alone and abandoned he actually felt. Now, as the king gazed gloomily toward the tower where Siddhartha was waiting, there was no return gaze. His son had flung himself on the floor, throwing off his suffocating robes and that absurd feathered turban. He buried his head in a pile of pillows, trying not to think of anything at all. His misery would have been simpler to bear if he had hated his father or wanted to thwart his will.

He had followed the dictates of his upbringing to the letter, had mastered the martial arts and excelled in mock battles. He had felt the exultation of downing an opponent on the field. So why did he feel like a coward, like someone who confidently marches to the edge of a cliff, only to find that he cannot take the last step? The last step was inevitable. Every day of his life had led to it. Siddhartha felt a sick dread in the pit of his stomach.

THE FEAST HAD GONE ON two full hours, the guests growing engorged and drunk as course followed course. Suddhodana alone drank nothing, and when he sensed that the time was right, he raised his goblet. "In my son's name I have spent half of my treasury on this day." He paused. "I have overseen every detail of your comfort and enjoyment. I personally examined every woman at court, and the ugly ones were banished to my friend Bimbisara's kingdom—" A burst of appreciative laughter. Suddhodana waited for it to die away.

"—where they are considered the most beautiful women in the land."

More laughter rose, this time raucous and mixed with applause. Even Bimbisara, the powerful ruler of Magadha, smiled and clapped, though his smile was tight and unpleasant to look on. He was one of the few guests who had come of his own accord, no doubt for concealed reasons.

When he was sure that the drunken guests were quiet and the astute ones were paying close attention, Suddhodana said, "I'm here to confess a precious secret, one that I have kept for half my reign." His voice rose dramatically. "Heed me, all of you!" He threw down his goblet with a clatter, ending the last few scattered conversations that had continued.

"After his beloved mother died, I summoned seers to Siddhartha's cradle. And they told me the most incredible news. About one who was destined to rule the world." Suddhodana paused and let the silence return. "This soul wasn't destined to rule a tiny kingdom. He was going to be given the world! Do you have any idea what that means?"

Suddhodana abandoned his throne and stepped down to his audience's level. The two chained leopards that flanked him followed behind until they reached the ends of their restraints and were jerked back. They growled, their tails twitching lazily.

"It means that it won't matter anymore that your lands are greater than mine," Suddhodana said, pointing to one of his peers, "or that your army is twice the size of mine," he pointed at another, "or that your father was a damned conniving murderer who tried to seize my father's throne."

The last man he pointed to recoiled. His hand dropped to the sword belted at his waist. For a moment he battled with his better judgment. Finally he broke eye contact and took his hand from his weapon. Suddhodana walked away, smiling in triumph. "Hate me all you want," he invited. "Plot all you dare." He turned back toward his throne. "My son will swallow all your kingdoms for supper. He'll buy and sell oceans, continents!"

The whispers of confusion and disquiet that trailed after Suddhodana subsided as his threats swept over the guests. Everyone was as superstitious of the gods as Suddhodana.

"Incredible?" he challenged. "No! I've seen it. I've seen all that will unfold."

At that moment a movement to the side caught his eye. Siddhartha was standing in the doorway, looking resplendent in his new bejeweled coat.

"Ah," Suddhodana cried, gesturing toward his son, "here he is." To himself he thought, *I've done all I can. Take the stage or pay the price.*

Siddhartha stared around him. Over the years he'd seen only a few of these faces. He took a step into the gathering. No one reached for his hand or made the slightest sound. He looked to his father for a sign and received an imperceptible nod. Siddhartha forced himself to go forward, wanting nothing more than to retreat to his room. His thoughts raced; they seemed deafeningly loud in the silence of the banquet tent.

"Come!"

His father called out for him, seeing that his son this time would not fail. Siddhartha began to notice those around him. The looks on some people's faces seemed wary, but other faces were stark; they spoke of awe and dread.

What did he say to them?

Siddhartha knew that anything was possible. His father was a man of great words when he wanted to be. Suddhodana held out his hand. "Come, great king, come!"

Feeling strangely as if he were watching someone else's body moving forward, Siddhartha felt his knees quiver, as if they would not hold. He took another step, and then another. When he was almost to his father, the king began clapping, slowly at first, then gaining speed. One or two guests joined in hesitantly, but Suddhodana didn't stop, and others now joined in, putting more heart into their efforts. The clamor built. Thunderous noise washed over the feast, drowning out all other sounds. .

When Siddhartha reached his father's side, Suddhodana gathered him in a fierce embrace and held him tight. The king was beaming with triumph.

"You've won your future," he whispered. "No one else could do it but you." He brushed tears from his son's cheeks.

Father, Siddhartha thought, *what have you done?*

IN THE TUMULT of cheering for Siddhartha, one man felt as much hatred as the king felt joy and pride. Devadatta bolted from the tent. His hands shook with the effort it took not to attack his cousin. For the first time in his life he realized how alone he was and how hopeless his situation.

The injustice of it was suffocating him. Hadn't he been trapped at court for ten long years, presenting a thousand opportunities for the king to compare his weakling son to someone who took ambition seriously? Unable to restrain himself, Devadatta shouted, "Fools! Bastards!" But his imprecations were drowned in the clamor of the celebration.

He collided with two servants bearing trays of honey wine, figs, and pomegranates, knocking them and their load to the ground. They cried out, and Devadatta's feet slid on a brown smear of fig pulp. He righted himself, barely noticing the havoc he'd created.

Both of them were idiots. The king and his make-believe warrior prince who would inherit the world. The prospect would have been sickening if it weren't so absurd.

Someone else had a stake in the evening's outcome. Mara had long ago invaded Devadatta's mind, had colored his jaundiced perceptions and fueled his resentment. Only one thing was missing. The captive prince had never invited him in, had never consciously allied himself with darkness. That might change now. Mara had the advantage, as all demons do, of knowing just how fragile reality actually is, built by the invisible hands of imagination and belief.

As long as Mara was merely a phantom, Siddhartha could keep him suppressed with other figments of his darker imagining.

Wisps of the mind, though toxic, are not mortal threats. Mara could not drive the boy insane; Siddhartha did not harbor the necessary seeds of delusion. To destroy him, the demon needed a completely dedicated ally, a vehicle for evil who had no thought of his own soul. Such an ally would be recklessly evil, but in that he would not be unique. His uniqueness would lie in remaining unmoved by Siddhartha's compassion; he would hate it and want it destroyed. Would Devadatta give him that precious opening?

Watching Devadatta continue his enraged progress toward the royal apartments, Mara decided to precipitate a crisis. He couldn't use brute force, but an enticing accident opened another way. Devadatta happened to pass by the room where a certain girl waited. She was unsuspecting and vulnerable. To bring forth a demon in the flesh, nothing works better than flesh itself.

It was no trick at all to turn Devadatta's rage in the direction of lust. Mara wafted a faint perfume in his nostrils, planted an arousing image of swelling breasts, whispered in Devadatta's ear that he could not rest tonight until he forced his will on somebody whose pain would bring him pleasure. Mara pushed the small switches needed. Devadatta barely suspected that he was being manipulated. He only knew that he had to have a woman *now*. The insidious mechanism, so subtle in its creation, so violent in its outcome, was set.

SUJATA STARED WITH LONGING out the high open window, placed close enough to the banquet tent that she could hear music rise and fall on the evening breeze. By the light of torches she saw Siddhartha approach in his resplendent outfit, and her fraught emotions made her believe that she saw him shudder as he entered. Catching sight of him made *her* shudder. She couldn't completely understand what this meant. She was only fifteen, but that's old enough to understand many things. For instance, she understood that she must never tell anyone her real story.

Kumbira had gathered Sujata with the other unmarried young women to watch the spectacle from a distance. This would be their sole participation until the secret hour when the men would be allowed near them.

"Here's a cream to rub out dark spots and lime juice to tighten wrinkles," Kumbira said, herding them around a table like an anxious madam whose girls must please if she wants to be paid. She had never seduced a man herself, but she was obsessed with the tricks of seduction. Buckets of snow bundled in straw had been fetched by runners from the mountains so the girls could dip their breasts in ice water to firm them up. "Those of you who are smart won't eat tonight, but if you are starving, no onions and lots of sweet fennel seed."

Only Sujata had held back, bored and detached from the excited preparations. She even considered paying a lower servant to sneak radishes and onions into her room since she didn't want to attract any men that night. Any but one. Their toilette complete, the other ladies-in-waiting sat on pillows near the balcony, dreamily feeding their fantasies. They wore gauzy sleeping gowns. Bowls of food covered the low settees in the center of the room. A few woman nibbled and gossiped lazily.

Was I ever so young? Kumbira wondered. She eyed them with envy and dislike. Scraps of conversation floated past her like eiderdown. "Did you see what she was wearing? It might have looked good on her ten years ago." "Do you suppose she knows?" "Knows? Her lover beats her and won't give her money for a thing." Kumbira couldn't remember being like that, ever, but she must have been. And now she knew as much about the empire as the king himself, although it would be her head if she ever told anyone.

Kumbira watched the young girl sitting apart from the others. She ate from a bowl of grapes, one at a time. Since she had arrived, brought to court at night in a ramshackle wagon with torches on either side, then rushed into the women's quarters without a proper introduction to anyone, Sujata had kept her own counsel. Kumbira hoped that the girl, whoever she was, had a strong sense of self-preservation. She must realize the danger in luring the attentions of a prince like Siddhartha.

The door curtains suddenly exploded in billows of velvet, and through them burst Devadatta. It was too early, and Kumbira saw immediately that he was in a state.

"Hush!" she warned the girls, who had started squealing and drawing together like startled mice. Devadatta brought danger with him, not seduction. Kumbira strode forward, putting herself between the intruder and her charges. "You're not allowed in here," she snapped.

Devadatta scowled insolently. "I didn't come for you, hag. I want one of *them*. That one." He pointed to Sujata.

Kumbira's first impulse was to let him take her. She couldn't turn him away, not aroused and angry. If she summoned the guards, provided they weren't too drunk to put up a fight, they couldn't lay hands on someone protected by the king. Perhaps it would be better if Devadatta used her and Siddhartha found out about it. That course of action would nip the prince's interest in the bud. The king wouldn't appreciate complications.

But Sujata drew back, eyes wide with fright and her hand to her mouth. Her pulse beat rapidly in the hollow of her throat. Kumbira's eyes weren't so old that she couldn't see that. She felt herself moved to protect the girl. And perhaps the prince as well.

Devadatta crossed the room. The other girls parted as if they were the wake left by his rage. He closed his fist on Sujata's arm. Terrified, she tried to pull away. She dared not struggle because striking a member of the royal family would put her in peril. Her fear made Devadatta's eyes glint. Even the small fight she put up brought a predator's smile of anticipation to his lips.

"Young prince," Kumbira said in a level tone that she hoped wouldn't provoke him. "I appreciate your lust. But not this one."

Devadatta glared at her. "Why not?"

Leaning close, Kumbira whispered, "It's her day of the month."

"You're lying." Devadatta studied Kumbira's face suspiciously. It wasn't in his nature to be blocked; there would be an outlet tonight, everything else be damned. "If she is untouchable, why is she here with clean women?"

But Kumbira had learned two generations ago to lie. She did it with a flat voice and no trace of defensiveness, maintaining eye contact. "She should be isolated, yes. But I'm old and softhearted, and this being a royal feast day—"

Devadatta cut her off. "Softhearted as a cobra, you old whore."

Kumbira held his gaze, not giving him any indication that she disapproved of the way he treated her. She knew how to follow up a lie. Devadatta turned away and grabbed another girl. This one went willingly, even though he almost yanked her off her feet.

Sujata turned to Kumbira like someone in shock. Without warning, she fell against Kumbira's breast, gripping her tight enough to hurt. "Thank you," she whispered urgently. "Thank you a thousand times."

The nakedness of the girl's feelings moved Kumbira. In her long life of tough resilience and calculation, only Siddhartha had ever had such an effect on her. She almost wrapped the girl, who had broken down in tears, in her embrace.

Then she caught herself and realized what she was about to do—with all the others watching, girls who had no pity for Sujata and would be deriding her the moment they were alone. Grabbing Sujata by the shoulders, Kumbira pushed her away. "You think I did this for you?"

A confused look filled Sujata's face. She wiped away her tears with the backs of her hands.

"What kind of ninnies are they sending to court?" Kumbira demanded. She reached into her sari and took out the gold coin Siddhartha had given her. "You're paid for," Kumbira said brutally. "By the prince."

"Oh." Sujata's voice was flat and weak.

"He'd never forgive me if I broke our bargain," Kumbira added. "Not without consulting him first."

The room was silent. The others knew they were witnessing a choice humiliation, fodder for backdoor gossips. Imperceptibly gaining control, Sujata drew herself up. "In two seconds you've been kind and cruel to me. What am I supposed to think?"

"Think yourself lucky," Kumbira snapped. "Try that." She turned her attention back to the others. "Now go back to your dinner, all of you. And don't stink up your breath," she warned.

Sujata remained standing there, her gaze locked on Kumbira.

Impudent girl, Kumbira thought. Still, she had some backbone, and the old woman wouldn't want that to be totally crushed. "You've got breasts like a suckled sow. Go to your room and take some ice water to firm them up with. It's going to be a long night."

There was general tittering, and Sujata gasped in embarrassed hurt. She turned and fled the room. Kumbira didn't watch her go. She had done Sujata a secret kindness by driving her away, and none of the others suspected it. Kumbira's role wasn't to bring Siddhartha and the girl together, but at least she could keep the greedy hands of other men off her.

Kumbira walked toward the window and wished she were watching Siddhartha in his glory. Cheers and applause rang once more from below. It must be past midnight. She smiled and thought of how proud the old king must be. And how drunk.

THE GREAT FEAST had wound down. The bulk of the guests had already retired or collapsed in a stupor. It was only a few hours before dawn. Siddhartha stepped over them and left the tent without his father noticing. The king sat in a heavy drowse, his head lolling on his chest. Siddhartha had made a show of drinking to every raucous toast but had actually sipped very little. He needed a clear head to make good his escape.

Tonight, after all the years of being kept like a nightingale in a gilded cage, he would be free. Excitement coursed through Siddhartha. He hurried back to his apartments and didn't bother lighting a candle. He'd lived all of his life inside these rooms and could make his way around them in the dark. Moving quickly, he packed a traveling sack, rolling a few clothes inside. He didn't know what to take or how much. He didn't want to be recognized as the king's son, so he packed rough breeches and shirts that he wore in the stables.

He slid his sword through his sash and secured it at his hip. All the travelers he'd talked to had agreed that the roads were dangerous. He'd share the common risk of being robbed, but if his identity were ever discovered, there would be the added one of kidnapping for ransom. He added some bread, dried fruit, and what few coins he possessed. Inside the palace walls he had never needed money; outside them he was genuinely poor. The coins came from Channa and various young nobles in games of chance or when he sold them trinkets he knew his father wouldn't miss.

Just as he was finishing, the ponderous closing of the main gates reverberated inside Siddhartha's room. He ran to the window and peered out. Moonlight burned cool against his bare skin. Below in the central courtyard the guards staggered to their posts, proving that the liquor had made its way to the barracks. The new arrivals shot the bolts on the gates; the noise was as loud as an ax splitting wood. Those portals had stood against armies who had fought against his father, as witnessed by the hacked scars that decorated their exterior.

Siddhartha heaved the laden sack over his shoulder and fled, going quietly down the stairs. A throbbing drummed in his ears. Only a short distance on, he paused and heard muffled voices through the walls. It sounded like men arguing. Siddhartha shifted the sack's weight and pressed on. He kept his hand on his sword hilt so it wouldn't strike anything. Dark shadows filled the hallway; the torches in their sconces had long guttered out.

Then a sudden movement in the shadows sent him into hiding against the wall. Siddhartha went flat and stopped breathing. The cold stone wall leached the warmth from his body. He watched intently for a while before relaxing enough to start breathing again. But as he started forward, the shifting shape returned like a shadow puppet against a dark screen. This time he saw that it was a woman. She was slim hipped and moved quickly on light feet. Her face and glowing eyes were visible for a fleeting second in a bar of moonlight.

Sujata?

She paused as if she could hear him thinking her name. What was she doing here? Siddhartha started to softly call out, but before he could, she turned and ran down the hallway as if in a panic. Siddhartha's escape plan vanished from his thoughts. He let his sack slide from his shoulder to the floor and ran after her.

As he rounded the next corner he saw the figure—he was certain now it must be Sujata—disappear through a doorway. He followed her into the royal gardens, not daring to call out, knowing that amours were taking place in hidden nooks among the camellias and roses. The gardens had been designed by his mother. Maya had intended them to be a place of eternal fascination, and the centerpiece was an intricate knot, a maze crafted with topiary dragons and elephants, along with fabulous sea monsters like the magan and the mythical karaweik bird of hypnotic song. The sweet smell of night blossoms thickened the air. Sujata paused at the entrance to the maze and looked back over her shoulder. Her expression was inscrutable.

"Wait!" Siddhartha raised his voice, more intent on the fleeing girl than on preserving his anonymity. He tried to use the tone of command that his father had mastered. Instead, Sujata vanished into the maze.

Siddhartha was helplessly drawn; he ran toward the entrance and ducked inside. The tall walls of the maze closed in around him, and the darkness became more complete. He ran, listening for her footsteps, shifting through twists and turns to follow the sounds she made. Then they stopped. If she had been as close as he thought, Siddhartha would have tripped over her by now. Footsteps sounded to his left, on the other side of the hedge wall. He tried to slip through the tangled growth, but the greenery was packed too tight.

"It's me, Sujata. Stay where you are. You're safe."

Siddhartha put his hand on the left wall of the maze. It guided him back to the last turn, and this time he took the route he'd passed up before. At that moment the moon disappeared behind a cloud, and in the darkness he ran into somebody blocking the way.

"Sujata?" he whispered.

Her voice came back, and it was very close. "How fitting. You're lost in the maze of your mind, and now you're lost in this maze."

Siddhartha was startled by Sujata's arrogant tone, but it was definitely her voice. "I saw you running away. Are you in trouble?"

"I'm never in trouble. I make trouble."

Sujata's voice had deepened, and despite his attraction to her, Siddhartha instinctively took a step backward. His eyes had adjusted to the dark, and he perceived that the figure before him was not the curved, slim-hipped girl.

"Who are you?" Siddhartha's hand went to the hilt of his sword, though he wondered how much use a weapon would be against a magician, if that was what he was confronting. Canki had told him that such beings existed and must be countered through ritual observances that made a person immune to spells and malevolent magic.

"I can be her if that makes you more comfortable. I can be whoever you imagine." The shadowy figure stepped closer, and there was no doubt that its voice was now a man's.

"Have you hurt her? Where is she?"

The stranger drew himself up; he smoothed his long-nailed fingers against the sides of his robe. "How do you know I'm not her? How do we know who anyone really is?"

"I'm going back." Siddhartha made a move to leave, but the stranger's voice spoke again with a peculiar allure.

"You think that if I take her shape she must be in danger? You could be right. The greatest danger she faces right now, however, is from you."

Siddhartha's temper flared. "Deceiver! Whoever you are, either fight me or leave me in peace."

The stranger's voice took on an aggrieved tone. "You mistake me, young sir. I've come to bring you peace, only peace. How can I convince you?"

The moon had come out again, and Siddhartha saw that he was confronting a tall young man, somewhat older than himself, who could have been his cousin, Devadatta. For a moment he almost called out Devadatta's name, but he realized that this encounter couldn't be anything but supernatural.

"Don't you recognize me?" the tall young man said. "I'm the son your father always wanted, the one you could become."

Darkness couldn't conceal the truth of what the stranger said. Siddhartha was looking at himself a few years older. "What is your purpose here? I am already the son my father wants." Despite his attempt to sound confident, the stranger laughed at him.

"Your father wants a son who steals away in the night without a word? I'm surprised. He has worked so hard to keep you here. But I understand. Fathers don't know everything. It's right that they shouldn't." The stranger's voice had a sinuous ability to shift between arrogance, familiarity, and cajolery. It stung and soothed at the same time. Siddhartha was feeling uncertain, and although the stranger made no threatening gestures, the mere sight of him drained Siddhartha's body; he felt slack and weak.

"You won't succeed, you know," the stranger said. "At escaping, I mean. This is your rightful place. We just have to decide how you are to occupy it."

The stranger was taunting him and making no effort to disguise it. "Tell me your name," Siddhartha demanded.

"Siddhartha."

"Then you are only a mocking demon, and I mistook you for someone of power."

The stranger's fingers curled like a cat deciding whether to use its claws or keep them retracted. "Don't be rash. I'm here because I know you. Don't act surprised, either. It's time to be frank, isn't it? A prince who is running away from a throne must be very confused, don't you agree?"

Mara watched Siddhartha hesitate in his reply. His bantering with the youth had not been for his own amusement. It went deeper than that. The shapes he took, the words he spoke were all part of a test. He wanted to find the best way to penetrate Siddhartha's mind, and so he circled it like a surgeon finding the exact place for the first cut.

"I didn't tell you my name because I was a little offended," said Mara. "You know me very well, and yet you offered no greeting. Is that any way to behave?"

Siddhartha shuddered slightly. He had never seen this shape before, but the voice in the darkness raised faint, troubled memories of a voice he had once heard in his head. Visions of his mother's lifeless body shrieked through his mind.

"See," Mara hissed. "He's starting to be convinced."

Then the demon's body jerked fitfully, twisting and bending in places where there were no joints. The tall young man became a floppy doll, which collapsed to the ground. Now its limbs folded into one another, turning into a crouched dwarf. Siddhartha froze in place, and the hummock became a formless mass that palpitated, waiting to take on whatever form his terror dictated.

Whether from horror or a reserve of strength that he didn't know he possessed, Siddhartha's mind became silent, without thought.

"Nothing to say to me? Really?" Mara taunted. "After all we've been through." Now Siddhartha saw a funeral pyre, a skull crumbling to ashes. His nostrils were filled with the stench of death.

Mara was confident that these reminders would create a crack, that riding the crest of terror, he could penetrate Siddhartha's mind. It was important to Mara that he do this, because to bring down the prince by his own fear was far better than using a tool, even one as talented as Devadatta.

"I don't know what you're talking about," Siddhartha said quietly. It was a deceptive quiet because inside himself he felt a battle being fought on the edge of awareness. It wasn't a battle of words or images; everything proceeded silently, like a creeping epidemic or like foul, noxious air seeping through a cracked windowpane.

This was no stranger. Siddhartha had known all along who he was and that his name was Mara. He felt trapped and helpless. All his life he had endured the demon's attentions on the periphery of his mind.

"What do you want of me?"

Mara offered his hand. "I want to teach you. I want to help." He smiled, but the taint of his intentions marred the effort. Siddhartha didn't take the proffered hand. He sank on the ground, burying his face between his knees. If he was the special target of Mara's intentions, there must be a reason. It could be great sin or great weakness on his part, but Siddhartha knew this wasn't the case. It was nothing he had ever done that attracted the demon. Therefore, it had to be something he *might* do. The fact that he hadn't defeated Mara in one night didn't mean he would always fail.

Mara scowled, watching the motionless youth crouched before him. It was a delicate moment. He could feel the workings of Siddhartha's mind; gradually the crack that Mara had found began to close up again. Siddhartha began to feel calmer. His mind had created a train of argument that he could believe in. He would vanquish the demon, not by resisting him but by finding a place that was already safe from him. Siddhartha didn't know where that place was yet, but with an uncanny certainty he knew it existed. Siddhartha looked up, seeing the full moon overhead, and he realized that no one was looming over him anymore and no shadow appeared except the one cast by the high walls of the maze.

Mara, who had shed his mortal form, watched the prince leave without pursuing him. The demon felt that a great secret had been stripped from him, and by someone so guileless and young. Siddhartha had figured out that demons enter the mind when we resist them. The stronger our efforts to fortify ourselves against temptation, the stronger temptation has us in its grip. Mara sighed. But his confidence wasn't shaken. He still had his allies. The coming battle would be interesting, which wasn't often the case. He was irked, but he wouldn't be defeated. Of that Mara could be certain.

8

The day after the banquet everyone's attention shifted to the king's entertainments and the part that his son, now elevated in the world's eyes, would play. No one saw the prince, however. The next morning Canki was summoned to Suddhodana's chambers, where he found father and son huddled together. Siddhartha looked away, lost in his own private world. Obviously his father had been hammering at him, with less and less effect.

"Tell him," Suddhodana commanded the moment Canki entered the room. "Put some sense in his head. He has to understand how serious this is."

"The prince knows his duties very well, Your Highness," Canki began.

Jumping to his feet Suddhodana erupted. "Stop it! I don't need a politician. The boy doesn't understand anything."

"What exactly is the matter?" Canki resorted to his most placating tone.

Suddhodana glared at him. "I've arranged mock combats for tomorrow. The army has been readied. I want *him*"—he pointed at his son—"to fight the way he's supposed to."

Canki turned to Siddhartha. "And you refused? I'm surprised."

Siddhartha kept silent. Canki already knew about the war games and the zeal that Suddhodana had put into them. The king didn't want to stop at creating awe among his guests. He wanted them to witness firsthand what would happen to anyone who had secret hopes of defeating the son after the father was gone.

It was like going back to old times. The army had been roused from its long, lazy slumber. "Tell them they're fighting for real," Suddhodana had ordered. "Three gold pieces to the bloodiest warriors at the end of the day. Nothing impresses like blood." Instead of dulling their swords and padding themselves with straw, his soldiers prepared to give and take real wounds. The only limit was that no blow should be deliberately fatal. "If you hit him and he doesn't get up again, consider your enemy dead, for this one day only," the generals instructed.

From the Shiva temple's perch on the hill, Canki had looked over the plain stretched before the palace, filled day after day with military exercises. Suddhodana rode among his troops, nodding with approval the bloodier the games got. Behind him rode Siddhartha, looking pensive but raising no objections. Obviously, however, when the time came for him to lead the combat, he had balked.

Canki didn't want to be caught between them, but he didn't dare disobey the king. "Are you afraid to fight?" he asked Siddhartha. The prince shook his head but didn't offer a word to defend himself.

"I've seen him with Channa. They go at it. No, it's something else, something he won't tell me," Suddhodana grumbled.

Ignoring the presence of the priest, Siddhartha threw himself flat on the floor and seized his father's feet. Suddhodana turned away, embarrassed by this show of humility, which to him expressed weakness. "For God's sake, get up!"

"I won't, not unless I can speak freely."

Suddhodana's eyes wandered the room in confusion. "Whatever you want. Just get up."

But Siddhartha didn't. His face touching the stone floor, he said, "I have never been what you wanted, and the more you demand, the less I am."

"If you're not what I wanted, then what are you?" the king said, now more bewildered than angry.

"I don't know."

"Ridiculous! I know who you are. *He* knows who you are." Suddhodana looked at Canki, asking for support. The priest was at a loss. Canki was in service to a warrior king, but at heart he despised violence and had contempt for those who used it to get whatever they wanted. Kings were no better than murderers, the only difference being that they had a legal monopoly on killing. The Brahmin's way was one of guile, patience, persuasion. To him, those were marks of superiority.

After a moment, he knelt beside Siddhartha and placed a hand on his shoulder. "Do what is asked of you. If you go one step at a time, everything will come easier. This is only a shadow, a charade of war. How will you know about yourself until you try?"

Skillful as he imagined himself to be, Canki had no effect on the prince, who ignored him and kept his eyes fixed on his father. "I want to go away," he said.

A chill passed through Suddhodana's body, a cold premonition of failure. "No, that isn't possible," he said in a flat, toneless voice. "Ask me for anything else, but not that."

The sudden weakness in his father's voice stirred Siddhartha, and he got slowly to his feet. "What have I said that makes you so disturbed? If you love me, let me see what lies beyond these walls."

"You know nothing about my love," snapped Suddhodana. He gazed into his son's eyes, and what he saw there couldn't be answered. Turning abruptly, the king left the room, pausing a moment at the door to signal to the high Brahmin. "No more words. Leave him be."

CANKI SAT IN HIS STUDY, a plate of sesame rice uneaten by his side. His mind was filled with the troubles to come when the world discovered, as surely it would, the rift between king and prince. The Brahmin's thoughts were interrupted by a soft knock at his door. He had to conceal his surprise when it opened and Siddhartha, unannounced and alone, entered.

"Tell me about the gods," he said.

Canki smiled easily. He pushed aside the plate of sesame rice, wondering inside if he shouldn't be worried. To side with the prince, or to even seem to, could soon be an act of treason.

"I attend to the gods," said Canki. "You don't have to concern yourself with them."

"But what do the gods want?" asked Siddhartha. "Why would they curse someone? Can a person sin and not know it?"

Canki cleared his throat to hide his momentary confusion. He had never known Siddhartha to confide in him, or to openly show anxiety. The youth was guarded, as princes should be. The priest decided not to ask why the sudden interest in curses.

"You want to know how to get into favor with the gods?" he said. "And so you should. It's commendable." Siddhartha, for the first time, placed himself at the priest's feet, in the classic pose of a disciple asking his master for wisdom.

"The gods allow great suffering—wars, famine, crime, and immorality—because the people have forgotten how to please them," Canki said. "Since no one can be perfectly good, there is much sin in the world. Rituals and sacrifices honor the gods and erase that sin."

"But everyone honors the gods, and not everyone is happy," Siddhartha pointed out. "Why does misfortune visit us?"

Canki waved his hands, pointing to piles of scriptures written on dried palm leaves and vellum, hundreds of scrolls lining the shelves of his cramped, airless study. "Every sin is a karma, and every karma has a precise remedy. It takes years to delve deep enough. You study and try to understand every detail. The invisible world is complex. The gods are fickle. Even then you may fail."

"Have you ever failed?"

Canki was taken aback. "Brahmins cannot fail. Every word in the scriptures was delivered to a Brahmin."

"And no one else? The gods have to find a priest or they don't talk?"

Canki had a ready answer. It was his job to know all the answers, but he hesitated, his mind searching for a solution. Despite all the king's efforts, his son was turning the other way. His deeper nature hadn't been diverted. Canki wasn't alarmed, however. Now he had a chance to influence Siddhartha, and it might be his last. He looked at the youth sitting at his feet and decided that the canniest course, for once, was to tell the truth. He said, "You are among the few who can understand. I've always sensed that, ever since you were a little child."

He leaned closer and put his hand on Siddhartha's shoulder. He had no real affection for his pupil, but experience told him that physical contact was a more powerful bond than words. "I want to tell you about the Golden Age." He ignored Siddhartha's puzzled look, pressing his fingers into the youth's flesh. "Just listen. There was an age, long, long ago, when the world was perfect. The scriptures tell us that no one had to struggle. There was no evil or wrongdoing. Abundance was the only life that people knew. But then decay gradually set in. This perfect world was only possible because the gods kept the demons at bay, unable to touch human beings and create mischief. Would you wish to bring back such an age?"

Siddhartha started. "Me?"

"It was prophesied when you were born that you could be the king of a new Golden Age. Your father knows this. Why else would he protect you so strongly, covet your safety above everything else?"

Siddhartha was hanging onto the Brahmin's words now, and Canki smiled knowingly to himself. The prince was listening so eagerly because he felt guilty. He thought he had committed some obscure sin, which was being punished by his imprisonment in the palace.

"Your father loves you, but he's also in awe of you. If he ruins the chance to bring back the Golden Age, how much guilt will he carry for the next hundred lifetimes?"

Siddhartha considered this seriously. "So he's not disappointed in me?"

"On the contrary, the failure he's anxious about is his own. You must prove to him that he has raised you as the gods and the stars prophesied. If you can do that, you will both be favored for the rest of your lives. If not—" Canki held his breath for a reaction. He had his private doubts about the destiny that awaited Siddhartha. There had been little evidence so far of a great warrior or a great saint in him.

"Tell me about demons," said Siddhartha abruptly.

Now it was Canki's turn to be startled. *Demons?* The Brahmin almost replied, "Have you met a demon?" Then Canki caught himself and realized that bluntness wouldn't work, not with a withdrawn youth just coming out of his shell.

"Don't worry about demons; they are indestructible and beyond your reach to defeat them. Worry about men who have taken evil to heart. There will be no Golden Age until they are defeated," said Canki. "You may find it impossible to believe that this all depends on you, but I am willing to risk that you can accept the truth."

Siddhartha stood up, his demeanor more serious. Canki could see that his words had sunk in. He had dangled a mystery before the youth, and few can resist a mystery, particularly one that features themselves at the very center.

SUDDHODANA HAD SULKED in his room, at first furious with his son, then gradually sinking into moroseness. To face rebellion from the prince just at the moment of victory was too galling to endure. Then moroseness changed to grief. Suddhodana was certain that he had lost his son.

That night the king awoke with a start. A shadowy figure had entered his rooms. Suddhodana fumbled for the table by his bed, reaching for a bell to summon the guards.

"Don't be afraid, father." Siddhartha's voice was soft in the darkness. "I will fight."

CANKI SAT IN THE GRANDSTANDS with the dignitaries, fanned by slaves waving palm leaves over their heads and charmed by veiled girls passing sweetmeats. He assumed that his talk with Siddhartha had turned the tide. But still there was danger. The prince had come around, but for how long? He was erratic, unpredictable.

The Brahmin remembered the king's threat from years ago: *Just live long enough to see what I'll do to you if this plan fails.*

As a public show of force, the mock battles were a success. The sheer bulk of Suddhodana's army, and the ferocity of his fighters, impressed the neighboring rulers and depressed their generals. There was a ripple of shock when one of the archers mounted on horseback was killed, but Canki had wandered away by then and witnessed nothing, not even the ladies-in-waiting who fainted and had to be carried from the scene.

By leaving early, Canki had missed the one part of the combats that in the end really mattered.

Siddhartha's surrender to his father's will was not a sham. He dressed himself early that morning in his armor, dismissing his father's grooms because he was ashamed to be seen donning so much padding and protection; he was the one fighter who couldn't risk being bloodied.

"Not that anyone is going to get near you, much less fight."

Siddhartha wheeled around. Devadatta had come in, not bothering to knock. He smiled maliciously. "They've got you pretty packed in. Why bother? You could go out there buck naked and nobody would so much as scratch you. Unless they want to be dragged out of bed tomorrow morning to kiss the chopping block."

Siddhartha clenched his jaw. "They have to fight me if I start it first. I'm not going out there just to watch."

"Of course you're not." Recently Devadatta had become more brazen in his contempt. He bent over and occupied himself with the intricate thong laces of his leggings.

"You can challenge me if you want," Siddhartha said quietly.

Devadatta burst out laughing. "You can't be serious."

"Why not?" Siddhartha stood up and faced his cousin squarely. The two were almost matched in height and strength by now despite the four years separating them. But Siddhartha knew he had one great advantage: Devadatta was so arrogant that he rarely practiced. He may have lost his fighting edge without knowing it or being able to admit it to himself.

"What weapon?" Devadatta looked intrigued now.

"Sword and dagger." Finished with his equipage, Siddhartha rested his helmet in the crook of his arm. "They're expecting me."

"Naturally. The carnival goes on."

The two cousins exchanged nods in mock courtesy, and Siddhartha left. When he got to the stables he found Channa holding the reins of his favorite white stallion. The horse had come to the king from the wilds, and at first nobody could tame him. But Siddhartha spotted the animal's fear and used it. Every time he brought a stick of sugar cane for the stallion, he would sit and wait as long as it took for the horse to walk over to him. He never approached on his own, even if it took an hour for the animal to calm down.

When he was tempted enough, the horse wanted to snatch the treat and run off, but Siddhartha made sure that his hand always touched the horse before he released the food. Gradually the white stallion began to accept being touched as part of being rewarded, until the day came when Siddhartha approached him in public and put a bridle on him, a feat nobody else had accomplished. From that point on it was only a matter of time before word went about that the prince had tamed an untamable wild stallion. On the day when the horse allowed himself to be mounted, Siddhartha named him Kanthaka.

Channa looked restless and disgruntled. "I hope you're not too bulky in all that gear. You need to ride properly, remember that," he grumbled.

"Don't worry." Siddhartha knew that Channa's resentment wasn't personal. Despite Channa's hours of military training beside Siddhartha, he was technically still a stable boy and not a fighter.

Channa said, "I assumed you wanted this one. The king isn't risking his best horses, but he didn't exactly say you couldn't. He'll carry you better than any of the others." Channa fixed his expert eye on the stallion's high shoulders and wide girth. Siddhartha nodded, stroking Kanthaka's flanks. The animal wanted his touch, and although Kanthaka had quivered nervously at all the neighing and galloping going on around the stables that morning, he calmed down and waited.

Channa managed to crack a smile. "I also assume you know that someone's staring at you. It's a mistake, I'm sure. She thinks you're me."

A girl had escaped notice following Siddhartha to the stables. Channa didn't know who she was, but as soon as he turned his head Siddhartha recognized Sujata. She stood shyly in the shadows of a large tree, but the moment their eyes met, she let the blue silk that half-covered her face drop. Siddhartha was at a loss. "What's she doing here?" he mumbled.

"I don't know. I guess she couldn't help herself." Channa laughed and gave Siddhartha a hit on the shoulder. "You've still got a little time. Go on."

"It's not what you think."

"It doesn't matter what I think. Go ahead." Channa was smirking now, and as happens between two young males who talk about everything except *that,* his look said, *You don't know all about women yet? You'd better believe I do.* They were both fairly sure that the other was still a virgin, but Siddhartha nursed a suspicion that Channa had more opportunities than he did belowstairs in the kitchen and scullery, while Channa suspected that Siddhartha had more chances than he did in the pleasure pavilion by the lotus pond. This unspoken doubt created a secret between them when there was no secret to begin with. Neither one dared to find out that the other knew almost nothing about women.

"Let her come to me if she wants to," Siddhartha declared. He hoped he could save face and at the same time not risk approaching Sujata—not now, with someone watching. Luckily, he didn't have to. She took a deep breath and came to him. Throwing aside the daintiness of court women who acted as if a stable was unholy ground, Sujata walked up to them with her eyes fixed on Siddhartha.

"I came to wish you well. Please be safe today," she said, her words coming out a bit too fast and too loud, as words do when they are practiced in advance.

Siddhartha cursed himself inside, knowing that Channa could see him blush. All he needed to say was "Thank you," but confusion made him stammer, "Why would you think I'm not safe?" His tone was brusque, and Sujata turned a deep scarlet. Humiliation took her breath away, and Siddhartha died inside that he was the cause. "I mean—" he said, and stopped. Nobody knew what he meant, least of all himself.

It's unclear whether Channa chose that moment for his first attack of chivalry, but he coughed and muttered, "I have to find a new bridle. This one's too loose." Then he was gone, and the two were left alone together. Embarrassment momentarily blinded Siddhartha, but as his sight cleared the first thing he became aware of was Sujata's beauty. It had been enough to make him notice her, then to chase her through the maze. A cloud passed over him with that memory. He took a step back.

Sujata had been looking for the slightest sign of approval, and this step crushed her hopes. "I shouldn't have come. If you can forgive me—"

"There's nothing to forgive. There could never be anything to forgive." Siddhartha had no idea why he blurted out those last words. But now that they were out, he took the plunge. "I've wanted to see you for a long time. I didn't know if it was right or not. But I'm glad you came today, very glad."

Although Sujata maintained her shy posture, head ducked down between fallen shoulders, she was thrilled. Something had kept her awake at night. She had decided to trust this something, and now Siddhartha was smiling at her. She became painfully aware of his lean, muscular body, disguised though it was under his armor. There are dams that crack and dams that break open without warning. Hers was the second kind. "I think about you all the time. I've come to your room at night, but then I run away. What can I do? This is too impossible. We can't be together, but I think about you all the time. Oh, I already said that. You must think I'm stupid."

"No, not at all." Siddhartha in fact was delighted with everything Sujata blurted out. When babble is like music, love can't be far away. He wanted to throw off his armor and embrace her, because he was as aware of her pale breasts and the soft flow of her hips as she was of him. Siddhartha had never heard of skin hunger, but he felt it now as strongly as he had ever felt anything. Instinctively his hand moved around to the side of his chest plate, fumbling for the leather ties. "Why can't we be together? My father doesn't have to know."

"Oh." A shadow suddenly darkened Sujata's face. Siddhartha seemed so eager, yet he was thinking about his father and the disapproval that would fall on them if anyone thought she loved a prince. Which meant that Siddhartha was aware, even at that moment, of the huge difference between them. "I can't stay," she murmured. She could already feel the sting of contempt that the court would direct at her. And then there was her secret, the thing nobody suspected.

Siddhartha grabbed Sujata's arm before she could turn away. "What's wrong? You look like you're going to faint. What did I say?"

"The king." With that, Sujata burst into tears and ran away. Siddhartha was confused and hurt, but at that moment Channa returned holding a new bridle. "Do you want this?" he asked.

"Of course not. You know as well as I do." Instead of thanking Channa for his discretion, Siddhartha sounded angry. He had made some kind of unwitting, disastrous blunder with Sujata, but there was no time to run after her. "Help me up," he said curtly.

Without a word Channa bent down and made a step with his two hands so that Siddhartha could mount Kanthaka with his full weight of armor. The layers of ox-hide padding creaked as he settled into the saddle. Siddhartha galloped off toward the field, not waiting for the equerries who were supposed to surround him in procession. His mind was preoccupied with the image of Sujata's pained expression and the guilt of knowing that he had caused it. However long he was lost in this mood, he suddenly became aware of his surroundings. People were gathered on either side of the tournament field, the nobles seated in a grandstand, the common people standing or sitting on the ground on the opposite side, unprotected from the sun. A cheer went up when the crowd caught sight of the prince; he automatically went through the motions of a well-rehearsed scenario.

The king was waiting impatiently for his son's arrival. The day had turned hot, the sun a fierce white disc burning in the sky. He rose to his feet as Siddhartha approached, and he had to admit to himself that the crown prince made a fine show on the white stallion. If only he kept his nerve and did what was necessary.

Siddhartha bowed. "I dedicate my victories to Your Highness and pledge that every glory in war, however many battles I am privileged to fight, will be for you and your kingdom."

Suddhodana returned a gracious smile and waved Siddhartha off toward the field of combat. He had written the speech himself, but the boy could have spoken it louder, and he had forgotten to rise up in his stirrups and swivel around to catch the eye of every noble spectator. *No matter,* Suddhodana thought, driving from his mind the fear that Siddhartha might fail him.

To his relief, everything went as planned. Blood was soon drawn in the hand-to-hand combats, just enough to whet the spectators' appetites. He had ordered that dangerous weapons could be used, the kind rarely used in mock battle. There was a knife-edged discus that could be thrown hard enough to decapitate an enemy, a lash with multiple barbs at the end that tore off any flesh it made contact with, a heavy two-sided ax capable of piercing any armor, even bronze, a nailed mace, and a rippled dagger that ripped muscles apart both as it went in and as it was pulled out. His soldiers wouldn't have thrown themselves into using these weapons of horror, but Suddhodana had made sure they were tempted with huge rewards, and in addition their food supply was allowed to dwindle so that every rice larder and meat chest was empty that morning, just in case they forgot who sustained them.

With these incentives, his men fought hard, and it was lucky, despite many gruesome wounds, that nobody was killed. Nobody, that is, until the time came for mounted archery. This was the most spectacular of the combats. Siddhartha had participated vigorously in sword fighting but had otherwise remained on the periphery. Now it was his turn to show his true mettle. On one side of the field nine archers were lined up on horseback. Siddhartha faced them alone on Kanthaka. One by one the archers would peel off and charge at Siddhartha, firing arrows as rapidly as they could. Siddhartha's goal was to knock each opponent off his horse while escaping the arrows.

The crowd grew hushed. This was a test of skill no pampered son of a king could pass unless he was born to fight, and although the arrows had been blunted enough not to pierce the prince's armor, he couldn't be totally protected. The spectators gasped when Siddhartha, in a show of bravado, took off his helmet and threw it to the ground. The crowd applauded, but then he went further and unstrapped his broad chest plate, letting it fall away. Everyone went into shock, including the king. Suddhodana leaped to his feet, ready to call a halt to the games, but he knew he couldn't. The humiliation would wipe out everything he had tried to achieve for the past week. Was Siddhartha desperate to show his worthiness? Whatever his motive, Suddhodana recognized the necessity of what his son had done: mock battles could only frighten people so far and no farther unless lethal danger was involved.

The first archer peeled off and rode at a hard gallop toward Siddhartha, who kicked Kanthaka in the side and charged to meet him. Both men shot their first arrow at the same time. The one aimed at Siddhartha grazed his leggings, while his arrow flew true—the horseman was hit in the middle of his chest and fell from the saddle. At that moment the second archer peeled off, raising his bow. Siddhartha quickly found a new arrow from the quiver over his shoulder and prepared to fire again.

In his mind he was clear why he had removed his helmet and chest plate. Only by exposing himself to real threat could Siddhartha feel he wasn't participating in a charade. If he was ever to be a real warrior, it must begin today. He fired, and again his arrow found its mark; the second archer toppled to the ground with a blow to the chest. Siddhartha wheeled Kanthaka around. The stallion wasn't panting yet, but there were seven more to go.

"Come at me harder!" he shouted across the field. "Anyone who draws my blood will be forgiven by the king, if he fights fair." This was a lie, but Siddhartha had seen the nervous glances being exchanged by the archers when he threw off his armor. Goaded on now, his adversaries wanted to prove to the king that they were the best. The next two men charged faster and aimed better.

But Siddhartha had taken his training seriously, and he had talent on horseback. When his next arrow missed, he kept his cool and fired again, unhorsing his opponent when they were within a few yards of each other. The crowd grew more impressed, and by the time Siddhartha was down to the last two archers, they were on their feet cheering in earnest.

Kanthaka's sides were heaving now, and Siddhartha felt a little giddy. He had eaten nothing that morning, and the constant wheeling and maneuvering were making his surroundings whirl. He braced himself because the end of the combat was the toughest part. The last two archers charged him together. Siddhartha had an arrow ready, but his nerves got the better of him and it flew well right of the man he aimed at. His hand fumbled for another arrow.

The bolder of the archers had already gotten off two shots, and the second one was lucky—it found a gap in the padded blankets that protected Kanthaka's front, deeply piercing the horse's skin. Siddhartha felt the animal rear and barely kept his seat. He pulled tight on the reins and closed his thighs around the animal, willing it to calm down and forget its fear. Kanthaka held on, galloping straight for the double enemy, who now closed in, one on each side.

They were too close for Siddhartha to get any arrows off. He heard a cacophony of hoofbeats against the packed earth, and his eyes blurred. He shook his head, and he saw Mara riding behind one of the archers, clutching his arms around the rider's waist. The demon was laughing, and then he suddenly disappeared. Siddhartha didn't have much time to refocus his sight. He ducked down close to his saddle as the two enemies whipped past him on either side. They fired, and Siddhartha was fortunate. The arrows flew over his body with a swish of air, missing him.

He wheeled around, and regaining his self-possession, he fired rapidly, first at the back of one horseman, then at the other. His timing was perfect. They were still struggling to turn their mounts around when his arrows hit them, and both men fell. Siddhartha had fired so rapidly that they seemed to go down simultaneously. The crowd roared. For the first time in his life Siddhartha felt exulted by battle; he rose in his stirrups and acknowledged the accolades. This was something, the first thing, he had earned for himself.

But despite his triumph, Mara's laughter rang in his ears. Siddhartha was disoriented, and he scanned the tournament field. Only one of the archers had gotten to his feet. The other lay on the ground writhing in agony. Siddhartha jumped down and ran over to him. He saw with horror that the man had been hit in the throat, the arrow's point coming out the back of his neck.

Arms lifted the wounded man to a sitting position, hands tried to dislodge the arrow. He groaned and almost passed out. Siddhartha's head swam in the confusion. He was dimly aware that someone broke off the arrow's tip so that the shaft could be pulled through the man's neck, but this caused a tremendous gush of blood, which shot so far that it hit Siddhartha in the chest.

"Do something," he pleaded, aware in the midst of everything that his voice sounded high and panicky, more a boy's voice than a man's. He looked up to see that the king had arrived. The soldiers parted for him. His father barked for someone to fetch a physician, but by that time the wounded man had lost consciousness, his head limply tilted to one side like a broken doll's. From the fountain of blood still erupting, but with weaker and weaker force, it was obvious he was lost. Suddhodana pulled out a silk kerchief and pressed it to the man's wound.

"Did you know him?" asked Siddhartha, although he had no idea why that would matter. His father grimly shook his head. The presence of death quieted the bystanders, until a new voice broke the silence.

"Amazing. Someone was actually hurt. Fire the stagemaster."

Devadatta pushed his way through the packed bodies surrounding the corpse. He stared at it coldly. "It's his own fault for missing his cue, isn't it?" He turned to Siddhartha, whose whole body was shaking. "You couldn't have fought for real, I can see that."

The bystanders were shocked, waiting for the king to explode with rage, but Suddhodana kept silent. His guilt told him that Devadatta was right—nobody was meant to get hurt when the prince was involved. He gazed at his son, and Siddhartha instantly read the truth.

Siddhartha willed himself to stop shaking and got to his feet. He drew his sword, glaring at Devadatta. "You said you wanted to fight me today. I accept your challenge."

"No!"

For a moment it sounded as if his father had shouted, but Channa stepped through the crowd. "No, I'll fight the bastard. It's about time." Channa took two strides, raising his fist to take a swing at Devadatta. But in his wildness he lost his balance, and the blow only grazed Devadatta's cheek.

Devadatta spit on his palm and wiped his cheek with a look of disgust, as if it were covered with excrement.

"I beg my rights, Your Highness." Devadatta dropped to one knee in front of Suddhodana. "This low-caste scum touched me. You all saw it. I beg my rights." The crowd stirred and became uneasy as the king remained immobile and silent for several seconds.

"The king acknowledges Devadatta's rights." Suddhodana finally spoke but not with his usual force. "He can decide the fate of any low-caste who has defiled him."

Devadatta smiled. "Death," he said.

Suddhodana scowled. "Think carefully. It was just a touch, young prince. Let me remind you, this is a cause for justice."

"I'm only looking for justice. This scum intended to catch me off guard, knock me over, and then stab me. See, his weapon."

By now two guards had grabbed Channa and wrestled the dagger from him. Pushed to his knees, Channa shouted, "If that's what I was going to do, let me finish it!"

Devadatta shrugged and held his open hands out to the king. "My case is proved. Let me have my rights, as you promised."

"No, let me have mine."

Without warning Siddhartha was kneeling at the king's feet beside his cousin, his voice on the edge of rage. "I have the right to fight in place of my brother, and Channa is my brother in everything but name. Everyone knows it, so why pretend? If any man of caste dares to defame Channa, I will fight that man, whoever he is."

This was the moment that Canki shouldn't have missed by leaving early. As high Brahmin, he had full authority, over even a king, to decide disputes of caste. These were many and complicated. Scriptures held, for example, that if the shadow of an untouchable fell across the path of a Brahmin, unclean contact had taken place and the Brahmin must return home to bathe. Food touched by someone of low caste could not be eaten by someone of high caste. This was clear enough, but what if the high-caste person was dying and the food was needed to save his life? Canki held court over these bewildering issues. But he had left the scene.

"Get up, both of you," Suddhodana ordered. With disgust he knew that Devadatta had more right on his side than the prince. Often in the heat of battle a low-caste's weapon had accidentally nicked a high-caste comrade's, drawing barely a few drops of blood. But this was enough to condemn the offender to death if the high-caste soldier demanded it. Channa clearly intended to draw blood; the waters weren't muddied until Siddhartha foolishly intruded. Suddhodana now had no choice.

"The two princes both have right on their side," he announced. "I will betray justice if I decide against either of them, so let Nature be the judge. The two princes will fight."

No one expected this judgment, but the first to recover from the general consternation was Devadatta, who gave a wolfish grin. Between arrogance and despair at his situation, he knew he had no future, not one befitting his worth. His fatalistic streak would be satisfied if he managed to kill this despised cousin who had led to his own imprisonment, or else got killed trying. "Sword and dagger," he said.

Siddhartha nodded grimly. Already free of helmet and chest plate, he began to strip off the rest of his armor for better mobility. But more than that, he wanted the fight to be decisive. The truth was that each of them—Siddhartha, his father, and Devadatta—was trapped by the others. Astonishingly, all three had come to this realization at the same exact moment, a moment from which there was no turning back.

9

The sky was divided between sun and clouds as the fighters circled each other. They had stripped down to cotton pants, their chest and feet bare. Siddhartha kept his eyes fixed on Devadatta's, because as tempting as it was to watch his opponent's hands, he knew that Devadatta's glance would give away his intentions.

Siddhartha felt he was moving in a dream. A part of his mind floated high above, looking down in wonder that a fight to the death ensued. But Siddhartha's instincts for survival were strong. He shook himself and made the opening lunge, his sword hand ahead of his dagger so that by warding off the first blade, Devadatta might open himself to the second one. Devadatta was agile and ready—he jumped to the side with a shouted "Ha!" and slashed with his own sword. Siddhartha went by too fast and wasn't hit.

Devadatta began a relentless round of parry and thrust, making Siddhartha counter blow after blow with his sword. Each time metal clanged on metal, a shock wave went up his arm. Siddhartha's muscles ached, and he knew that Devadatta had an advantage over him. This was his cousin's first combat of the day, while Siddhartha had been fighting for hours. He had to win quickly or his energy would fail. Knowing that Devadatta was following his eyes as well, he made a feint, glancing right, taking a half step in that direction. When Devadatta's dagger followed him, the move opened up his body, and Siddhartha stuck his sword into the exposed midriff. It was incredible luck. If the blow had struck home, it would have been fatal.

But in the instant before the blade entered Devadatta's body, Siddhartha heard his heartbeat thud in his ears with long stretches in between the strokes. He felt the breeze blow the hairs on his forearm slowly, delicately, back and forth, and each blink of an eye was like a door closing, leading to blackness, before it opened again and the world reappeared.

He felt very different from before—calm, free of anger. Out of the corner of his eye he could see that the mood of the king had shifted. Suddhodana was returning to reason, and as he did, the thought of loss of his only son was intolerable. Suddhodana was within half a breath of stopping the fight. He had yet to register that Siddhartha was about to win. The last thing Siddhartha's eye caught was his sword inching closer to its perfect target.

Suddhodana shouted, "Stand back, a fighter is down!" He wanted to run forward and embrace his son. The prince stood over Devadatta's fallen body, panting hard.

"Get up," he said. Devadatta was shaking his head. Instead of delivering a fatal wound, Siddhartha's sword tip had been deflected, slicing the skin over his heart. He spat out the dust he'd swallowed going down, aiming deliberately at Siddhartha's feet. Siddhartha's eyes fixed on the slimy spot it made.

He held out his hand to Devadatta. "You win, if it pleases you."

Devadatta refused the hand with contempt. "It's not going to be that easy, boy," he hissed. Siddhartha ignored the jibe and turned around.

"I quit this fight," he said in a loud voice, keeping his eyes away from the king's. "I can't prevail over a better man. Give the honor to my cousin."

Suddhodana shook his head. "You have prevailed. The contest is over," he shouted, but few heard him. Screams rent the air because, at the moment when Siddhartha turned away from him, Devadatta lifted his dagger and raked its rippled blade across the small of his opponent's back. Siddhartha staggered. Devadatta brought back his arm to strike straight up into his enemy's stomach as he doubled over.

Siddhartha never gave him the chance. He reached out and grabbed Devadatta's hair with one hand while batting the threatening dagger away with the other. The gash it made across his palm was insignificant; rage canceled out the pain. He banged Devadatta's skull into the packed dirt. The first time was enough to make his opponent half senseless, but Siddhartha repeated the action twice more. Devadatta's eyes betrayed panic when he realized that he was alone and defenseless. The second time his head smashed against the ground, his eyes glazed over; the third smash, and they rolled up into his head.

Siddhartha paid no attention. He lifted Devadatta's limp body off the ground in a wrestler's hold around the chest, squeezing the breath out of him. It was remarkably easy to do, as if he were shaking a rag doll. Siddhartha locked his arms into a vice and leaned back, his face to the sky. Inside a voice said, "*This* is freedom. This is what the gods feel like when they mete out death." Siddhartha believed the voice and waited for the moment when he would let Devadatta's body fall.

As his face turned up to the sky, which was still divided between sun and clouds, his arms felt Devadatta's body grow more and more still.

Surrender, and be free.

For the first time since he could remember, a voice came to him from another place. Siddhartha's grip weakened just a fraction.

Surrender, and be free.

When the voice came back again, Siddhartha could hardly keep from shouting back, *Haven't I already surrendered?* He had conceded the fight to his enemy, yet instead of freeing him, it had opened him to treachery. What was this new surrender? Where would it take him? Siddhartha felt seized with fear. If he let go of Devadatta, their old enmity would be twice as strong; he would have failed his father and turned victory into humiliation. None of that mattered now. Deep down he knew what he had to surrender. The voice wanted him to jump into the abyss, a place deep inside and completely unknown to him. It was the only way out.

Devadatta quivered and softly moaned. Siddhartha dropped him without being aware of his action. He walked to the edge of a cliff—the image in his mind was as real to him as anything he'd ever seen—and leaped. He saw his arms fly up and the yawning gulf, like a monstrous mouth, below him. His first impulse was to shriek, so dizzying was the sensation of plummeting into emptiness. *This must be like dying,* he thought. He couldn't feel his body anymore; no sights or sounds reached him from the outside world. But his worst fears were unfounded. The void was not a place of destruction and chaos. No, it was very different.

He saw his mother holding a baby in her arms, and her face was the sun. He saw Mara sitting on his throne surrounded by swarming, buzzing entities, and his face was the night. He saw his father, an infant swaddled in a suit of armor, crying to be let out because he was suffocating. He saw Sujata, the stars, Channa riding the white stallion Kanthaka. The spectacle whirled and slipped past him like painted gossamer, and Siddhartha laughed, feeling exhilarated. The things that had meant so much were as thin and fragile as tissue.

He kept on falling. The tissuelike images flew apart. It was like watching the wind scatter leaves, and the leaves were his life. As this life evaporated before his eyes, Siddhartha felt a shiver, as if someone had ripped off his winter coat and left him naked in the cold. But he wasn't naked, and far from dead. Instead of the mask of images and memories, surrounding him on every side was something pure and free: life itself. He couldn't remember who he was. There was nothing left of his fears and dreams, nothing to do, nothing to want. He was simply alive, the breath of the breath, the eye of the eye.

The falling sensation ended. Siddhartha was held in suspension, an invisible spider dangling from an invisible thread. It would have been wonderful to remain like that. It would have been everything. Then a low throbbing could be heard like distant thunder, and it rolled toward him, a wave of thunder that boomed in the night until the muffled boom turned into a word.

"Son?"

Siddhartha opened his eyes. His father's stricken face covered the sky. *I'm all right,* he wanted to say, seeing the sick worry in the king's eyes. No words came out. They were stifled by Siddhartha's emotions. He reached back in his mind, trying to return to where he'd been after he leaped into the abyss. There was nothing there.

He felt his father lifting his head; other arms were under his legs and torso. They lowered him onto a litter, and then he was jounced up and down as the bearers ran with him toward the palace. He was returning to his right mind now, full of images and memories once again. What had he done to Devadatta? What would happen to Channa? His whole body felt heavier; it was being tied to earth again by a thousand threads. Siddhartha struggled, desperate to break free. Then a physician's soothing voice said, "Try to calm down. Quit fighting." Someone pressed a cold slimy thing to his forehead, and the last thing Siddhartha saw before passing out was the painted ceiling of his father's bedroom, in the image of the sky.

"HEAT STROKE, THAT'S ALL. Did you see his face? He was sweating like mad, then he turned white as a sheet before they carried him off. He could have died."

"He went crazy. It was bound to happen. Don't you know the pressure he's under? You'd crack too."

"The wretched boy's cursed. My wife has a maid who can see demons. The one she saw around him almost scared her to death."

The rumor mill at court hummed with excited speculation. No one could make their favorite theories stick. They were too bewildered over Siddhartha's sudden outbreak of violence. Would he ever be himself again? The gods of gossip were not sure. After three days the leeching was over, and the royal physicians, squeezing clotted blood between their fingers, declared that the worst poisons had been extracted. The astrologers sounded guardedly optimistic about the transit of Mercury coming to an end after it had combusted with the sun. In their eyes, malefic forces had taken over Siddhartha. Suddhodana didn't believe any of it. But no one had died, and if his guests went away thinking he had raised a half-demented son, it was better than thinking he had raised a gentle one.

Even though Devadatta's dagger had drawn considerable blood, and losing more was dangerous, Siddhartha felt no distress over the leeching—not compared to the shroud of sadness that would not unwind from his heart. His father refused to leave him unattended, but late at night when the nurse's head lolled on her breast—Siddhartha made sure she was given a double cup of liquor with supper—he crept out of bed and paced the floor. In his mind he would approach the edge of an abyss again, but when he jumped, nothing happened. It was simply his imagination.

Siddhartha got reluctant permission to have Channa admitted to his room. He breathed a sigh when he set eyes on him. He was still alive. Siddhartha's relief was too enormous to disguise. Channa was embarrassed; he raised his voice and talked about the whole affair with bravado. "No one's going to kill me. I have friends everywhere. I'm protected." But Siddhartha noticed welts on Channa's shoulders, and when he pressed him for an explanation, the truth emerged.

There was consternation on the field of combat when Siddhartha and Devadatta had both been carried away. The king ordered the massed fighters to remain in place, which added an air of threat to the confusion, but he wanted to make sure that every guest realized that his army was always at the ready. No one had time for Channa, who ran back to the stables and packed his best saddle horse to leave. As he was stuffing food and blankets into leather bags, he sensed that someone had entered the stall.

"Father?" He turned around expecting to confront Bikram, who would never forgive him for touching a high-caste. But it was the king, who had not forgotten Channa for a moment. He brandished a whip in his hands.

"I expect you to take what's coming to you and then keep your mouth shut."

Without waiting for a reaction, Suddhodana struck the youth across the chest with the lash's iron-tipped barbs—there were three, a gentler version of the deadly seven-tipped whip used in battle. The pain was excruciating; Channa fell to the ground and rolled over, which was fortunate, because the king was in a genuine rage and vented it by striking him, over and over, across the back and shoulders instead of his face.

The only way that Channa could keep from passing out was to force himself not to count the blows. *This one's the last,* he thought every time the iron hooks raked his flesh. It never was the last, however, or so it seemed. Then he became aware that the searing pain was coming not from the lash anymore but from the wounds he already had. Channa risked looking up, and he saw the king stooped over, panting hard with the whip dropped to the stable floor.

"Walk around, make sure everyone sees your wounds. Don't dress them for two days." Suddhodana was focused on him, but not with rage or implacable cold hatred. Channa could almost read sympathy, as if he'd had to punish his own son. "Then have Bikram hide you for a month, somewhere far away. Somewhere a hired assassin won't look. They're lazy; they won't go very far to find you. And never go near Devadatta again, understand?"

They both knew that Channa was being let off easy. By rights he should have been turned over to the priests, who would have meted out maximum punishment as a show of power over the king. As Suddhodana turned away, Channa mumbled, "Thank you."

The king looked back at him, and now his eyes were stone cold. "Your father was a horse thief when I met him. That's a hanging offense, and if I ever have a whim to kill him, why not take the son along too? Just to be sure."

Channa related only the bare bones of this incident to Siddhartha. The prince was troubled enough by the welts he could see; the worst were hidden under Channa's tunic. Several days passed before Siddhartha told Channa about his own mysterious experience.

Channa was amazed. "You turned into a god. What else could it be?"

Siddhartha didn't know whether to be shocked or amused. But when Channa's face remained serious, even a little awed, he said, "I shouldn't have told you. I should just go to old Canki and get him to purify me."

"I wouldn't. Not until somebody purifies *him*." Channa's contempt for the Brahmin was open, despite the risk he was running if the priest should find out. "How long have I been getting school from him? Ever since any of us can remember. You think that matters? He'd see me stretched out on a rack as soon as look at me. He thinks I'm an animal, and he has scripture to back him up."

Siddhartha looked grim. "And I'm not much better."

Channa was stunned; the color rushed to his face. Siddhartha rushed ahead. "I mean, caste keeps my life perfect. That's the word you used, right? It doesn't matter if you're stronger than me or smarter or braver. The fact that we embraced when you walked in the door today could mean a death sentence if my father decreed it."

Channa straightened up. "I am stronger than you, that part's true."

"The rest is true too." Siddhartha couldn't help smiling.

Channa said, "You can change the world when it's yours to play with. The rest of us have to live in it."

"You think I'm going to get the world?"

"It's just what they say."

Siddhartha knew it was better to let the whole subject die. He had lived a long time with the knowledge that even his best friend, at some level that reason couldn't touch, regarded him with superstitious awe. It wouldn't matter that Channa had seen the worst of Siddhartha, watched him cry, run away, complain bitterly about his father. It wouldn't matter that the prince was a creature of flesh and blood or that Channa had often in the heat of sword practice drawn his blood. Being the friend of a royal gave Channa the special status and protection that he enjoyed. But there was a limit to royal protection with an enemy as cunning as Devadatta.

The realization came to Siddhartha that he had always regarded his cousin with anxiety. Devadatta had been like a blade held lightly against his throat. That's what was now missing. Fear. Siddhartha couldn't bring back the old sense of threat.

If he wasn't afraid of Devadatta anymore, what else wasn't he afraid of? Siddhartha reached inside and opened the hidden trunks of memory, expecting that phantoms of dread would fly out. But the trunk was empty. He had been a death-haunted child, a boy full of fears without a mother.

Tears were rolling down his cheeks now. It was the first time in his life that truth had made Siddhartha weep. That's what had changed when he jumped into the abyss. He exchanged illusion for truth. He felt purified, and yet some part of him couldn't rejoice in it. What would it be like to be the only man who wasn't afraid? His father was afraid despite his battles won; Canki was afraid despite the favor of the gods; Channa was afraid despite his bravado. None of them would be able to grasp this change in Siddhartha. They might even hate him for it.

• • •

WITH THE CURTAINS CLOSED and one candle guttering to a spark, Sujata's room was almost dark. She lay in bed staring at the ceiling. In her mind she kept going over what she should have said to Siddhartha. Everything had gone wrong. Even when she got her heart's desire and he showed that he wanted her, she had run away. Sometimes when she woke up in the middle of the night, all Sujata could think about was the fact that Siddhartha had looked at her with longing. She fixed that look in her mind and swore she would never let it go.

The simple truth is that Sujata was waiting for Siddhartha to come to her on his own. So when she lay half asleep and the door creaked open, Sujata was instantly wide awake. She trembled under the sheets and widened her eyes to see him in the dark, to make sure this wasn't another phantom of her imagination.

She saw the outline of a strong young man moving toward the bed, his bearing erect, moving quickly because he desired her so strongly. Fear and exultation fought wildly in Sujata's breast. If only her bed could have been prepared properly for love, with scattered flower petals, rose water, and sprinkled spices known to make a man aroused.

For a fleeting instant Sujata thought of her mother and wondered if she had been in the same situation. She banished this thought as soon as it came. She didn't want to think about anything when Siddhartha's hand took hers; he was bending over her, lowering his face to kiss her.

"Hold still. If you scream I'll kill you."

Scream was all she wanted to do, in that instant when she realized this wasn't Siddhartha and horror had entered her sanctuary. The man's hand came over her face, covering mouth and nose so that she would be too breathless to cry out, even to think. But panic had already seen to that.

"You've been waiting for me a long time. I've seen your light. I wanted the moment to be perfect, sweetheart."

It was unmistakably Devadatta. He tore open her bodice with quick efficiency and began to knead her breasts with his hands, roughly and without consideration for how it hurt her.

Please stop. . . . I'll do whatever you want.

With her breathing cut off, Sujata didn't know if she actually spoke those words or if they were a desperate prayer. Devadatta had opened her dress against her feeble struggling, and she felt his hand opening her legs. Half-suffocated as she was, she couldn't sob. Devadatta was having her, and his thrusts were violent signals of his savagery and disdain.

She went limp, hoping that her rapist would spare her more violence. Devadatta suddenly stopped what he was doing to her. "I know who you want!" he said, and the menace in his voice should have warned her. But Sujata, knowing she was dead, felt a flood of relief.

The only mercy remaining to her was that Devadatta acted swiftly in the dark. She couldn't detect him pulling out his rippled dagger. "Remember that the last thing you ever saw was me," he growled at the instant that the blade swept across her eyes. Sujata heard a shriek that must have been her own, then the searing pain came, and she stopped breathing. She was spared the spectacle of Devadatta rolling off her body with a groan. He tried to control himself, but his hands were shaking.

Devadatta realized his predicament: someone would come sooner or later, and there was no time to waste. He seized hold of himself and started the work in front of him. He wrapped Sujata in bed sheets and tied her shrouded body with curtain cords. He easily slipped past the guards and found a sentry's horse tethered by the gates. He loaded the corpse on its rump and rode quietly toward the river. Mara was already there; he stood by while Devadatta, still not speaking, strong enough that carrying the body didn't make him groan with exertion, approached the water.

"Weigh her down with stones," Mara ordered. Devadatta shot him a look of hatred and dumped the bundle into the water. The bed sheets were not securely tied, and they billowed out over the surface of the river, a spectral white like sails in the moonlight. They retained enough air in bulges and bubbles that Sujata didn't sink immediately, and the fast current carried her away. Devadatta didn't wait. He wanted to forget that Mara was beside him.

"Not beside, dearest. Inside," Mara said with satisfaction.

Devadatta trembled in despair. He had no doubt that the gods didn't exist. But at that moment he understood why, when the horror of life finally reveals itself, somebody had to invent them.

10

Sujata's disappearance wasn't discovered for several days. The first day a maid ran to Kumbira with the news that the tray of food left outside Sujata's door was untouched.

"She's always pouting. Wait till she gets hungry enough." Sujata's staying in her room hadn't hid her plight from Kumbira, who knew well enough that she was lovesick. But when her food was untouched the second day, Kumbira knocked on the door and entered. What she saw made her react quickly.

"Run away. Now."

Kumbira pushed the maid who had followed her out the door, hoping that the drawn curtains hid the sight of blood on the stripped bed. But the frightened girl certainly saw something, which left Kumbira very little time before palace rumors would spread like wildfire. She immediately went to the king and laid before him everything that had happened between Sujata and the prince.

Suddhodana took the news more calmly than she had expected. And if the king was concerned about Sujata's fate, it certainly didn't show. "She was too ashamed to stay. Send a few men to search where she went. Not too many." It wasn't even half an hour before Channa carried the news to the prince, who immediately ran to Sujata's room. Kumbira had been swift enough in having the bed removed; even so, Siddhartha was alarmed at Sujata's sudden disappearance.

"I've sent my men out," Suddhodana told him. "What else do you expect me to do? She wanted to go home. Somebody should have kept her from getting so lonely."

Siddhartha was stung by his father's implication. The pleasure pavilion had been open to him since he was sixteen, but in those two years he hadn't gone there. Suddhodana was offended by this show of chastity. "I didn't put those girls there so you could pray with them," he had once taunted.

Stymied by his father's indifference to Sujata, Siddhartha ran to Channa. "We have to find her."

"Do we? Stop and think," said Channa. "There's a good chance your father is behind it himself. He wants her gone."

"You think she's like an old horse?" Siddhartha said coldly. He was well aware that his father caused people to disappear from sight after a certain age, no different from what went on in the stables.

Channa didn't argue. He put a saddle on his favorite mount and started to lead it outside. "Don't tell anyone I'm gone," he said. "You're staying here." He saw Siddhartha flush a deep scarlet. "Go ahead, blame me," said Channa. "You can't risk leaving."

Siddhartha was all too aware that if he rode past the palace gates in search of Sujata, no one could predict his father's reaction. Every person at court had connived to keep him prisoner. But that wasn't going to stop him. Siddhartha strode over to the saddle rack, took down a saddle, and began to cinch it on Kanthaka. The stallion usually stood still for him, but it shied and almost bucked.

"Easy," Siddhartha whispered.

When he had mounted, Siddhartha headed toward the woods, leading the way. On their hunts Channa had once pointed out a stream that ran steeply down a hillside and more than once, despite the king's soldiers on patrol, the prince wondered if it was an escape route. Channa had said, "There's a dry gully at the bottom. If I ever wanted to leave without anybody knowing, I'd take the horses through the stream first to kill the scent. It's even steeper beyond. Nobody bothers to patrol it."

They headed that way now because if he was gone even an hour a scouting party would be sent out after him. That much was a given. The stream was easy to find; it was steep and rocky enough that both riders kept quiet, concentrating on the horses' footing. The dry gully, as Channa had promised, got even steeper. They decided to walk the animals down. Under the black jungle canopy of tangled trees and vines, the sun struck their skin in dappled spots, but each speck felt searing at high noon. It wasn't the way Siddhartha had envisioned his break to freedom. Reality dictated otherwise.

Channa began talking again, letting out his sentences in short bursts as he negotiated the scree-strewn slope. "My father swore me to secrecy about what happened when you and I were still sucking at the breast. The king sent them all away. All the old, sick ones. It was a bad time."

Siddhartha had come to that conclusion on his own. After his mother's death, it was the grimmest fact about his birth. Channa stopped talking, trying to calm his horse as the slippery ground slid out from under its feet. The gully led to an overgrown bamboo thicket, the space between the trees too close for a horse to squeeze through.

"There's an old road just beyond. They took some of them that way."

"Who?"

"Some women. Ones the king didn't need anymore."

Channa was recounting the past in a clipped, flat voice, like a physician noting the cause of death. "He told Bikram to take them out a secret way, the one we're following. He didn't want anybody to see."

Siddhartha had a realization. "You hate him, don't you?"

"You really want to know?" Without turning around, Channa lifted up his shirt, exposing the full extent of his wounds from the whipping. "A king's no better than a criminal." Silence followed until they reached the end of the thick bamboo. Channa stopped his horse and faced Siddhartha. "You can turn back, you know. Nobody would be the wiser."

"Why would I?"

Channa looked more thoughtful than Siddhartha had ever seen him. "Your father may be a bastard, but he could be right, doing what he did. He kept misery away from you. Isn't that a good thing? I try to work it out in my mind."

"He wasn't right."

The determination in Siddhartha's voice caught Channa's attention.

"Three years went by. One of the women had a baby. Life was too hard, and she died. The baby survived. So your father sent guilt money and food, year after year."

"Until she was old enough to bring to court," said Siddhartha.

"Just be glad she's not your half sister." Channa's tone was indifferent now. He'd taken the weight off his shoulders. "So, their village is up ahead. That's where we have the best chance of finding Sujata if she did run away. Not that I believe it."

Siddhartha didn't ask Channa what he did believe. He had his own premonitions. He couldn't escape the fact that he hadn't seen Devadatta in the past few days. It would be like him to kidnap Sujata for revenge. Far better if the king had packed her off in the night instead.

Siddhartha gazed down at the village, which looked normal from a distance, a single dirt street winding between low bamboo huts, the only oddity being the parched wastelands and untended fields on the outskirts. *Why aren't the farmers tending their crops?*

"Come on. You can't really see much from here," said Channa. He led the way down a narrow rutted trail. Weeds grew up to the horses' stomachs. Channa pointed them out. "Nobody comes this way. They probably haven't seen visitors for half a year."

"Why not?" There was no plague in the area, and the lushness of the undergrowth meant there had been no recent drought.

"Because this is 'the forgotten city.' That's what everyone calls it. I like 'the king's city' better. Don't ask me any more," said Channa.

In half a mile the trail leveled off, and soon they were riding past the first few huts on the village fringe. Their roofs were rain-stained gray, the wood jambs falling down around the sagging doors. No one seemed to live inside, or else they were used to hiding from strangers. The next clump of huts was just as dilapidated. Siddhartha caught a glimpse of faces at the window that withdrew as soon as he spied them.

"Here," said Channa. He dismounted in front of a hut more ruined than the rest, its door stolen and the carved ornaments of gods and demons stripped from the eaves. "This was hers, the mother's."

Sujata couldn't be here, living like this, Siddhartha thought. But he got down and followed Channa into the bleak shell of a house. The evidence of vermin and gaping holes in the floor told him that no one had entered in months. A torn scrap of red silk over the back window and a cracked teapot beside the charcoal hole used for cooking were the only signs that a woman could have made a home there.

"Let's go back. I'll demand that my father tell me where she is," Siddhartha said, his heart sinking. He sensed a truth he couldn't face.

When they stepped outside, things had changed. People had emerged from nowhere, like rabbits from their warrens. A clutch of men surrounded the horses.

"Stop! Hey, stop!" Channa shouted. A few of them were trying to uncinch the saddles. Channa was armed and they weren't, but when he drew his sword, Siddhartha held his arm back.

"Who are they?" he asked grimly.

The people, perhaps a dozen in all, were starving and dressed in rags that hung from their bones. All had gray hair, sometimes only a scrap left over their exposed skulls.

"They're the forgotten," said Channa. "We've come to their city."

"And my father sent them here?"

Channa nodded. The decrepit old men who tried to steal their saddles had fallen to the ground, prostrating themselves. The women came forward and mutely held their cupped hands out for food. "Give them what we have," said Siddhartha. There were bits of provisions in the saddlebags. He looked away when Channa produced bread and meat to hand out; he couldn't face the sight of beggars clawing for scraps.

The scuffle drew more attention, and now Siddhartha could see others approaching from the main part of the village. "Let's go," urged Channa.

"Why? They're not dangerous." This went without saying since the newcomers were as old as the first ones they'd met.

Channa was restless nonetheless. "I could knock them all down with one swipe of my sword," he said. "But it's still not safe."

"Why not? What's wrong with them?"

Channa didn't know how much Siddhartha was oblivious of, so he spoke as if to a small child. "These people were at court when you were born, and even then they were too old to be kept around. Those over there, walking with crutches, they're lame. They've been sick, but nobody treated them. The ones who are coughing with their mouths covered over with cloth, don't touch them. They're sick; they carry disease, and we could get it too. I'm still young and healthy, thank you."

"We'll become like them?" asked Siddhartha, genuinely puzzled.

"Someday."

"All of us?"

"All of us," said Channa. Ignoring what Siddhartha would think, he kicked at a barefoot old woman who had crawled on the ground to touch his sandals.

Siddhartha was muttering words to himself that were never spoken around him. *Old. Lame. Sick. Diseased.* How could he ever have imagined that he had suffered? Not compared to this.

"How do they stand it?" he murmured. Now the gathering crowd's mood had changed. Their hollow faces darkened, and there was angry muttering.

"They realize we've come from the court," said Channa. He and Siddhartha were dressed in plain white cotton, but the mounts' trappings were stamped with the royal insignia. "Get on your horse. We're going."

Siddhartha climbed up again, but instead of turning Kanthaka toward home, he kept riding into the forgotten city. The streets were lined with haggard ghosts, and eyes bulging from hunger stared at him. Siddhartha prayed that his aunties hadn't been banished here when they had disappeared from court.

There was one building better repaired than the others, and no one stood in front of it. For some reason Siddhartha stopped, his attention drawn to its covered windows and a Shiva statue at the door decorated with wilting wildflowers. "I want to go inside," he said.

"No, you don't," Channa said.

The smell coming from the building was unmistakable. Siddhartha had come across that smell in the woods where a rotting deer carcass lay. He dismounted and pushed the door open. He stepped into a dim, moist, fetid room. In the watery beams of light coming through the shutters Siddhartha could see someone sleeping on a table, naked except for a light sheet across the torso. No, not sleeping but lying motionless. The man's face was gray-white, eyes closed, and his slack, sagging mouth made him look both angry and sad.

"What is this place?" Siddhartha asked. He could guess well enough, but talking helped him avoid getting sick.

"The house of the dead. Don't get close. They're not blessed."

As his eyes adjusted to the light, Siddhartha saw that there were other corpses on the floor, laid side by side and covered with burlap; the worst smell came from them. The man on the table must be newly dead.

Siddhartha wasn't aware that he had moved closer. He reached out and touched the corpse, eerily certain that the old man would wake with a start. The coldness of the flesh surprised him; it felt colder than the air in the room. Despite the fact that the man was dead, Siddhartha wanted to apologize. He hadn't asked permission to touch him, and they were strangers.

"Is this all for them?" he asked. "Do the dead live in their house?"

"No, they'll rot if they stay here. Bodies are burned," explained Channa.

Siddhartha winced. "So one day you might burn me," he murmured. Channa had lingered by the door, and his reaction to Siddhartha's curiosity was a growing impatience.

"What's wrong with that? I'm glad if they burn me. My ashes will go into the river. When there's nothing left for demons to grab on to, I'll go to heaven. You'll have to break my skull with an ax to let my spirit out first."

If Channa intended to shock Siddhartha, it didn't work. Bemused, Siddhartha muttered, "Is that how it's done? Then why are they still here? Don't they have axes?"

Channa shrugged. "There's no wood and nobody strong enough to cut some. They probably wait for wandering monks to come through."

Channa's impatience wouldn't allow them to stay any longer. Siddhartha took the hand of the corpse, which had fallen limply to its side, and replaced it across the man's chest. When he came out of the house of the dead, the crowd outside looked angrier than before.

"Prince?" someone called out. "Are you the king's son? Do you like what you've done to us?" He hadn't counted on being recognized. A sense of shame kept him from speaking.

I will try to help you, I promise, he thought. Muttered threats surrounded Siddhartha as he walked up to Kanthaka. An old woman spat on the ground while an unseen voice said, "Better your mother had died sooner, you hear me? Why were you ever born?"

"Stop it!" One of the old men stepped forward, raising his hands and shushing the others. His starved body was wrapped in dirty hemp cloth, but underneath Siddhartha glimpsed saffron rags, the color of Canki's robes.

"The gods, not this noble youth, have brought such misfortune on us. We should give him money to take back and make offerings for us." Scorn greeted the old priest's suggestion; he wriggled his way through the crowd. "Blessings, blessings," he muttered as he edged closer to Siddhartha.

The old priest smelled almost as bad as the corpses. He smiled toothlessly, and Siddhartha was ashamed of himself for drawing back. "Bend close, young prince, and let me whisper a special blessing in your ear."

Siddhartha forced himself to lean over, closing his eyes against the old man's fetid breath. "I accept your blessing," he said politely.

"And I curse you to hell unless you take me back with you." The vehemence in the old priest's voice was like cobra venom. Siddhartha jerked back. Without a word he jumped into the saddle. He felt the priest's tight, bony grip on his ankle, but he kicked free and galloped off. Behind him the population of the forgotten city jeered and catcalled. Others cried out piteously, and when he could no longer hear any of them, Siddhartha stopped. Kanthaka's sides were heaving; so were Siddhartha's. He leaned over and whispered, "Forgive me," into Kanthaka's ear, even though he hadn't driven him that hard.

Channa caught up where the road was starting to slope back upward and become a mountain trail again. Siddhartha waited for him. "How often have you come here?" he asked.

"Once or twice. But you're not coming back. What's here for you? Your father won't let you save them, and by the time you're king they'll all be dead. Face facts. One strong wind this winter is all it would take."

Siddhartha hated these words but didn't argue. The sun was still mercilessly hot, and they had given their goatskins of water to the old ones.

Channa's right. It should be called the king's city. His conscience searched for what to do. Should he go back and farm the fields himself with a few slaves from the palace, against his father's wishes? Would it do the slightest good to send them to the forgotten city? Underneath all this was Sujata, who haunted him now more than at the moment he had learned she was gone. For a fleeting instant he could see her on a table in the house of the dead.

It was at that painful moment that Siddhartha caught a glimpse of someone. A naked hermit was hidden in the thick underbrush, crouching on his heels. His sun-brown skin made him nearly invisible against the ground except for his beard, which was nearly white. If Siddhartha hadn't happened to turn for a last glimpse behind, he would have missed him.

"Asita!" Siddhartha called out, jumping down from his horse. The sudden motion must have frightened the hermit, who scurried away into the thicket out of sight. "Wait, don't you know me?" Siddhartha was baffled but plunged into the underbrush, heedless of thorns and snakes. The hermit was escaping as noiselessly as a deer. Siddhartha stopped, straining his ears to catch any telltale sound. Channa came up behind him. "What's wrong?"

"You didn't see him? It was Asita."

"If it was, he's a million years old. I thought I saw an old man, that's all. Probably following us from the village," said Channa.

But they both knew an old man couldn't keep up with horses. Siddhartha was too excited to stop and convince Channa. "Asita!" he called.

Siddhartha set a direction upslope and followed it, telling Channa to wait below. There was no trail to follow anymore, and after a moment he was immersed in deepest jungle. Scarlet parrots scolded him from overhead; a lone monkey scouring the ground for fallen fruit was startled and leaped up a tree with a scream. Siddhartha pressed on with more energy, even though he knew he was running aimlessly, fueled by what he wanted to find rather than what he would. Then, just when it was undeniable that the jungle had swallowed up all traces of the hermit, he stumbled on something.

Hidden in the dense growth was a small clearing, so shaded by trees that it felt like a green cave. Panting, Siddhartha stopped and looked around. Someone definitely lived here. From a fire circle, wisps of smoke arose. A bamboo lean-to nestled in one corner with moss spread for a bed. His eye was caught by a pile of rocks made into a shrine. On top was the only sign that anyone but a primitive called the place home: a small picture of Shiva painted in jewel tones, like the forlorn one he'd seen at the house of the dead.

But this god was well tended, with fresh pink wood orchids at the base. Shiva was sitting in lotus position, a tiger skin wrapped around his shoulders. His eyes were closed; a mysterious smile played across his face. Gazing at him, Siddhartha felt exhausted. He had no idea where he was and no longing for anywhere else. Perhaps the faint memory of a rose-apple tree when he was a boy came to mind. He felt his legs give way, and he sat on the ground facing Shiva. He folded his legs in the same position as the god's and closed his eyes.

The green cave was cool and soothing. Siddhartha felt that he belonged here, but there was little time for thinking. A kind of seductive silence wanted to pull him in. It softly surrounded him, and he gave in to the embrace. He could feel his breath moving in and out of his chest, growing fainter and fainter. A fly landed on his arm, and it was as if he could feel every step of its feet before it flew away again.

Nothing changed for a time—how long, he couldn't judge—and then Siddhartha's eyes opened. Before him squatted the old hermit on his heels. It wasn't Asita, but the two were made from the same mold. The hermit had deep brown eyes whose calm belied his weathered skin. Neither of them moved. Then the hermit raised a finger to his lips, and Siddhartha nodded imperceptibly, letting his eyelids close again, sinking back down into the silence. Now he clearly saw the image of a boy sitting under a rose-apple tree while the anxious world swirled around him. How had he forgotten Asita's advice back then, that there would always be a place for him to go when he was in trouble?

With a deep sigh of relief, Siddhartha knew he was back. He hadn't remembered the silence, but *it* had remembered him. And waited. It would be so easy to sit forever. A gentle current flowed through his body, and when a thought chanced to arise, it escaped like a dandelion puff blown away in the breeze.

Before time and space disappeared like thieves in the night, he had a fleeting perception. Something he couldn't identify—a cloud of golden flecks? a ghost wearing a smile? a god?—was hovering a few inches over his head, just where the current had escaped. The cloud or god shimmered for a second. Siddhartha had the distinct feeling that it was watching him.

Then without any warning it began to descend.

PART TWO

GAUTAMA THE MONK

11

The skies had given plenty of warning all day. Clouds with sagging gray bellies almost touched the treetops. Night fell quickly, before shelter could be found. The young monk was curled up under a sal tree in the forest when the rain hit, not with a few warm droplets but all at once, as if mischievous monkeys in the trees had overturned a bucket on his head. The monk awoke with a sputter. He squatted in the mud, shivering, soaked to the bone. Being Prince Siddhartha had filled up twenty-nine years; being a penniless monk had filled up barely a month.

He noticed something nearby. A small clutch of men had built a campfire whose flicker peeked through gaps in the jungle. The monk crept near and saw that they had found protection in the mouth of a cave. It was dangerous to intrude on them. They might be *dacoits*, bandits who had no scruples about killing a holy man simply for his sandals. Also, asking for help wasn't part of the rules. If a wandering monk appeared at their back door, householders were obligated to bring food out to him and offer shelter for the night; sacred duty demanded as much. But the beggar at the door had to remain silent. Only his presence could speak for him, no matter how hungry he might be, even starving.

Sitting in meditation while your nose filled with the smells of rice and lamb cooking over a fire was pure agony. A warrior's discipline, by comparison, was child's play. The young monk always lost focus: he salivated; his stomach growled. But this particular night he didn't have to beg. One of the men sitting around the campfire noticed him and took pity. Siddhartha was startled to see him carrying an ax as he approached, but then he realized the men were woodcutters.

"*Namaste*," he murmured, bowing his head. The woodcutter, a lumbering, thickset man, made no reply. *Namaste* was the simplest form of hello, but from a monk it was also a blessing: *I greet what is holy in you.* Siddhartha noticed that without thinking, he had put a harmless tone in his voice. So in a single word he had said, "Hello, I bow to your sacredness. Please don't hurt me."

"What are you hanging around for?" the man said gruffly.

"I saw your fire," said Siddhartha. "I should have headed for a village, but it got dark too soon."

"Someone like you isn't going to get very far." The man was scowling now. "What's your name?"

"Gautama." Siddhartha held his breath. He had taken on his family name, which was known everywhere. But for centuries it had also been a clan name, and many common people carried it.

"Well, you didn't get any food today, Gautama, that's clear enough."

The young monk had practiced saying the name in his head—*Gautama, Gautama*—but this was the first time another person had used it. Losing his old name was the start of losing his old self. He felt forlorn and victorious at the same time.

"You'd be better off with an honest living that doesn't depend on another man's sweat," the woodcutter said.

Gautama hung his head. If this was a taunt, it was better not to look him in the eye. Exhausted or not, Gautama still knew how to defend himself like a warrior. (When suspicious characters would stare at him and wait by the road while he passed, his hand had reflexively reached for his sword hilt before he remembered that it wasn't there.) He forced himself to have humble thoughts. *You're a holy man. Let God protect you.*

Now the stranger was holding out something. "Take it. You can't expect any food without a bowl, can you?" He pushed forward a smooth hollow gourd, split in half and filled with steamed rice and potatoes. "I'd ask you to the fire, but some of the others—" He nodded in the direction of the group huddling in the mouth of the cave. None had turned their heads to look at the stranger crouching in the mud. "They've had bad run-ins with monks."

Gautama nodded. In the month he had been wandering, he'd heard tales of criminals and madmen who assumed the disguise of monks so they could roam the countryside undisturbed.

"A blessing on you, brother." Gautama said this with complete sincerity, and he continued looking into his benefactor's eyes rather than diving into the food. He knew that his accent gave away that he was high-caste. He touched the man's arm in gratitude, and the woodcutter was startled. Sometimes, very rarely, a high-caste warrior or noble might take up the life of a wandering monk, but they never touched anyone of low caste, even as beggars.

"And a blessing on you," the man said. He got up and walked back to the fire.

As a *sannyasi,* one who has completely renounced the world, Gautama was allowed no possessions other than his saffron robes, a walking stick, a string of prayer beads around his neck, and a begging bowl. A monk ate out of his bowl, and when he was done, he washed it in the river and wore it as a hat to keep off the sun and rain. The bowl was what he drank from, and while he was bathing in the river he rinsed himself with it. Gautama turned the gourd around, admiring its simplicity.

Once he had eaten the food the woodcutter gave him, Gautama got to his feet, trying not to groan from the cracked blisters on his soles. He took a last, longing look at the fire—the men were drinking and laughing loudly now—and began slip-sliding through the mud toward the road. You couldn't sleep too near the roads because of bandits. As he walked, he wrapped his arms around his thin frame for warmth and tried to find resignation. *It's just rain. This is nothing important. I accept it. I'm at peace.* But resignation was empty peace, with no real satisfaction. What else could he try? Reverence.

Holy gods, protect your servant in time of need.

Repeating a prayer felt better, but his mind wasn't fooled by reverence, either. It injected an ironic aside: *If the gods wanted to protect you, why did they leave you out in the rain?* Gautama was astonished at how many ways his mind could plague him. It blamed him for everything—for his blistered feet, for getting lost in the forest, for making a bed from tree boughs that turned out to be full of lice. Hadn't Prince Siddhartha's mind been calmer before he left home? Sick of arguing with himself, Gautama began to count his steps.

One, two, three.

It was a feeble trick to keep his doubts from attacking him. But he had too many memories, the kind that he couldn't escape on the longest road.

Four, five, six.

The worst memory was of leaving his wife, Yashodhara. She had refused to watch Siddhartha ride beyond the gates. "Go at night. Don't tell me when. It would be like having my heart broken twice," she said. Her face was careworn with the tears she had shed. The two had been married almost ten years. It was such a love match that they had never spent a single night apart.

Yashodhara kept silent the first few days after he made his intention known, but they shared a bed, and one night she found her voice, softly, next to his ear. "Isn't love enough, being here with me?"

Siddhartha wrapped his arm around her. He knew this question cost her an effort. If he said no, she wasn't enough, Yashodhara would feel like a widow when he left. If he said yes, he had no argument for leaving. After a moment he said, "You are enough for this life."

"Are you looking ahead to the next one?" she asked.

"No, not that. This life is only part of who I am. I need to know everything, and I can't by staying here." His expression was deeply serious, although she couldn't see his face in the dark. "How can I know if I have a soul? Ever since I was a boy I've assumed I did because everyone says so. How can I know if the gods are real? Or that I came from them?"

"Knowing everything is impossible," she said. Siddhartha sighed and held her closer. "It won't be forever," he promised. Yashodhara tried to believe him despite her experience. Everybody knew of husbands who ran off into the forest and never came back. Becoming a sannyasi was a holy act, but respectable men left it for old age.

Many men waited until they were seventy, especially if they had money, and the richest built lavish summerhouses that were a mockery of spiritual retreat. But all kinds of ne'er-do-wells ran away early. It was something you did if life got too hard or you had too many mouths to feed.

Yashodhara realized that some monks had a genuine calling. One day, despite her sorrow, she told her husband, "I know you have to go. I'm your wife. I feel what you feel." But scandal burned her cheeks anyway; a prince of the blood deserting his kingdom was worse, infinitely worse, than some farmer deserting his barren rice fields.

Seven, eight, nine.

Gautama's mind wasn't falling for the feeble trick. *You nearly killed her,* it said with bitter accusation.

Ten, eleven, twelve.

People can die of grief. How would you feel then?

Gautama winced, remembering how much Yashodhara had suffered as his departure neared. Every night made her dread that she would wake up alone in the morning. There was nothing she could do for him, not even to pack little things for his new life. On the other side of the palace gates a beggar's existence awaited.

Suddhodana, now enfeebled with arthritis, had mustered up a brief, reproachful rage, as in the old days. "You can't give me one good reason," he shouted. But the lit fuse sputtered out, and after that his father ignored the whole subject.

When it was finally time, the prince performed two farewell rituals. He went into his wife's chamber and kissed her while she slept, a bar of soft moonlight across her lips. This was a familiar ritual from the days when he had first begun to ride out before dawn in order to reach poor, faraway villages. The forgotten city had shriveled to nothing, its last feeble cast-offs taken under the prince's personal care. He had knelt by the bedside of those who had cursed him the first day he rode into the village.

There was one, a withered scarecrow of a woman named Gutta who was as old as Kumbira, a former ladies' maid overjoyed to come back to the palace. She knew she was there to die. Siddhartha sometimes imagined that Gutta might have been an auntie to him long ago. During her last days he sat vigil, and one night he trusted her enough to ask, "Does it hurt to die?"

She shook her head. "Not as much as you're hurting."

"Why am I hurting?"

"How should I know?" The withered old maid had always been crabby, he knew, and dying hadn't sweetened her temper. After a moment she said, "I'm luckier than you. I'm throwing off my burden, but you keep adding more to yours."

"Is that what you see?" He had heard that the dying told the truth and even had prophetic powers.

She snorted. "Everybody does. Just look at you. You're kind, but you think it's not enough. You give to the poor and sick, but you don't feel happy from it." Her voice grew softer. "You mourn a dead girl there was no hope of finding."

The prince had looked away, feeling a pang from every word. His mission of mercy began while he was searching for Sujata. It became his custom to lead a pack mule loaded with food, crop seeds, and clothing behind his magnificent white stallion, and the three became a familiar sight in the countryside. For the sake of safety, an armed guard rode behind, but he had made sure that the men kept far back, out of sight.

"What does it say if I ride into a village with soldiers?" he asked his father.

"It says nobody better lay a hand on you," replied the old king, who wanted to send half the garrison with him.

But his son couldn't stand the idea of showing people mercy with one hand and a sword with the other. Soon his kindness was the thing that kept him safe. The local thieves and bandits belonged to their own caste of dacoits. Many of them benefited from the food he took to the starving villages, since dacoit families and dacoit relatives lived in them. The younger, headstrong thieves argued that they still had a right to loot any gold a traveler might be carrying, but the elders knew he carried none.

"His type can't stop himself. If he lays eyes on one colicky baby, he'll throw all his money on the bed if he has any," they said, quieting the hotheads.

Siddhartha's second ritual of farewell had been to kiss his baby son. The boy was four, old enough to have his own room. The prince had taken a candle and tiptoed in. Rahula slept, not curled up in a ball like most children, but facedown with his limbs spread-eagled, as if he was prepared to take flight. He lay like that now, and his father looked at him a long time, then turned away without kissing him. Resolved as he was, regret would have its way. *If he wakes up and sees me, I'll never go.*

That night of departure Channa drove a chariot to protect Siddhartha, but instead of standing behind him the way he would in battle, the prince rode Kanthaka, who was old but still strong.

When the gates of Kapilavastu closed behind them and they hit the main dirt road, Kanthaka's hoofbeats became a dull thud, like muffled drums at a funeral. They moved slowly toward the river. Channa's back was rigid with anger; he refused to break his sullen silence. By sunrise the prince was bathing in the green, slow-flowing river. He stepped out and wrapped a saffron skirt around his waist.

"What do I do with those?" asked Channa. He pointed at the embroidered robe and silk shirt hanging from a tree limb. There was no need to give him instructions—royal finery was burned after it was discarded. Channa just wanted an excuse to pick a quarrel.

"It's a waste to burn them if you're really coming back," he said. "Or did you just tell her that?"

Siddhartha ignored the jibe. "Do what you want. They belong to someone who isn't me anymore." He took out a short-bladed razor and began to cut his long hair as close to the scalp as he could.

"Isn't you anymore?" Channa shook his head with disbelief. He had no idea why Siddhartha had gone crazy, only that he had.

Siddhartha continued quietly cutting his hair. He hadn't reckoned on how much sorrow he would create around him by deciding to leave. His father fumed and screamed at the servants. Channa whipped the chariot horses too hard. Smiling court ladies acted vaguely as if they'd been jilted. What they really felt, deep inside, was that he had died.

Siddhartha held out the razor to him. "Do you mind?" he said. Channa looked startled. "You've done so much for me, friend. This is the last thing I'll ask." Siddhartha pointed at the back of his head, where he had made a mess of cutting his hair. Channa reluctantly took the blade. He squatted beside Siddhartha on his heels and began to cut. He was expert at it. This was something that women didn't do. Barbering was left to men, and on the battlefield soldiers would trim off hair that was too long to fit under a helmet.

At first he was rough, and Siddhartha, saying nothing, gave him a questioning look. "Sorry," Channa mumbled. After a moment he began to settle down. The intimate act distracted him from his grief. Channa knew, as everyone at court did, that only he was allowed to touch the prince—tapping his shoulder to make a point in argument, brushing dirt off his hunting jacket, embracing him when Siddhartha rode off to the villages—but no one openly spoke about this breach of caste rules.

"That's enough." Siddhartha took the razor from Channa's hands. "I don't want anyone to think I have an expert barber."

"No, you're just another monk with hardly a stitch to wear," Channa said.

They parted there by the river as the sun came over the treetops. Channa refused to say farewell; he kept his arms tightly pinned by his side to deflect Siddhartha's attempt to embrace him. As Siddhartha walked away, he trained his eyes straight ahead for the first hour. The jungle canopy was fairly dense, even though trees had been cut down to make the road. For a while he hardly knew how he felt, except in the most basic physical ways. His body felt lighter; the slightest breeze ruffled his thin silk shawl and passed coolly over his skin. Being without long hair and heavy robes was exhilarating and unnerving.

Having been a hunter, he knew how to forage for fruit and wild greens; in the past few years he'd spent days on long treks without provisions. But it wasn't the physical necessities that worried him. To really be Gautama, he would need to find a teacher. There were forest hermitages scattered over the countryside, most of them near big villages and towns. Saffron-robed beggars had become a common sight on the wide streets of cities beyond the kingdom of Sakya. Their increasing numbers baffled people, and the priests muttered about shiftless pretenders. Some kind of spiritual ferment was taking hold. Before he left home, Siddhartha was intrigued by this new movement, which didn't even have a name yet.

"It's young rascals, these so-called holy men," a silk merchant complained. "They fear work like the plague. They're abandoning the farms and turning away from their parents. Nothing seems to hold them back, certainly not respect."

The merchant kept his own son tied close to his side with constant demands and a trickle of money, not enough for him to leave or to get married before the father arranged a match.

"How do they live?" Siddhartha asked.

"Like any other lazybones. I wouldn't leave meat hanging in my front yard," said the merchant. "You never know when the gods might want it."

Siddhartha ignored his cynicism. "Who teaches them?"

"You call it teaching? What are the temples for? Not that the priests are much better, mind you." Siddhartha pressed the point, and the merchant eventually realized that he wasn't there simply to reinforce high-caste prejudice. "I'm amazed that you care, Your Highness. From what I can tell, the young ones seek out the older ones. They move around the forest from camp to camp, and the day they arrive at some makeshift school, they bow down before the teacher and ask about the *Dharma*, whatever his angle happens to be. Dharma? The priests filled us with enough of that." *Dharma* could mean many things—a man's occupation, the rules of proper conduct, a person's holy duties as outlined by scripture. In this case it was a philosophy, a particular teaching that disciples committed themselves to learn.

"And which Dharma is attracting the most followers?" Siddhartha asked.

The merchant shrugged. "Who can say? The young ones keep wandering. They're restless and never stay anywhere very long."

Other travelers that Siddhartha came in contact with were just as hostile. They would have been shocked if they could have penetrated Siddhartha's defenses and seen what lay behind his hospitable smile. He belonged to the same young, restless breed that disappeared into the forest for years at a time. With each passing day he became more and more aware of his calling. Yet, time was pressing. If he stayed in the palace for just a few more years, the king would be old enough to step aside and bequeath Siddhartha the throne. He couldn't let that happen. Not love, not family, not his own conscience could force him to betray himself.

And this is what you call being true to yourself?

Gautama's mind wasn't convinced. The rain continued to pour from the sky, and the road was so dark that more than once he slipped into the gully on the side. There was no use arguing with his mind, which seemed untamable anyway. Gautama wondered if he was alone among mortals, wanting to abandon all that was good in order to suffer the torment and uncertainty of the wild world. He'd add that to his long list of questions to ask his teacher once he found him. If he found him.

12

Gautama passed several travelers on the road who could have directed him to one of the forest ashrams where teachers were located. He greeted them humbly, letting them decide to accept his company for a few miles or not; a handful offered him food for his bowl. But he was reluctant to throw himself into the midst of a band of disciples. Gautama wanted to learn, but he didn't want to give up who he was. His only model for a spiritual teacher was Canki, who had a hidden motive for everything he said.

It wasn't long before he ran across a wandering monk, a thin, sunburned man who seemed old enough to have had a family with grown children. Gautama expected that the sannyasis he met would be very serious or very eccentric. But this monk, who gave his name as Ganaka, turned out to be cheerful and sociable.

"I've been away for twelve years now, lad," he said as they walked along the road. "You meet all sorts. But now the local people know me, and I'm treated pretty well. Your first holdup's a shock, though. The dacoits like you to know who's boss."

"Do you belong to an ashram?" Gautama asked.

Ganaka shrugged. "I've visited them. You get too hungry sometimes."

"What Dharma do you follow?"

The older monk gave him a look. "Is that what you're after? I didn't know you were one of those." He had nothing more to say for a while, and Gautama wondered with some puzzlement if the word *Dharma* had offended him. How could you be a monk without a teaching? When he decided to speak again, the older monk said, "Don't let them fool you."

"Who?"

"These teachers who promise enlightenment. Listen to the voice of experience. I'm not enlightened, and you won't be either. They'll feed you a pack of high-sounding ideas, you'll work for them year after year, and then when they've worn you out, you'll leave with the taste of ashes in your mouth."

There was a lot to read in Ganaka's bitter tone. In a sympathetic voice Gautama said, "Tell me your experience. I want to know."

Ganaka sighed. "In that case, you'd better have some of my bread. I was going to save it until you were out of sight." He reached into his shawl and pulled out a large round roti, or flat bread, folded into quarters. He ripped off half for Gautama, but not before blessing it. "I see myself in you," the older monk began. "I left home after my wife died. I was a vendor of ghee and spices in a village, never rich enough to own a proper store but not poor either."

"And you were devout?"

"Oh, yes. Raised by a strict father who sent us to the temple for lessons as soon as we could walk. As a child I believed. Even when my dear Bhadda died in so much pain, moaning pitifully for her suffering to end, I believed. I gave away all my earthly possessions, and with the blessing of the priests I set out on my journey."

"I think you're still devout," said Gautama. "You bless your food. Even when no one is watching, I imagine."

"Habit," the older monk said curtly. "Anyway, the road is a hard life. I went to visit the forest ashrams, eager as a bridegroom the night after the wedding. I sat at the guru's feet and waited, mouth open like a gaping fish. That's why I see myself in you. You want them to drop their wisdom into your gaping mouth. You're probably a philosopher. No offense, but I can tell by your accent that you never sold rubbish from a stall in the open bazaar."

"I can't disagree," said Gautama diplomatically, caught between smiling at the older monk, who clearly had been dying for someone to talk to, and worrying about the tale of disillusion that was about to unfold.

Ganaka tore off a chunk of roti with his yellow teeth. "They're shameless, these gurus. The garbage they spew as truth! Do they think we're fools? They must, as I found out the hard way. I took some of the younger disciples aside and joked with them a bit. Little stuff. Does this guru get paid by the yarn, like a wandering storyteller? Does he think you can feed cows on moonbeams? Next thing I knew, I got thrown out bodily, like I came to steal their shoes. Hypocrisy." His voice trailed off mournfully as he ran out of spleen. "Moonbeams and hypocrisy."

"What did you decide to do?"

"I couldn't go home. I'd given almost everything to the priests, and they don't give back. But you've got some sense, you could see that I'm still devout. I pray, and I have a circuit of householders who feed me and let me take refuge from the storm."

"Pardon me, but aren't you simply waiting to die?" asked Gautama.

Ganaka shrugged. "It's a life."

Before Gautama could pose another question, they heard a commotion up ahead. A man was screaming curses, a woman was crying. Gautama's steps quickened, and when he rounded the next curve he saw what the trouble was. A laden bullock cart going to market had run off into the ditch. Several bags of grain had spilled out. A woman was crouched on the ground trying to scoop up the scattered grain with her hands, while over her stood her furious husband.

"Are you an idiot? You're putting dirt back in the bags. Stop bawling!" he shouted. He began to beat her about the shoulders with his bullock goad.

Gautama came toward them. When he saw a monk, the husband sullenly lowered his stick. "Is your animal hurt?" Gautama asked, noticing that the bullock, which was old and blind in one eye, had fallen onto its front knees.

Without answering, the man began to apply the goad heavily to the bullock, who lowed mournfully as it struggled to regain its footing. Out of panic it pulled the wrong way and tilted the cart farther over; more bags spilled out, and the woman began to weep loudly. Beside himself now, the man couldn't decide which one to beat next, the bullock or his wife.

"Wait," begged Gautama. "I can help you."

"How?" the husband grumbled. "If I have to give you a bag of rice, you're cheating me."

"Don't think about that, just try to calm down," Gautama coaxed.

Once he got the husband to back off from his rage, Gautama helped him free the bullock from its yoke and unload the cart. Then he and the man shouldered the cart from the rear and with considerable grunting and groaning rolled it out of the ditch. While they sweated in the hot sun, the wife sat in the shade holding the bullock's tether and fanning herself with a palm leaf.

"There." Gautama stood back after the last bag of grain had been put back into place.

Without a word the man got into the driver's seat. "Are you coming or not?" he said sourly to his wife.

She put her hands on her hips. "Why? So I can go home with a man who beats his bullock into a ditch and is so stupid it takes a monk to show him how to get it out again?"

Gautama could see that the man wanted to hit her again with the goad, but his shame kept him from doing it in front of a holy man. He bit his lip while his wife climbed into the cart, flashing a contemptuous smile at the young monk. The cart began to trundle off. Over his shoulder the man said, "Whatever rice you can pick out of the road is yours. Namaste."

Gautama turned around to find Ganaka standing a dozen yards away laughing, and he was clearly laughing at him. "How long have you been standing there?" Gautama demanded, feeling the blood rising to his face.

"The whole time," said the older monk nonchalantly. He was chewing a stem of sour grass he'd plucked from the roadside.

"Is there a stream nearby? I need to wash my face," Gautama said curtly. There was no point, he thought, in asking why Ganaka hadn't helped or if he had heard of the monastic vow of service. The older monk led the way to a fresh rivulet in the forest. Gautama poured water from his begging bowl over his head and shoulders while Ganaka watched, squatting on his heels.

"Those people didn't love you for what you did," he pointed out.

"I didn't expect them to," Gautama replied. The stream was shallow enough that the water he poured over his back felt as warm as bathwater. His tense muscles began to relax.

Ganaka said, "If you didn't want them to love you, at least you wanted gratitude. You're just too proud to admit it. And angry that I laughed at you. Imagine, here you are being a saint, and a monk, no less, ridicules you for it."

Hearing the truth stung, but Gautama was too exhausted to work up heavy resentment. Instead he said, "Was I ridiculous in your eyes?"

"Why would it matter? A saint has to rise above ridicule. Maybe I was trying to teach you that."

"Are you my teacher now? I thought you hated teachers." Gautama knew that he had let childish pique creep into his voice, but he didn't care.

He expected Ganaka to keep on mocking him, but the older monk's voice grew suddenly serious. "I'm part of the world. If you want a teacher, turn to the world."

Gautama stepped out of the water, feeling cooler but still sore with the sense of having been badly used. "The world's wisdom is contained in you? Congratulations."

"Not all the world's wisdom, but a piece of it. The piece you need to hear," said Ganaka calmly.

"And what is that?"

"Are you free enough of anger to listen?" Ganaka asked. He met Gautama's stare. "I didn't think so." He sat under a tree and watched Gautama as indifferently as he had watched the husband and wife in trouble. Gautama could have walked away, but after a moment he felt settled enough to sit down beside the older monk.

"Everything you say is true," he admitted.

"Only it shouldn't be. That's your position, isn't it? That when you act like a saint, you should be loved, and whoever sees you doing good works should be inspired to join you."

"All right, yes," said Gautama reluctantly. "What's your position? That you can be my teacher by standing around and letting me do all the work?"

"There was no work to do."

"I think there was," Gautama protested.

"Then tell me where I'm wrong. The man would have calmed down eventually and figured out how to unyoke his animal and empty the cart. He and his wife were strong enough to push the cart out of the ditch, and if they weren't, they could walk back to their village and get help. So by helping them, you kept them from helping themselves."

"Go on."

"If you thought you were preventing violence because the man stopped beating his wife, all you really did was shame him. He will not only resent you for that; he will beat his wife extra hard tonight to make a point. He is master, she is slave."

"And no one should try to show them a better way?"

"Maybe, but why should it be you? They had parents and priests who taught them right from wrong. They must know families where the wife isn't beaten every time the husband loses his temper. Or maybe they don't. Why should it be up to you? You're a wandering beggar," Ganaka pointed out.

Gautama was too tired to argue in the face of the older monk's certainty. "I'm sorry you feel that way," he mumbled.

Ganaka laughed with a hint of scorn. "You can do better than that. I can tell what you're thinking. You're highborn, so that makes you right. No question about it."

"Do you always goad people like this?" Gautama asked, resolving not to make himself the butt of this irksome cynic.

"Is there any other way to learn?" Ganaka replied. "If you don't want the world to have more shame, helplessness, and slavery, stop doing what you did today. All you did was increase it." He got to his feet, as indifferent as if they'd been talking about the possibility of rain, and looked around for the shortest way back to the main road.

"Thank you for the bread, and the company," Gautama said, forcing the words out.

Ganaka shrugged. "I may not be enlightened enough to suit you, my idealistic lad. But I'm far from being a fool. Don't pretend you're a saint. Experience tells me that they might not even exist."

THE OLD KING mourned the day he saw his son ride out the gates of Kapilavastu, but he didn't send guards to break into the Shiva temple and arrest the high Brahmin. The writing had been on the wall a long time before their plan finally failed. Canki realized that fate had turned against him, and he decided to appear in the king's chambers one morning unannounced. He bowed without prostrating himself on the floor.

"I hope you don't have the gall to try to console me," Suddhodana grumbled. He had taken to sleeping late, and more often than not there was a young courtesan on the pillow by his side, the only consolation Suddhodana wanted these days.

"I'm only a priest, bringing the king's wishes before the gods," Canki said.

"I had only one wish, and you failed to make it come true. Your presence is distasteful to us. You should stay home."

They had hatched their conspiracy almost thirty years earlier, and Suddhodana wasn't one to look backward. He placed little faith in the promise that Siddhartha would return. "Return as what?" he said. "He'll never come back a king." The last part he didn't voice aloud to anyone, just as he didn't voice a secret intention he had, to name Devadatta as his successor. The notion had come to him in a dream. He often revisited old battles in his dreams, but not as he had fought them. Instead he was a wanderer among the dead.

Night after night Suddhodana saw himself asleep in his tent, still dressed in armor. He would wake up feeling stifled, suffocating for air. He would throw aside the tent flap, and scattered around him in the moonlight would be bodies, thick on the ground in poses of agony. He didn't weep over them; he hated them for troubling his peace.

However, this dream was different. He wandered the dusty field listlessly, head bowed. He came across a shallow grave. A body lay faceup, arms crossed over its chest. A cloud passed away from the moon, and he recoiled to see Siddhartha's corpse. A cry erupted from his chest, and Suddhodana leaped into the grave. He embraced the corpse, which was horribly cold. Suddhodana was wracked with sobs, so strongly that he was sure it would wake him up. Instead, the corpse moved. Suddhodana clutched it tighter, praying that his own life could seep into his son and revive him.

The corpse's head was beside his ear, and a voice said, "The prince is not the king." These were Siddhartha's words, and the moment they were spoken Suddhodana woke up in a cold sweat, but not before he got an instant's glimpse of the face again, which melted into dust.

He turned now to Canki. "You've been released. That's why I'm not going to kill you," he said.

"Released?"

"From our plot. I'm not heartless. I know what I've done, to my son and to all those people who suffered."

Canki had never heard the king talk this way; remorse wasn't in his nature. In fact, the high Brahmin had intruded in the royal chambers to remind Suddhodana that his son still had a great destiny ahead of him.

"You must have another plan. I will aid you however I can. I sense that you've found a ray of hope. True?"

Suddhodana gave a derisive snort. "So, you're not in your dotage after all. I thought priests softened when they saw heaven coming closer." He didn't wait for a reply. "What if Devadatta is king? Do we trust him?"

"Is that really necessary?" Canki said coolly. After Sujata's disappearance Devadatta had fallen under a cloud, yet he might be a necessary tool, and for that reason the king hadn't banished him.

"Explain yourself," Suddhodana demanded.

"The boy came here as a prisoner. He turned into a schemer. You have no idea if he really loves you or simply fears you. For myself, I don't think anyone could find out the truth. But it doesn't matter. What matters is ambition. If you promise Devadatta the throne, two purposes will be served. You will put out the fire of his hatred. And you will give your kingdom to someone as vicious as you are."

Heaven had to be close indeed for anyone, let alone a Brahmin, to risk those last words. Suddhodana looked at Canki, who had lost much of his imposing bulk. His haughtiness seemed to have shrunk with his body.

"You call it vicious, I call it being strong," Suddhodana said.

Canki and the king bent their heads together, rethinking every aspect of the new plan, mulling over every possible point where it might go wrong. Conspiracy was their only bond, and now that new blood flowed into it, the king felt alive as he hadn't for a long time.

• • •

SUDDHODANA WOULD NEVER KNOW if a demon or a god had sent him his prophetic dream. But a demon wanted Devadatta to be king. Of that there was no doubt. For almost ten years Mara had been bored by mortal affairs. He had watched Devadatta and Siddhartha like twin horses trying to break the yoke that bound them. He hated the way humans clung to indecision.

Devadatta had grown more violent over the years. His night excursions into the poor parts of the city ended as often in murder now as in rape. Since he was protected by caste, no one dared assassinate him for fear that they would be damned in the afterlife. So the common people set up watch, and when Devadatta's horse was spied, or if he showed his face in a tavern, word spread quickly and doors were locked. He found himself lurking deserted streets, and in time his great problem wasn't his obsessive urge to hurt—it was loneliness.

His only escape these days was to go out riding, either to hunt deer or race his mount mile after mile until both rider and horse were totally spent. This reckless sport injured and crippled several fine horses, but it was the only way Devadatta had found to forget himself. One day soon after Siddhartha left to become a sannyasi—a decision Devadatta considered criminal for a prince of the blood but one that he rejoiced in as well, for now he had an opening, an opportunity to seize control of the kingdom—Devadatta had left the main road in order to force his horse to gallop where the trees were thick, adding to the thrill of his excursion.

Suddenly he smelled smoke in the air. He stopped and rose in the stirrups, casting his eyes over the trees until he saw the thin wisp of a campfire. Normally he wouldn't have cared. Fires were set by woodcutters and other workers, never women. But Devadatta heard a faint whisper in his ear, and on impulse he rode toward the fire.

Sitting by the fire with his back turned to him was Siddhartha, and he hadn't become a monk at all. He was still wearing his princely robe and embroidered skirt. His cousin had simply run off for some secret reason. In the next instant, however, Devadatta's horse stepped on a twig with a loud crack. The man by the fire turned his head, and Devadatta saw that he was mistaken. The man smiled nervously, and his cracked teeth and stubbled beard betrayed that he was a beggar. Devadatta could see that he was roasting a dead parrot he must have scavenged on the forest floor.

"Friend, can I help you?" The man stood up, smiling anxiously.

"Don't call me friend," said Devadatta coldly. "Where did you steal those clothes? Did you kill someone for them, or are you with the dacoits?"

"Kill?" The man looked alarmed now as Devadatta slowly rode toward him. "I couldn't be no killer, or no dacoit, sir. As Your Worship can see, I'm all alone."

It was true that forest thieves always traveled in packs. "What if I believe you? You still have on royal clothes, anyone can see, filthy as they've gotten," said Devadatta, making his voice as menacing as he could.

The man started to strip Siddhartha's robes off. "You can have 'em, sir. I never been to court. I knew they was fine clothes, but I never suspected them of being royal. Not for a minute, I swear."

The poor man was too frightened to run and had no chance of escape if he did. Devadatta had already seen what must have happened in his mind's eye. A wretched beggar lying in a ditch. His fool of a cousin taking pity—hadn't he already wasted years ministering to the poor? No doubt he lifted the beggar up and gave him the clothes off his back. Devadatta shook his head.

"Stop trembling," he said. "And put your clothes back on. You think I'd touch them?"

"Thank you, sir." The beggar mumbled his gratitude and with one eye glanced over at the fire, where he had dropped the parrot. His meal had roasted to a crisp, and he looked pained.

"It's ruined," said Devadatta, nodding toward the fire. "Forget it. I'll make sure you don't need to beg anymore."

The beggar's smile would have turned to a look of puzzlement, but he had no time for that. It took a matter of seconds for Devadatta to draw his sword and even less, given his years of practice with the weapon, to chop off the beggar's head with one swipe.

That evening Suddhodana heard women wailing outside his rooms. Something in their cries was heartrending. This wasn't another funeral formality for an aged courtier. He opened the door to see every lady at court kneeling along the entire length of the main corridor.

"Out of my way!"

He strode through the mass of female bodies, bent as low as hummocks in a meadow, with little care that he was stepping on them. In the main courtyard of the palace the court men formed a dense crowd, some murmuring in low, grim tones, others shouting oaths and imprecations. The crowd was a thick, angry mass like a single creature. By now Suddhodana's blood was cold. It could only be one thing. The crowd parted when he was spotted, and all but the most senior advisers and generals prostrated themselves on the cobblestones, which were still hot as cooking stones so soon after sunset.

"Where is he? Where is my son?"

Suddhodana followed the eyes of the men around him. Their gaze formed a path, and at the end stood Devadatta. He had dismounted. Over his tall horse, whose sides were panting from a hard ride, a body was draped. It took a second before the king recognized his son's clothes hanging off the corpse. The head had been cut off, leaving a grisly stem.

Suddhodana recoiled in revulsion. He had no desire to come closer or to take a second look. He turned and put one foot ahead of the other until he had reached the security of his darkened rooms. The heat of the cobblestones seeped through his sandals. The old king felt it, and somehow his hot shoes stuck in his mind, the way trivial things often do, as the first thing he remembered on the long road of suffering that stretched ahead forever.

13

The moment Gautama stepped into the small clearing, he knew that he'd found what he was looking for. A crude thatched lean-to faced him from under the shade of an old tree. The shadows were deep, but he could see a hermit sitting in lotus position. There was no trail of footprints or telltale smoke in the air to lead Gautama to this place. He had been away from home for three months now, and he was an adept forest dweller himself. No longer did he wake up with a start in the middle of the night fearing danger from the snap of a twig. He could let his footsteps wander where they wanted to, and now here he was.

He crossed the small clearing and stood over the hermit, who could have been Asita—slender, wiry build, nut brown skin, thinning hair with a long beard. Gautama moved as silently as he could, and he didn't speak in greeting to the old ascetic, who made no motion, not even the flutter of an eyelid, to acknowledge his visitor. Finding the shade of a nearby tree, Gautama sat under it and folded his legs. For ten years now he had been meditating, and just as Asita promised, it had become his refuge from the outside world.

At first he had found it hard to settle down completely. As the scriptures say, the mind is like a runaway coach, and the driver never stops whipping the horses. But from inside the coach a voice whispers, "Please stop." At first the team and driver ignore the voice. It is very soft; it never insists. Over time, however, the voice wins obedience, and the driver and horses stop wildly galloping. Bit by bit they slow down until the mind is at rest. Thus Siddhartha learned a basic lesson: whatever can run can also stand still.

Gradually the tree shade moved away, and he began to sweat. He could see an orange glow in his eyelids and knew, if it was this near sunset, that hours must have passed. Gautama took a peek, but the hermit was still motionless under his lean-to. There was no guarantee that he possessed any wisdom or could be a useful teacher. But Gautama had promised himself that he would seek out someone like Asita. How can freedom be taught except by someone who is free?

Darkness descended, and still there was no sign of activity. Gautama got to his feet and headed toward a stream he'd crossed near the clearing. Stooping to drink, he realized that waiting could take longer than he'd thought. He collected some fruit from the trees and headed back to the clearing. He fashioned a bed of boughs and went to sleep. The hermit became a black outline against the nearly black night sky.

In this way three days passed. The hermit's ability to remain as still as one of the Shiva statues outside Canki's temple impressed Gautama deeply. His own body ached from the hours he had put in sitting and waiting for something to happen. He fidgeted, obeyed the call of nature, ate and drank when he had to. Like a force of nature, the wiry old man remained immobile. Once or twice Gautama gave a soft cough to make his presence known. On the second day he ventured to say "Namaste" in a quiet voice. On the evening of the third day, he walked over to the ascetic, squatted on his heels beside him, and said, "Sir?"

The hermit opened his eyes. "You talk too much," he said. His voice was clear and alert; the trance he was waking up from was no ordinary kind.

"Can you teach me?" Gautama asked, wanting to seize the

moment before the hermit retreated back into his deep *samadhi* once more. But he was too late. The hermit closed his eyes, and soon the sun set. Gautama stretched out on the ground for the night, having no idea if he'd made any progress. Apparently he had. When he woke up the next morning the hermit was standing over him.

"Maybe," the hermit said.

Gautama sprang to his feet. "What shall I do first?"

"Be quiet."

The hermit went back to his place under the lean-to and resumed his meditation. Gautama suspected that he wouldn't open his eyes for another three days. It took four. In the meantime, however, the new disciple wasn't bored. Gradually he began to be filled with his teacher's presence. It happened invisibly. Gautama was obliged to meditate along with his master. Imitating the guru was the main path for a disciple: you ate when the guru ate, slept when the guru slept, listened when the guru spoke. Yet the greatest teachers, so Siddhartha had been told when he interrogated visitors to court, taught in complete silence.

Apparently Gautama had run into one of those, for whenever he closed his eyes, something new would happen. He found stillness, as before, but now it was vibrant and alive, as if a shower of sparkling white light were falling inside him. Its effervescence caused his body to tingle gently, a delicious sensation that made it effortless to sit in meditation for hours at a time. In between, when Gautama found that his limbs were too stiff and his body too restless to sit any longer, he puttered around the clearing, sweeping away debris, placing a gourd of water beside his master, gathering fruit and firewood for the night. He was eager to ask the hermit how he managed to enter a disciple and fill him with his presence. Then he remembered his master's rebuke about talking too much. On the evening of the fourth day the hermit surfaced from his samadhi.

His first word was, "Well?"

Gautama prostrated himself at the hermit's feet. He could have said, "I am satisfied," but his gesture of obeisance was enough. His teacher had given him a taste of all that was to come, and when he said, "Well?" he meant, "Do you accept me?" The bond between a guru and a *chela,* or disciple, exists deep in the heart. Gautama had become so sensitized that this one word, "Well?" said everything. It said, *This is how things will be. If you want praise and smiles, go to someone else. I'm not here to flatter you.*

The routine at camp was soon established. The disciple performed the small duties that kept the necessities of life going. Most of the time the two of them simply sat, facing each other across the clearing like two life-size icons abandoned by a sculptor in the forest. Then the face of Yashodhara began to appear in Gautama's mind. She was smiling, and he couldn't help looking at her smile. The scriptures give permission to meditate upon various divine images, so why not his wife? If love is divine, can't a woman also be? Yet the moment Gautama fixed his mind's eye on Yashodhara's face, her body appeared, and it was not clothed. The young monk squirmed, praying that his master didn't see the physical reaction this caused, which wasn't his fault.

He fought his reaction. Meditating on arousal wasn't in the scriptures. Yashodhara's face changed; it began to mock him. Her hands moved down her body. He fought harder. Perhaps if he focused on the purity of his love for her. Gautama thought about the day he chose her to be his wife. She was sixteen, he was nineteen. He had given up on finding Sujata but was far from losing her memory. When it was announced that he was to be betrothed, eager fathers drove a long distance to present their daughters in faraway Kapilavastu. Nobles, princes, and kings of neighboring domains crossed the border with elaborate entourages of slaves and horses. Siddhartha sat on the ramparts looking down at the scene with Channa.

"If the interviews are too much for you, I can always take a few off your hands," Channa said. Some of the younger girls were barely twelve; it wasn't expected that he would live with them immediately—arrangements would be made. But delay was only temporary. Suddhodana couldn't be put off.

"Choose a girl who plays with dolls, choose an old maid of nineteen," the king said. "But you can't walk away without choosing someone." They both knew that the future of the dynasty was at stake.

On the ceremonial day when all the hopeful brides were assembled at court, Siddhartha entered the hall in the same elaborate coat and plumed red turban he had worn when he turned eighteen. Each girl was prostrate on the floor, and as the prince walked down the line, he would catch a fetching or shy glance, a glint in one eye that promised sensual delight, in another a darting shyness that spoke of innocence and even bewilderment. Only one girl didn't look up at him, keeping her veiled face to the floor. She made Siddhartha curious.

"A great day!" declared Suddhodana in a loud, jovial voice. But when his son walked into his embrace, he whispered in his ear, "None of your tricks. They're not here so you can pray with them."

Siddhartha knelt. "I know my duty, father." As he turned around, a chamberlain ran up and handed him a garland of gold necklaces. Siddhartha pulled out a strand and approached the first girl.

"You are very beautiful. Why do you wish to marry me?" he asked, lifting her from the floor. Her direct gaze told him she wasn't shy.

"Because you are kind and good. And handsome." She gave him a seductive look, one that was well practiced. Siddhartha knew it was called "the assassin's knife" in the manuals of love that noble girls were given to read. He bowed and handed her the gold necklace. He returned a smile that was gracious, but Siddhartha wasn't practiced at hiding his feelings, and the girl knew she had no chance. Her father would be furious.

To the second girl he said, "If anyone could be even more beautiful, it's you. Why do you want to marry me?"

The second girl had kept close watch on what happened to the first. She said, "To give you sons as magnificent as yourself." Her voice had the ring of sincerity, but Siddhartha suspected that she was simply better trained. The love manuals taught that a man must always feel that he is making his own decisions while at the same time being carefully manipulated. If a woman was skillful, and applied eros when it was useful, he wouldn't even know what was happening. Siddhartha bowed and handed the second girl a necklace. She put it on with a haughty toss of the head as he moved on.

The king felt anxious. "He doesn't like any of them," he whispered to Canki.

The high Brahmin was unruffled. He knew that discrimination can hold out against desire only so long. "Patience, sire. He's a young man. When peaches are ripe, no one leaves the market without buying one." But nothing about Siddhartha's manner looked promising by the time he had reached the last girl. She looked up at him but didn't remove her veil.

From behind the girl, her father nudged her with a fierce whisper. "Go ahead. Get up and look at him!" She took a moment before rising. Now Siddhartha remembered who she was. The one girl who had made him curious.

"I cannot tell if you are beautiful," he said. "What's your name?"

"Yashodhara."

"May I see you?"

She kept her veil on. "Is my appearance the only thing that would make me worthy? If so, don't look at me. My face might conceal a false heart."

Siddhartha smiled. "A good answer. Then tell me: Why do you wish to marry me?"

"I'm not sure yet. I don't know you, and you haven't made any pretty speeches, the way you did to the others."

Siddhartha was intrigued by these words, but he also had to see her. He lifted Yashodhara's veil. She wasn't beautiful in the way the first girls had been, modeled from the pages of the love manuals. But instantly he knew how he felt.

"You're wonderful, because you were made to be loved."

Up to this moment she had had the advantage, but now Yashodhara blushed. "That was a pretty speech, but too short for me to make up my mind. My father will be so disappointed if I come away empty-handed. Can I have a necklace?"

She held out her hand and Siddhartha frowned. "Was that a good enough reason for you to come here?"

She replied, "Sire, I live in the deep woods, four long days' journey from here. My father is very anxious that I marry you. But a gold necklace can feed a hundred of my starving people, those I left behind."

"Girl!" her father rebuked.

Siddhartha held up his hand. "It's all right." He bowed to Yashodhara. "With your first words I found that you are honest, and now I find that you are also kind. What more can I wish for?" He took her hand and led her to kneel before the king as the hall rang with cheers. There was no need for a long betrothal. Just as Siddhartha said, Yashodhara was a woman who existed to be loved, and their union was as real as Suddhodana's with Maya. Yet it was known to both of them, if to no one else in the world, that Yashodhara had wept inconsolably on their honeymoon night.

Siddhartha turned red. "If I was clumsy or did something wrong—"

She put a finger to his lips. "No, don't."

"Then why are you so unhappy? An hour ago you seemed to be in love."

"An hour ago I didn't realize that you are going to leave me one day."

He smothered her with kisses to reassure her and chided her gently about being a superstitious girl like the maids who ran to the temple for a good luck charm if they spilled the milk. Yashodhara's words were never repeated between them. Ten years wasn't enough to erase the memory, however, and when it came to pass that her husband did decide to leave her, Yashodhara was crushed by seeing her premonition come true.

All these memories danced before Gautama's mind along with the image of his wife. The recollection of her sorrow was the only thing that enabled him to defeat his arousal. Gautama's back slumped, and he wondered for the first time since finding his master if abandoning his family wasn't an unforgivable sin.

Suddenly Gautama felt a stinging pain on one cheek. He opened his eyes to see his master standing over him, hand raised. Sharply the hand came down and slapped the other cheek.

"Why did you do that, sir? What did I do to offend you?"

The old hermit shrugged. "Nothing. You smelled like a man who sleeps with women. I knocked the stink off."

This incident stuck in Gautama's mind for two reasons—because it permanently banished any images of Yashodhara from his mind, and because it was the most words in a row that the hermit had spoken. But his master wasn't setting a precedent for garrulousness. Weeks passed, the monsoons came, and he said not another word. This became a time of great peace for Gautama. One day he went for firewood but couldn't find any that wasn't soaked from the rains. He recalled a cavern formed by fallen boulders where perhaps some dry logs might have lodged.

Walking through the woods, he felt the rain coming down, but the monsoons were warm and he was toughened by months of exposure. His body didn't shiver or his mind complain. Yet as he kept walking, Gautama noticed that he started feeling chilled, and a hundred yards farther on he was shaking badly. By the time he reached the cavern of boulders, he felt quite uncomfortable and his mind was attacking him mercilessly. *Go home. This crazy master is going to turn you into his slave or a crazy recluse like himself. Run!* It was as if he'd been taken back to his first day on the road.

He found an armful of dry kindling, and when the rain abated he headed back to camp. Now the process reversed itself. The closer he got to the small clearing, the better he felt. His mind calmed down, and the shivering in his limbs subsided. As he set foot in camp and saw his master again, perfect peace descended like a curtain over his whole being. Gautama stared at the old hermit in wonder.

"Mara."

Gautama was startled. "What?"

"Mara is interested in you." Gautama opened his mouth, but the hermit shook his head abruptly. "You know it's true. You knew it before you came here."

Gautama trembled, sensing that a gulf was opening up between himself and his master. He was surprised at how afraid this made him feel. "I haven't thought of Mara in years," he protested.

"And so you kept him away. For a time."

The hermit breathed a deep sigh, as if he had to remind his body how to return to the physical world before he could say another word. A few agonizing moments passed. Siddhartha felt his heart sink. *If he can smell that I have a wife, what must a demon smell like?* he thought.

The hermit said, "Mara will keep away from me. He has no interest in feeding when the bowl is empty. You are different."

"What interest could he have in me?" asked Gautama.

"You don't know?" The old hermit saw the look of bafflement in his disciple's eyes. "There's something he can't let you find out. You must go beyond anything I can teach. That's the only way to rid yourself of the demon," his master said.

Gautama felt panicky. He bowed to the ground and seized the hermit's gnarled feet. "At least tell me what I'm looking for."

When he got no reply, Gautama glanced up to see that the old hermit had closed his eyes again and was far away. The disciple could barely sleep that night. When he woke up before dawn he saw no dark outline against the night sky. His master had left.

Grief overwhelmed Gautama, and yet deep down he wasn't completely shocked—his master could only do the right thing. That was their bond, and he would never betray it. At that moment leaving had been the right thing.

Gautama could have hung around camp for a few hours or perhaps a day to see if his abandonment was only temporary. But the storm in his heart and the return of despairing thoughts told him something definitive. His master had withdrawn his protection; therefore, their relationship had come to an end. Carefully the young monk tidied up the camp. He swept the ground and put a fresh gourd of water beside the place under the lean-to where the hermit sat. Then he bowed to the grass mat that had been his master's only throne and departed.

As it turned out, one shred of their relationship was left. As he trudged back to the main road several miles away, Gautama fell to musing. He saw the hermit's face and its look of pity. He heard his own desperate plea, "At least tell me what I'm looking for." The hermit turned implacable; he closed his eyes and refused to speak. Only this time the answer came silently in Gautama's mind.

There is one thing Mara can never let you find out: the truth about who you really are.

14

Gautama wandered down the road, his whole being churning with what the hermit had told him. Before he left his father's kingdom he had fought against Mara the only way he knew how—by trying to alleviate suffering and want wherever he could. Saints persevere even though the tide of suffering rolls back in despite their compassion. Mara had survived a lot of saints. What was one more?

But a strange new element had been added. The forest hermit implied that the demon was afraid of Gautama. But why? Demons are immortal; they can't be harmed physically. The riddle went even deeper. Gautama seemed to be the *only* person Mara feared.

These thoughts kept turning over in Gautama's head like wheels within wheels. How remarkable that in one day all the peace he had gained with his master in the forest had come undone. Why even seek a teacher if the same thing would only happen again? Gautama muttered the only words of consolation that he could remember.

"Surrender and be free."

"Did you say something, brother?"

"What?" Gautama looked up to see another monk about his age. "How long have you been standing there?"

"A few minutes. Care to join us? You've got a hungry look about you. There's a well-off farmer up the road, and his wife doesn't exactly hate me." The young monk spoke with a half smile and a sense of assurance. Gautama rose and followed him down the shade-dappled dirt road. At the next bend he saw a patch of brilliant saffron flash through the trees, and when a small band of monks rounded the bend, the one Gautama was with waved to them. "Press on!" he shouted.

Gautama remained silent, melting into the group like a stray fish merging back into its school. The monk who had gathered him in was taller and older than the others. "Where are you headed?" he asked.

"East." Gautama replied. There were big towns toward the east, and with large populations there would be more ashrams and all the famous teachers. He'd ask for help with his dilemma.

"Who are you?" the taller monk asked.

Gautama gave his name and the taller monk gave his: Pabbata.

"We'll take you as far east as we're headed," Pabbata said. "You'll be safer in a pack. These four scruffs are my cousins."

"You all wanted to be monks?" asked Gautama with surprise.

Pabbata laughed sheepishly. "We all wanted to see more of life than a quarter-acre field that the jungle tries to take back every year." His cousins nodded in assent. They began to chat among themselves, ignoring the stranger, and it didn't take long for Gautama to take their measure. These were typical young men, all but Pabbata still adolescents, who needed to get out and stretch. They eyed every pretty farm girl who passed by on the road, joked with anyone who spoke their dialect, eagerly asked for news and gossip if they were lucky enough to meet a villager from near their home. Gautama didn't have to close his eyes for the disguise of saffron robes to vanish.

"Have you found a Dharma?" he asked Pabbata when there was a lull and the group fell relatively quiet. He expected the taller monk to answer indifferently or with a joke, but his face lit up.

"I think about the Dharma night and day," he said.

His cousins laughed, and one said, "He's the serious one. We let him think for the rest of us."

Pabbata's spine stiffened. "Without a teaching, we're no better than shiftless beggars." This rebuke, mild as it was, irked his cousins, who sped up and left Gautama and Pabbata to trail behind. Gautama was glad to see them go.

Suddenly Pabbata asked, "Do you know why I stopped for you?"

"You seem kind."

"Maybe. Fat lot of good that does you on these roads. No, it was something else. I was trudging behind my cousins, cursing the heat, thinking about someone I left behind, if you know what I mean. All at once I felt this cool breeze, and when I looked in the shadows, there you were. You understand?"

"No."

Pabbata looked disbelieving. "You're putting me on, right?"

When Gautama didn't reply, the taller monk's eyes widened. "You mean you don't know? It was you. I felt your presence."

Siddhartha could feel himself flush a deep scarlet. "That's impossible. Let me assure you—"

"Assure me?" Pabbata guffawed. "I had a feeling you were high-caste. Look at you, even saying that makes you go red."

Gautama was drawn to the tall countrified monk. He said, "I've been with a saint in the forest. I felt his presence. Every day, every minute. It made me—I don't know what it made me."

"Drunk, maybe. That type can throw you off your head, that's for sure." Pabbata stopped for a second and then replied, "So you must be a saint too. Like attracts like, isn't that how it works?"

"Not in this case."

Pabbata shook his head, frowning. "You shouldn't talk about yourself that way. Karma is shy. It's easy to drive the good kind away." He sped up to rejoin his cousins. Gautama lagged behind, and after a moment he heard loud laughter and banter. He was tempted to fade back and lose the other monks, but he didn't. Pabbata looked over his shoulder and saw Gautama a few yards behind them.

"Don't be shy, princess!"

The jibe, like everything Pabbata said, was good-natured. Gautama could do worse than travel in such company. Maybe the next town or the next teacher could offer him some answer. And so the saffron-clad sojourners walked on together for several days. Gautama lightened the time between farmhouses by finding fruit and fresh water that the others couldn't spy; in return, they were much more persuasive beggars and flirted with the country wives for extra roti and rice. "This one makes good mango pickle. It's worth a kiss behind the barn," one of the cousins said with a wink.

One morning Gautama had gotten up before dawn, as he was accustomed to do with his master, and meditated in the faint blue-gray light. He washed himself in a stream and shaved his beard with the sharp shell of a freshwater mussel. As he walked back to camp, he felt a strange sensation. After a moment he realized a cool breeze was tickling the back of his neck. The morning was already heavy with heat, and he stopped. He raised one hand and could definitely feel a cool current of air around his head. Gautama had felt such a sensation around his master without comprehending why.

Gautama turned his steps and headed back toward the main road instead of to camp. He hadn't met a better person the whole time he'd been wandering. And yet he couldn't stay now, not if it meant being turned into a false god.

Emerging from the thick jungle growth, Gautama saw that the main road was crowded with travelers. He ducked his head and kept as close to himself as possible. But he couldn't help becoming part of the passing parade. Farmers' carts were a constant sight, trundling to market and home again. There was the occasional merchant caravan, usually surrounded by armed guards to protect the precious bales of silk and spice stowed in a horse-drawn wagon.

Gautama regarded them all with troubled eyes. They were like phantoms to him, no longer made of flesh and blood. They were dream images that he could pass his hand through if they came close enough. As their bodies faded, he saw something else more clearly. Each person carried an invisible burden. The young monk was amazed that he hadn't seen it before. Everyone walked or rode with their lives on their shoulders, a pack of memories that spilled over with disappointment and sorrow. This one had never recovered from losing a wife in childbirth. That one was afraid of starving. That other one fretted over a runaway son who may have died in battle. And always there was the pall of age and sickness, the endless worry over money, the unceasing doubts about the future.

"Look!"

A small child, bolder than the others, pointed at Gautama, then jumped down from the cart he was riding in. He ran up and tugged at the monk's saffron skirt with a smile. The boy didn't beg for anything; he just held on to the skirt and walked beside Gautama. Instead of scolding him or calling him back, the parents nodded benignly.

"I have to find my brothers again," mumbled Gautama. He removed the little boy's hand and turned around. Walking away, he could hear the child crying behind him, and this, as much as the stares people were giving him, distressed Gautama. He'd heard children crying like that many times, when there was no food or the kind Prince Siddhartha had run out of coins for them. But Gautama had given this child nothing and taken nothing away. Except himself.

Gautama found the path that had led him to the main road, and soon he was swaddled in the protective gloom of the jungle. The five cousins would still be in camp. They were never eager to travel in the heat of the day. Once he found them, Pabbata looked puzzled over why Gautama had been gone so long, but he kept this to himself. Solitude was a monk's privilege, one of the few. Gautama had taken the precaution of gathering some mangoes on the way, which placated the other cousins in case they had questions to pose. He lay down under a tree, gazing up at the dappled light that filtered down and made small white circles on the forest floor. He couldn't find a way to fall asleep as the others dozed off.

Own nothing. Give everything.

It was all he could think about.

"DO YOU RECOGNIZE ME?"

Gautama lifted the sick man's head and brought a water gourd to his lips. The man had been unconscious when the novice monks, the *bikkhus,* found him. Only Gautama thought he was still alive. He ordered the bikkhus to put the body in his tent and leave the two alone. They obeyed without question. First, because wherever Gautama went, from camp to camp, ashram to ashram, he was revered. He had emerged from the forest only a year before, yet many of the novices whispered that someone like him, a man of stature and power, should be master, not a worn-out old yogi.

There was a second reason too. If the man they found in the forest actually was dead, Gautama might bring him back to life. Miracle stories swirled around him, and no amount of discouragement on Gautama's part could make them die down.

"Do you recognize me?" Gautama repeated when he saw the old man's eyes flutter and then open.

"I—I'm not sure."

Hunger and dehydration had made the man's mind weak. He looked around the tent, baffled at how he had gotten there. Then his gaze returned to Gautama's face and stayed there. "Ah," he said. "The saint."

"That's what you called me, Ganaka. But don't worry. Didn't you also tell me that saints don't exist?"

Feeble as he was, Ganaka summoned a cynical smile. "You waited this long to prove that I'm wrong?"

His head fell back; he struggled with another wave of delirium. Ganaka had been found deep in the forest, sheerly by accident when the bikkhus were chasing down a deer with bow and arrow. "I didn't ask for your help," he mumbled. "It's my life. Who are you to save it?"

"Weren't you about to give it away?"

Gautama had sensed such a possibility. Someone as experienced as Ganaka didn't just wander away alone unless it was to die. The careworn monk turned his head away and refused to answer.

"We'll talk later," Gautama said. He placed water and fruit beside the cot and departed. Outside the tent his eyes saw dozens of huts in the large clearing. It was spring, and the younger bikkhus were feeling the effects—they exercised, argued, talked in secret about girls they had left behind. Some missed home too much. Every day the weather was fair, a few more failed to show up for evening prayers. Spring had more power over them than God.

Gautama walked among the campfires. By now he had explored every city in the kingdom and those that lay far to the east, but he had avoided the temptation to set foot inside the gates of Kapilavastu. As the word spread and scores of villagers and farmers traveled out to find him and receive his blessing, some were from Sakya and remembered him. If they murmured "Prince" or "Your Highness" when they prostrated themselves before him, Gautama took no notice, gave no hint to acknowledge who he once had been. Four years had made Gautama into Gautama.

Of course he could still conjure up the old faces. But they didn't return on their own anymore. In order to see images of Channa or Suddhodana, he would ask to see them. "Learn to use your memories," he told the younger bikkhus. "Don't let them use you."

Ananda, a monk around his own age of thirty-three, ran up. He looked vexed and excited. "Another miracle, brother. What should I do?"

Gautama frowned. "What marvel did I supposedly perform this time?"

"There's a cripple just come to camp. Hobbled in on crutches, then he fell on his knees and called out your name. He gave a few twitches, and now he's walking again."

"Aren't you impressed, Ananda? You'd think with all my powers I could prevent my feet from getting blisters when we walk down a rocky trail."

Ananda was too exercised to smile. "He's just one of those cheats who wants a free meal."

"Don't we give food to anyone? Even cheats?"

Ananda bit his tongue. No one was closer to Gautama in their travels, thanks to his sincerity about God and his total devotion to Gautama. Recently, though, the short, stocky Ananda, who exuded stubbornness as much as loyalty, had become like a sergeant or an aide de camp as more and more responsibilities fell Gautama's way with the bikkhus.

"I think I know what to do," Gautama said. He sat down by the central campfire on a rough-hewn bench. Whenever they stopped for any length of time the bikkhus bestirred themselves to build huts and stools and such from forest timber. "Feed him well. Then say that I need his crutches to help another lame man. If he hesitates to hand them over, tell him to come and personally tell me why. I imagine he and the crutches will both be gone in the morning."

At last Ananda found a smile. "He'll never hand them over. He needs them for his next miracle down the road."

"I think so."

Although he wasn't the senior monk, Gautama had been relieved of chores around camp. He attended to the guru's major affairs instead. "I wouldn't burden you," the guru said, "but you are cursed by your gift."

"And what is my gift?" asked Gautama.

"The bikkhus think you're their father."

"Shouldn't you be their father?"

The guru shrugged. "I already got rid of my curses."

This master's name was Udaka, and he was the second luminary Gautama had found in his wanderings. The first, who was named Alara, had been a quiet, reclusive scholar, a Brahmin but nothing like Canki. Alara paid no attention to caste. He immersed himself in the Vedas and wouldn't bother to eat unless someone placed a plate of food beside his study table. When he first walked in, Gautama immediately attracted Alara's attention. His head, bent close over a sacred text, whipped up, and his eyes squinted as if looking into a bright light.

Instead of saying hello, Alara asked a question. "Stranger, if the scriptures tell me to avoid violence, is it enough that I walk past a fight and not enter into it?"

Gautama, who was prepared to prostrate himself at the master's feet to beg for instruction, was taken aback. He opened his mouth to say, "Tell me the answer, wise one," but what came out instead was, "Merely avoiding violence shows virtue, but it shows much more virtue to help end the fight and bring the combatants to a state of peace."

"Ah." Alara looked pleased. He patted the rough plank floor next to him, signaling for Gautama to sit close by. He even shifted the small prayer rug that he occupied so that his new disciple would be more comfortable. The next two months were nothing like the silence Gautama had shared with the forest hermit. Alara was a *gyani,* or philosopher. He thought and he talked.

"What is the mind for if not to find God?" he said. "The scriptures assure us that this physical world is a mask, and yet the mask isn't physical. It's made of illusion, and illusion is created by the mind. Do you understand? What the mind has created, only the mind can undo."

Gautama threw himself into a study of the Vedas, the ancient scriptures, and what Alara had said was holy writ. Every person has two selves, a lower self that is born of flesh and tied to the illusions of the material world, and a higher self that is eternal and unborn, with no attachments at all. The lower self craves pleasure, the higher self knows only bliss. The lower self cringes from pain, the higher self has never felt pain. If that was true, then Gautama had to find his higher self or be lost in the endless quicksand of the mind's deceptions.

"You found me just in time," said Alara. "Never mind that ordinary people are wasting their lives in foolish dreams of finding lasting happiness. To the ignorant, pleasure and pain appear to be different, but wisdom tells us they are the right and left hands of the lower self."

For months Gautama focused on nothing else, praying, meditating, and studying to find a path to his higher self. It was not difficult to believe in the teaching of illusion, or *maya,* because he continued to see ordinary people as ghosts, weighed down with care and suffering. Alara also looked like a ghost, but there was no pain lingering around him. For his part, the old gyani had never met a pupil like this one, and every day he delighted in him more and more.

One day, however, a young man of about twenty came and sat beside the front door of Alara's hut. He was thin, almost emaciated, and his face was one of the saddest Gautama had ever seen. As it happened, Alara stepped out of his hut just as Gautama was about to hand the young stranger a bowl of rice. With a swift, abrupt swipe, Alara knocked the bowl out of his hand, and the rice scattered on the ground. Before Gautama could speak, his master grabbed his arm and pulled him away.

"Don't look back," he said sharply.

Behind them Gautama heard the young man cry, "Father!" At this Alara's neck stiffened, but he kept his eyes straight ahead. When they were out of sight of the hut he said, "Yes, he's my son.

I do not greet him or encourage him. You shouldn't either." Alara saw the baffled look in Gautama's eyes. "My lower self once had a family. They are of no concern to me, just as this whole world is of no concern."

"I understand," said Gautama, lowering his eyes.

"No, Gautama, I can see you don't. I have been on the verge of telling you that there's little more I can teach you. But a true gyani must live what he's learned. How can you hope to reach your higher self if you remain tied, even by the slightest thread, to this vale of illusion? Maya sets traps everywhere."

Gautama didn't argue. But he wondered, *How would the sad young man at Alara's door feel to know that he was an illusion, another trap to be avoided?*

Two days later Gautama came into Alara's room, but he didn't take his accustomed place on the floor beside him. The gyani didn't look up from the page. He said, "I'm almost sad that you're leaving. That's what you're here to announce, isn't it?"

"Yes."

It could have ended there, simply, without a rupture. But Alara's hand shook, and he threw down his scrolls. "Just who do you think you are?" he asked irritably.

"A disciple."

"And since when does the disciple dare to teach the master?" Alara still hadn't looked at Gautama, who could see the veins standing out in the old man's neck.

"I didn't mean to disturb you this way," said Gautama.

"Insolence! I cannot be disturbed. You haven't learned that by now?"

Gautama knelt on the floor without coming closer.

Alara was unable to disguise his cold fury now. "If I need a demon to shake my faith, I'll call on a proper one, not a disciple who smiles and smiles, only to betray me."

This outpouring of blame didn't shake Gautama. He had lain awake thinking about how his master, for all that he knew about illusion, had fallen into a trap. The scriptures were his illusion. They led him to imagine that he was free just because he could describe freedom out of a book and think about it with his subtle mind.

"I didn't come here to harm you," said Gautama. "I no longer believe in the higher self. I wish that I could. But it seems nothing more than a fine phrase or an ideal no one ever attains. You are good and wise, but you became so by study—isn't it the lower self that reads the Vedas?"

These words, intended to be mild, had the opposite effect. Alara hurled a scroll at Gautama's head, then jumped to his feet, looking for a stick.

"Get out, scoundrel!"

Gautama longed to say, "Who is so angry with me right now? Your higher self?" But Alara's eyes were bulging already. Gautama backed away quickly.

For weeks he had wandered on until he found Udaka, his next teacher. Udaka wasn't a philosopher but a pure yogi, devoting his every moment to achieving divine union. Because he sat in silence most of the day, Udaka felt more like the forest hermit, yet he fathered the bikkhus around him every night and spoke.

"Some of you are new here, some have traveled with me for years. Which of you has met God?" he asked. A few of the older bikkhus, after some hesitation, raised their hands.

"You new ones, look around and pay attention. See those with their hands up? They are the greatest fools, and you must never listen to them," said Udaka. Somebody gave a sharp laugh; the older bikkhus stirred uncomfortably.

"How can you meet God when God is invisible and ever-present?" Udaka asked. "If He is everywhere, you cannot meet God, and you cannot leave Him, either. So how many of you are seeking God right now, with all your hearts?"

This time a great many of the men sitting around the campfire raised their hands. "Take a close look at yourselves," said Udaka.

"You too are fools. I just told you that God is everywhere. How can you seek what is already here? If someone came up to you and said, 'A thousand pardons, sir, but I am seeking this mysterious thing called air. Can you tell me where it is?' you would mark him down as a fool, wouldn't you? Yet you follow like sheep somebody's word who told you that you must seek God."

What Udaka taught instead was redeeming the soul, or *atman*. "Your soul is just as invisible as God, but it belongs to you. It's your divine spark, hidden and disguised by restless desires. Your atman is always watching you, but you do not notice it. You notice your next meal, your next argument, your next fear. It is always drawing you closer to the divine, but you do not heed it. You heed a thousand desires instead. Be still and know your soul. Seek it, and when you meet your soul, seize it for yourself, because it's worth far more than gold."

Gautama, who had been disillusioned by the higher self, felt a sympathy for this new teaching. For one thing, it gave him time in seclusion, where he could meditate and sit in the cool silence that he considered his real home. Udaka knew that the other bikkhus held the new arrival in awe; they vied to sit next to Gautama because his mere presence deepened their meditations. The guru put Gautama on his right hand when the group next sat together, and this unspoken gesture was enough to raise him above even the most senior monks, who were not so holy that they enjoyed being displaced.

"Let them hate you, let them love you. It's all a waste of time," Udaka said indifferently. Gautama believed him. He'd grown up in a world torn apart by worse things than petty jealousy in an ashram.

"But if another monk hates me," asked Gautama, "why can't he see that he is being distracted from his purpose?"

"He might. His soul could send him a message," Udaka said.

"But not always? He could go on hating me a long time, then."

"Yes."

Gautama felt a disquiet. "But if the soul is always loving, why doesn't it tell him immediately not to hate me? What reason does it have to hold back?"

"You're asking me to be wiser than the soul," said Udaka, with a trace of irritation. "Don't be so clever. I've never seen anyone think their way to heaven."

Now Gautama knew what his disquiet was about. He had lost the forest hermit and Alara. If he kept on this way, Udaka would fall away next. Disciples without masters are like fallow fields where no rain falls. He couldn't do without nourishment. Udaka knew this too; he gave Gautama a hard look. "You have something more to say? Perhaps you want to ask me about humility."

"No." Gautama kept his composure. "I wanted to tell you that I've been having a vision. My wife comes to me. She says that I deserve compassion. Can you tell me what that means?"

"Ignore it."

Udaka said this without the slightest sign that he cared about such things. Gautama wouldn't be put off, however.

"Master," he said, "many of the disciples have left homes and women they love. Their children are forgetting their father's face. Can't a devoted wife be part of my soul?"

"No one belongs in your soul but you," said Udaka.

"Then perhaps her image is a message. You said that the soul sends messages."

"But it doesn't send dreams. She's the figment of an ignorant mind," Udaka said curtly. "What if you caught a cold? Would you want me to tell you what the soul means when it sends you a cold? Get over her as you would get over any other disease." Gautama's master had never been married, and like many yogis he made a sour face whenever women were mentioned. Udaka's revulsion bothered Gautama. *Does he imagine that women have no souls?* But the discussion was over. Gautama bowed and left without another word.

That night he returned to his tent, where he found Ganaka sitting up eating a bowl of millet gruel. "Why so worried, saint?" asked Ganaka, looking up.

"You must be feeling better."

"Much." Ganaka began slurping the last bit of gruel from the bowl. "I should be strong enough in the morning to leave."

"Where will you go?" asked Gautama.

"Deeper into the jungle. I don't intend to be found a second time."

Gautama was shocked. "You're going to try to kill yourself again?"

"Of course. It's my Dharma." Ganaka looked perfectly calm and serious, speaking without a trace of cynicism. "Strange, isn't it? I have to eat to get the strength to go out and starve myself."

"I can't let you," Gautama blurted out. He was so shaken that he wanted to pace back and forth. Instead, he forced himself to sit on the ground with his hands folded in his lap. His heart pounded.

Ganaka said, "There are two things even a saint can't stop. One is being born, and the other is dying." He waited for Gautama to protest. It was hard to miss who in the tent was calmer and more collected.

"Killing yourself is a sin," said Gautama, then he stopped himself. Ganaka wasn't a fool or ignorant of scripture. "Please explain what you mean," Gautama said.

Ganaka burst out laughing. "Excuse me, but I just can't help myself, little saint. Look at you. You wanted to jump out of your skin when I told you what I'm going to do. But you didn't. Oh, no, you controlled yourself. You know how a holy man acts, and I must say you've gotten it down. I wish I could train a monkey half as well."

Gautama felt the heat creeping up his face. "That's unfair."

"Who cares? I'm going to die tomorrow. I can say what I want." The strange thing is that Ganaka wasn't speaking harshly; his tone toward Gautama was almost kind. "I once told you that you reminded me of my younger self. Has it occurred to you yet that I might be your older self?" Seeing the scowl that Gautama was trying not to show, Ganaka broke out into laughter again. "You're like a traveling show. I can see at least five or six people fighting inside you. Quite a spectacle."

"Stop it!" Gautama jumped to his feet and began pacing as anxiously as he'd wanted to since entering the tent.

"Good," said Ganaka. "Even a cat is smart enough to thrash its tail when it's disturbed. Most people aren't."

This show of implacable honesty caused Gautama's heart to sink. "You're making me so sad," he said, half pleading.

"Then I'll stop," said Ganaka. "Wisdom is never sad, and you want one last word of wisdom, don't you?" He stood up and placed his hands on Gautama's shoulders to stop him in place. "Dharma is worthless unless it teaches one how to be free. I have listened to all the masters, read all the scriptures, bathed in all the sacred springs. I found freedom in none of them."

"And killing yourself will set you free?"

"When all else fails, whatever is left must be right," Ganaka said with serious simplicity. He let go of Gautama and turned away for a moment. "What is freedom, little saint? It's the end of struggle. Is not death the same thing? I want to meet God, but my efforts have failed. Not just failed, but made me more unhappy than when I was married and lived with a loving wife. I do not say your seeking is a fraud. Perhaps you must walk as many paths as I did before you reach this point."

He turned back and fixed Gautama with a clear, unflinching gaze. "You can shed your tears now."

"I won't weep for you," said Gautama mournfully.

Ganaka sat back down on the cot. It was very late, and he was ready for sleep. "I meant weep for yourself. Whatever I am today, you will be tomorrow."

He lay down and turned his back on Gautama, who sat vigil for hours. He wanted to be awake in case one last plea would dissuade Ganaka when he woke up. But time stands still in the dark. The next thing Gautama knew he woke up with light in his eyes and his head lolling on his chest. He looked toward the cot with faint hope. It was empty.

15

One morning Ananda didn't find Gautama in his tent. Several days had passed since the disappearance of Ganaka. None of the bikkhus were told anything about him, and only Ananda learned the grim truth. In the vastness of the jungle there was no possibility of searching for him, wherever he had gone to die. Gautama was badly shaken.

"How can we believe in supernatural powers, Ananda? No power in heaven protected him, or even cared," said Gautama. "Ganaka had fallen into despair, and I couldn't save him."

"Why should it depend on you?" Ananda asked.

"Do you know who Buddha is?"

"No." Ananda shifted with embarrassment.

"Buddha can protect people," Gautama said.

"Better than this?" Ananda held up an amulet he'd been given as a baby by his parents, who purchased it at a temple with half a year's income from their farm.

"Yes, much better than that. Don't ask me how. I'm the last person who'd know. I should have protected Ganaka."

Mention of Buddha puzzled Ananda, but he took heart that this god, even if he'd never heard of him, was helping his friend. That was how he understood Gautama's words. Ananda believed that the gods never let anyone out of their sight. It bothered him that Gautama didn't respect the gods anymore. Sometimes he spoke of God, who was like the soul of the universe or a spirit that permeated everything. As a child Ananda had been brought up to believe that the gods were different faces of one God. But lately even that God was on shaky ground with Gautama.

"We can pray to Buddha together," Ananda said. "Or I can make an offering in the fire tonight." Perhaps that would lift Gautama from his gloom.

Instead of answering, Gautama closed his eyes. This was his way of getting out of reach. None of the other monks could go as deeply into samadhi, and when he was in this state, Gautama heard and saw nothing. Ananda departed, and then rain came during the night, turning the trampled ground of the encampment into a mud slick.

Thunder rumbled overhead. Ananda's shawl was soaked and useless for warmth, but he pulled it close to fend off a growing disquiet. Every monk was pledged to serve the master, but he had pledged to serve Gautama. He had done this silently, in his own heart. To him, Gautama was already a great soul. He kept that to himself too.

Ananda frowned as he hurried through the rain to peer into all the makeshift shelters. When he was sure that Gautama was nowhere in camp, Ananda took a deep breath and knocked on Udaka's door. Disturbing the master could result in something more physical than a rebuke. There was no answer, though, and Ananda turned back. After all, he had no proof that anything drastic had happened.

He was only a few steps away when the guru's door flew open, and Gautama stepped out. He looked pale and drawn, and when he set eyes on Ananda, he could have been looking at a stranger. Ananda's heart pounded.

"What's happened?"

Gautama shook his head and walked past. He offered no protest, though, when Ananda followed him into his tent. The lowering gray skies made the interior oppressively dark. Suddenly Gautama had something to say.

"I have no faith anymore," he said. "I'll be gone by tonight. Dear friend, don't try to follow me. I'll come for you when it's time. Be patient."

Ananda's lip trembled. "Why can't I come?"

"Because you'll try to stop me, as I tried to stop Ganaka." The comparison filled Ananda's face with alarm, but before he could say anything Gautama went on. "I'm not going to kill myself; don't worry. But something may happen, something severe."

"You've told the master?"

Gautama shook his head. "Only that I'm taking a journey that may be long or short. If he lives by his own teaching, he won't sorrow over losing one disciple. If he gets angry, then I'm right to stop serving him. I'm only sorry to say good-bye to you."

Heartsick, Ananda fell into a gloomy silence; the two sat in the gray light listening to raindrops pelting the roof of the tent. Gautama placed a comforting hand on his shoulder.

"There's no reason to keep secrets from you. I was brought a message," he said. "A traveler came to camp this morning, and I stumbled across him in one of the huts. I knew from his accent that he was a Sakyan, so I tried to leave, but I wasn't fast enough."

"Fast enough for what?"

"To not be recognized. The stranger threw himself at my feet and began to weep. I entreated him to get up, but he wouldn't. The bikkhus in the hut began to murmur and exchange looks. Finally the stranger looked up and told me that I was supposed to be dead."

"Dead?" said Ananda. "Because you left everything behind?"

"Worse, much worse. I have a cousin named Devadatta. He's filled with jealousy and has always set himself against me. When I left home my fear was that he would gain influence at court. Now he has, and in the most terrible way."

Gautama told Ananda what he had just learned about how Devadatta had found a beheaded corpse in the forest wearing Siddhartha's robes. "Everyone believed him. The head was never found. Probably Devadatta committed the murder himself. He's capable of it." Gautama's voice died away mournfully. "I caused this disaster. Everyone I loved has been plunged into suffering."

"But it's a fraud," Ananda protested. "Send a messenger home and tell them."

"If I do that, Devadatta will be arrested and executed. I didn't sacrifice my family's happiness for that. Killing him would make a mockery of my search. I have to push on. I haven't done enough."

"But they'll suffer even more to think you're never coming back," Ananda said.

Instead of persuading Gautama, this seemed to harden him. "The person they once knew is never coming back. If that's what they wait and hope for, then I might as well be dead."

Hard as he tried, Gautama could not conceal the anguish in his voice. Ananda reached out and grabbed his hand. "Go home, put everything back in order. I'm not brilliant like you, but if I caused so much pain to my family, I would consider it the same as betraying God."

This speech moved Gautama, but as he considered what Ananda had said, his face grew darker. "You're condemning me to a trap, my friend. I set my whole heart on meeting God. I abandoned everything for his sake. If that is the same as betraying God, my situation is hopeless. So is yours, and everyone's here."

There were more arguments that afternoon, more pleas from Ananda, but Gautama had made up his mind. The skies were so dark that they blended seamlessly into nightfall. Gautama didn't permit Ananda to keep vigil beside his cot until dawn; he recalled how much it had hurt when he woke up to find Ganaka gone.

"Before we part, I want you to understand something," he said. "I was raised in a palace, but I was a prisoner there. I had only one friend, so I spent hours alone or with the servants. What most fascinated me were the silk weavers. I discovered them bent over their looms in a tiny upstairs chamber. The room was full of the smell of indigo and saffron. The weavers didn't talk among themselves; all I heard was the clack of shuttles running back and forth.

"There was one old woman, stooped and nearly blind, who did something I couldn't understand. If a thread snapped, she would unload her loom completely and start over again. I asked her why she destroyed a week's work over a single thread. She answered me in a word: *karma*.

"Karma keeps good and evil in balance. Karma is a divine law. When the law is violated, however innocently, it can't be undone. One snapped thread alters the whole design; one misdeed alters a person's destiny."

Ananda listened carefully, wanting to remember every word from Gautama in case they never met again. "So the thread of your life has been broken," he said.

"I thought it broke the day I left home. But I was naive. When I ended as Siddhartha, his karma continued to follow me. I feel as troubled as the day I left my wife and child a year ago. My hunger is for freedom, but the trap keeps closing tighter. Instead of attacking me directly, the demons sow discord everywhere around me. There's only one thing left to try." Gautama had skirted the truth, that the demons actually feared him.

"But what are you going to do?" Ananda pleaded, trying not to think about how alone he would be after this night.

Gautama wanted to protect his intentions, but he relented a little. There was a good chance that he would fail, and if that happened he would return home, not try to find the next guru. "Death has been stalking me since the day I was born. Eventually, no matter how hard I struggle, death will win—the hunter will kill his prey. But until then I have one chance to turn the tables. If I move quickly, I may be able to kill death first. There's no other way, not if you want to be free."

• • •

IN A COUNTRY where villages were a day apart and travelers hugged a strand of road winding through miles of uncharted wilderness, Gautama could disappear into the green world and never be seen again. He set out to do just that, but it was too dangerous to go alone. Tigers don't mind eating idealists. Therefore, once he had left Udaka's camp behind, Gautama searched for more rigorous company. They would have to be monks. They would have to be willing not to talk for days or weeks at a time. Finally, they would have to push their bodies so far that only two choices remained: bursting through to freedom or perishing in mortal form.

Gautama made the same proposition to every monk he encountered: "Come with me and defeat your karma once and for all. Death is playing a game with us. It's a long game, but in the end the outcome is certain. Now's your only chance to defeat the pain and suffering that became your inheritance the day you were born."

These words were not strange; every holy man knew that the world was an illusion. The Vedas talked about it endlessly. But each monk who heard Gautama shook his head and looked away guiltily. "Your truth is too harsh, brother. I'm already living a life that ordinary people consider impossible. One day I will meet God, but if I try to force his hand, the only reward I may get is that I kill myself."

Some put it this way, some another, but no one braved Gautama's challenge. The more eloquent he grew, the more reluctant they became. "You look holy, but you may be a silver-tongued demon," one old monk reminded him. Eventually Gautama did find company, but not with his words. He ceased to eat more than a handful of rice a day. His body wasted away, and as his skin became a taut, translucent membrane clinging to his bones, Gautama acquired a glow. His hands, which he held out to bless anyone who asked, looked larger, as did his deep brown eyes.

This aura of saintly emaciation attracted five other monks, and once the band had gathered, Gautama led them upriver into the high country, where they found a large isolated cave.

It was a breathtaking place to suffer in. The sentinel peaks of the Himalayas ringed the far horizon. The air was crisp and cold as the first ice crust on a pond in winter. Gautama would wake up with supersensitive hearing. The faint air currents sweeping up the valley sounded like the breathing of the world. But rain made his bones ache, and thunder split his head open—it would throb with pain for days. For some months he and the five monks sat in their cave, doing the minimum of speaking, collecting roots for food, filling their gourds from a stream.

At first Gautama was worried that he was indulging himself, because no matter how austere the conditions, he loved the life of austerity. Perhaps too much. He tried sitting in the snow for hours to see if he could make his body hurt so much that it would give up all its hopes for pleasure. Day after day he repeated this, and then a miracle happened. Through the heavy falling snow he saw a stranger walking toward him. At first he was only a blurred dark shadow against the whiteness, but as he came nearer, Gautama saw that it was not a man who had braved the storm but the god Krishna. He had the most serene and beautiful face; his skin was a deep blue-purple that was all but black.

Gautama prostrated himself in the snow. "I have waited to meet you all my life," he murmured. "I have abandoned everything for you."

"I know," Krishna said. His voice rang among the mountains like dull thunder. "Now go home and don't do anything so stupid again."

The god turned his back and walked away. At that instant Gautama woke up, shivering and starving. The skies were clear; there was no snowstorm. He returned to the cave but said nothing to the five monks. Maybe he'd only had a dream; maybe Krishna was real. In either case Gautama was determined not to heed a delusion. But he needed some kind of sign that his war against death was succeeding. All he got was that his mind started to rebel. At first it complained of being lonely and afraid. It argued that Gautama was hurting himself needlessly. In this phase the voice Gautama heard in his head was whining and weak, like a small child's. As the weeks passed, however, his mind grew fiercely angry.

Gautama wanted to hasten its surrender, so the more his mind ranted, the more he deprived himself. He would sit naked all night on a frozen lake while his mind screamed in agony.

If you want to kill me, do it now, Gautama said defiantly. He didn't know who he was addressing, exactly. Perhaps not his mind but Yama, the lord of death. When dawn came and he wasn't dead, Gautama exulted. He had gotten his sign, because the cold and the elements had not defeated him. He was still alive, which proved that he was stronger than sun, wind, and cold.

Bolder now, he wanted to push further. More extreme austerities lay ahead. He could pile rocks on his chest or pierce his cheeks with sharpened sticks. There were legendary yogis who tore their own arms off and threw them into the fire. But the five monks resisted. They had been given no signs of their own. Gautama knew that he had to preach conviction into his brother monks. Otherwise, he would open his eyes one day after a cruel austerity and find that they had vanished.

"You doubt my methods, don't you?" he said.

"Yes," said the eldest monk, who was named Assaji. "If you could see yourself, you would be frightened. Why do you think that inviting death is the way to defeat it?"

"Because when everything else has failed," said Gautama, "whatever is left must be the answer. I've done nothing yet to earn your respect, but believe me when I say that I have tried everything to become free. I learned the Dharma of the higher self, but I never met my higher self or heard a word from it. I learned the Dharma of the soul, which was supposed to be my speck of the divine, but no matter how blissful I might feel, the time always came when I was overwhelmed once more by anger and sorrow. Much the same must be your experience."

The five monks said nothing, which Gautama took to be assent.

"In time I concluded that my struggles could last a lifetime, and to what end? I will still be a slave to karma and a prisoner in this world. What is this karma that visits us with so much suffering? Karma is the body's endless desires. Karma is the memory of past pleasure we want to repeat and past pain we want to avoid. It's the delusions of ego and the storm of fear and anger that besieges the mind. Therefore, I have resolved to cut karma out by the roots."

"How? You think you know something that no one else knows?" Assaji asked. His rail-thin body already showed the effects of years of austerity.

"Myself, no. But you live the ascetic's life. Haven't you already spent years sitting in silence, repeating your prayers, contemplating images of the gods, reciting a thousand and eight names of Vishnu?" The eldest monk nodded. "Has any of it made you free?"

"No."

"Then why should you continue to do more of what doesn't work in the first place? The temple priests taught you how to reach God—priests who have not found freedom either, but who claim title to the holy teachings the way a farmer puts a brand on cattle." Gautama had eaten nothing for days and barely slept. He wondered briefly if he sounded delirious.

One of the younger monks interrupted. "Tell us your way."

"On the road I met an old sannyasi named Ganaka, and he told me something important. *Let the world be your teacher.* I couldn't understand what he meant at first, but now I do. Every experience that traps me is a worldly experience. The world is seductive and hard to interpret for what it really is. Yet this world is nothing more than desire, and every desire makes me run after it. Why?

Because I believe it's real. Desires are phantoms, concealing the grinning face of death. Be wise. Believe in nothing."

It took many nights around the fire, but Gautama and the five monks came to an agreement. They would give their bodies nothing to live for in the world, no desires to fulfill, no cravings to become a slave to. They would sit like statues facing a wall, and no matter how many desires arose, each one would be coldly turned away. "Even if we are tied to our karma by ten thousand threads," said Gautama, "we can break them one at a time. When the last attachment is gone, karma will be dead instead of us."

He believed every word. Perhaps the five monks didn't, but they followed him. They sat like statues facing a wall and waited. Gautama was so fervent that he expected to reach his goal soon. Assaji wouldn't commit himself. "Unhappiness is born of expectations that don't come true," he reminded his brother monk. "Even to expect nothing can be a trap."

Gautama bowed his head. "I understand." But this gesture of humility disguised the fire he felt inside. In legend, other yogis had found immortality. They were great aspirants, and Gautama saw himself as nothing less. He chose a spot away from all shelter, sat down on a patch of rocks without clearing them away, and waited.

"If you must go, then go. I don't need a reason," said Assaji. He looked on Kondana with mild eyes that held no reproof. Kondana was the youngest of the five monks, but he had proved the toughest in the end.

"You already know my reasons. Look at him," Kondana protested. He pointed at a gnarled carving lying on the jungle floor, which was so close to looking like weathered wood that at times he had to remind himself that it was actually a living person—Gautama.

"I can't stay and watch him kill himself," said Kondana. "It's like watching a corpse decay while it's still breathing." He had already stayed longer than three of the five monks. None were impatient. Since vowing to follow Gautama, they had pursued enlightenment for five years.

"He never moves anymore. I wonder where he is," said Assaji.

"I think he's in hell," Kondana said mournfully.

The years of austerity had caused many things to happen. They had all gone through experiences in meditation that they never dreamed possible. Assaji himself had visited the home of the gods. He had watched Shakti, the sinuous consort of Shiva, dance for him, a dance where every step shook the worlds and the tinkle of ankle bells turned into stars. He had conversed with the greatest sages, like Vasishtha, who had been dead for centuries. Only Gautama never told such tales, and after winter settled in among the Himalayan peaks, it was a matter of survival to force him to find a place where they could be more protected. Reluctantly Gautama agreed, but only on the condition that he would continue his austerities and that the five monks would make no contact with other human beings.

An emaciated man whose skin has toughened into cracked brown hide and who has subsisted on a tenth of the food given to a newborn baby is not a sight for ordinary eyes. Some people would consider him a fraud, others a madman. The superstitious few would call him a saint. "I do not know who I am anymore," Gautama said. "But I am blessed, because it has taken me only five years to know who I am not."

Now Assaji walked over to Gautama and with Kondana's help set him upright again. He had fallen over during the night, and these days he was lost in a samadhi so deep that nothing registered from the outside world. It was up to the other monks to feed him by opening his mouth and placing a handful of chewed rice in it. They carried him to the river to bathe him and moved him out of the worst of the searing sun. All this made it appear that Gautama was helpless and paralyzed. But Assaji knew that appearances were deceiving. Gautama was on a quest the likes of which went back almost before time.

Kondana put on his sandals and tucked some dried berries into the corner of his shawl. "Will you come?" he asked Assaji.

"No."

"You still think he has a chance—he might succeed?"

"I wouldn't say that."

There was nothing more to talk about. Kondana bowed down before Gautama and placed a pink wild orchid at his feet in reverence. He no longer felt guilty over losing hope; he was too exhausted to feel much of anything. As he left camp, Assaji touched him on the shoulder.

"When the time comes I'll send for you. The five of us should carry the body back to his people."

That was the last word Assaji said or heard for the next three months. Spring came, and every day brought a shower of creamy white blossoms falling from the sal trees that blanketed the northern forest. Gautama had not altered. At times he showed more signs of life than at other times. Assaji would hear him at night walking out of camp for the call of nature, but that was rarely. The water level might dip in the gourd Assaji placed by his side.

What eventually broke was Assaji's own body. He got sick alone in the jungle; for all he knew it was a sign. Wrapped in his shawl, he suffered the delirium of fever for five days and nights. When the fever broke, he shivered with cold sweat. Slowly his body returned to health, but with it came an unexpected change. Assaji grew hungry again. He craved a real meal and would scour the jungle floor for a dead parrot to take back and cook.

If I am reduced to unwholesome food, my quest is over, he thought. He wasn't willing to sink to a subhuman level, no matter how enormous the goal of enlightenment might be. He decided to tell Gautama. One morning he crouched in front of his motionless brother, wiping away the dirt from his face with water from the gourd.

"I'm going," he said. Gautama showed no signs of hearing him. "I must think about my soul. If you die and I let you, my sin is as great as murder. You shouldn't be responsible for that. I'm ashamed to speak of sin to someone like you, but there's no shame in it if you decide to come with me."

Assaji's guilt made him feel that he'd said too much already. Like the others, his faith had been worn down too far. Assaji lingered around camp a few more days. He piled fruit next to Gautama and a week's supply of water. How strange that this immobile icon should still be alive and that behind his mask he was fighting such a huge battle. *Face the wall like a statue and give them nothing.* Assaji remembered Gautama's rallying cry, but he couldn't follow it anymore. He left camp before dawn without a sound.

Gautama didn't hear him depart; he had heard nothing since he became aware—and then only at the farthest edge of his mind—that Kondana was gone. It didn't matter. He had come to realize that he was walking the path alone. Two journeys had to be made without companions: the journey to your death and the one to enlightenment.

In his meditations he had arrived at heaven before the others, but he said nothing about it. There was dazzling beauty; golden celestial beings materialized all around him, but then he took a route the other monks would not. Gautama turned his back on the celestial beings. "I've already known pleasure. What good does it do me to feel more?"

"This is heavenly pleasure," the celestial beings said.

"Which I can enjoy forever only after I die," said Gautama. "Therefore it's as good as a curse." He walked away and asked to see more suffering.

Thus he arrived at the gate of hell, where Gautama saw the terrifying torments that lay beyond. But no demons came for him. Instead he heard these words: "No sin brings you here. Do not pass."

He entered anyway, of his own free will. *I've known fear,* he thought. *And fear is death's chief weapon. Let me experience the worst torment, and then fear will lose its hold over me.*

The phase of hellish torment lasted a long time because every morning his broken bones and flayed skin grew back. "Where is Mara?" Gautama asked. "I need to see the worst that he can do too." But for some reason Mara hung back and never appeared. Gautama wondered if this was a trap, but after a while the torments became routine, and his mind grew bored. One morning the demons failed to appear, and then the scenes of hell disappeared, giving way to dark, motionless silence.

Gautama waited. He knew he had defeated every form of suffering he could imagine. His body no longer felt pain; his mind gave rise to not a single desire. And yet no sign came that he had reached his goal. Like an endless, calm night, the silence bathed him. Gautama decided to open his eyes.

At first there was only a dim sensation of being wrapped in a blanket, which after a time he realized was his body. He looked down. It was midday, but someone had positioned him under the jungle canopy where no sunlight ever penetrated. Surveying himself, Gautama saw two crossed sticks. Legs. Two dried monkey paws. Hands. He noticed a pile of rotting fruit beside him, covered with ants and wasps. Suddenly he realized that he was thirsty. He reached for his water gourd, but the last inch of liquid inside was green and filled with mosquito larvae.

He could feel, as he grew used to being in his body again, that it could endure no more. Yet all he could think about was finding the five monks to tell them that he was enlightened. Gautama tried to uncross his stick legs and get up, but when he moved them an inch, the wasted muscles screamed with pain. He stared at them with a slight frown of disapproval, like a new father who feels helpless when the baby cries.

Gautama felt no sympathy for his body, but it would have to be dealt with. He willed his limbs to move, and slowly he began to crawl along the forest floor. It felt damp and hot; there were vermin that slid under his skin, and fungi and rocks. He could hear running water nearby. He sensed his body's desperate thirst. Maybe he would get to water in time, maybe not. He kept crawling, but the forest floor barely crept beneath him now. He could practically count each beetle that his weight crushed. A small snake, colored brilliant red, slithered away at the level of his face. The air became very still, and moving any farther, even at a crawl, became impossible.

Lying there, he never expected that enlightenment would be the last thing to happen before he died.

PART THREE

BUDDHA

16

While he lay motionless on the ground, Gautama became dimly aware that a shadow had fallen over him. When it moved, he assumed it must be the outline of a large animal, a predator drawn by his smell. The animal would most likely be hungry, yet it made no difference to Gautama how his time on earth ended.

"Please don't die."

The girl's voice caused his eyes to look up, almost against his will. She was startled and moved back shyly. She must have been all of sixteen, and alone. Gautama closed his eyes and waited for her timidity to send her away. Instead, he felt soft warm hands on either side of his face. The girl raised his head slightly and wiped the grime away from his cheeks with a corner of her sari. It was faded blue and threadbare, a poor girl's sari.

"Here."

She pressed something to his mouth. A bowl, and its edge hurt his cracked dry lips. Gautama shook his head, and a croaked word came out of his throat.

"No."

The girl said, "Are you a god?"

Gautama felt a wave of delirium; her words sounded meaningless. The girl said, " I've come to the river to be blessed by the god who lives there. It's my wedding day in a month."

A god? Gautama couldn't even smile. He shook his head slightly and let his face fall back to touch the warm jungle floor. But from wasting away he had become weaker than the girl, so he couldn't resist when she turned him over and held him upright in her arms. She did this effortlessly.

"You must." She held the bowl to his mouth again. "Don't be stubborn. If my offering is good enough for a god, you're not better than him, are you?"

Now a smile rose inside Gautama. "Go find your god," he mumbled. He clenched his jaw so that she couldn't pour the contents of the bowl into him. There was no purpose in her being there.

"I won't leave you here," she said. "I can't have people saying that Sujata did something like that."

In the midst of his torpor, Gautama's mind suddenly became alert. What she said didn't seem possible. "Tell me your name again."

"Sujata. What's wrong?"

The girl saw tears streaming down the dying man's cheeks. His emaciated body began to tremble in her arms. She felt terribly sorry for him. Weakly he opened his mouth, and Sujata poured a little food into it. She had cooked sweet rice in milk for the river deity. The dying man accepted more. His stubbornness had vanished, though the girl had no idea why.

In a stricken voice he mumbled, "What have I done?"

"I don't know," said the girl, confused. But she was no longer shy or frightened by him. "We have to get you home. Can you walk at all?"

"In a little while." Gautama ate the rest of the sweet rice with painful slowness. Then Sujata left him for a moment and returned with some water. He drank it greedily, his cracked lips bleeding slightly as he opened his mouth.

"I'll carry you as far as I can, and then I'll get my brother," Sujata said. Gently she lifted Gautama to his feet. His brittle legs looked like they might snap. He couldn't walk, but he was light enough so that the girl could prop him against her shoulder. Together they hobbled their way up the narrow trail she had taken to the river. They arrived at a road, and Sujata placed him under a tree, propped up against the trunk like a limp doll.

"Wait here. Don't let anyone move you."

Tears started rolling down his cheeks again. Sujata found it hard to watch; she hurried away and soon disappeared around the bend. Gautama wished she hadn't gone. He suddenly felt alone and desolate. *Sujata.* He hadn't heard that name in fifteen years. But he had not forgotten her. This was the cause of his weeping, because five years of austerity hadn't wiped out his memories. It all came back in a flood: his first sight of Sujata on his eighteenth birthday when his robes were gaudy enough for an elephant. Winding his red turban. The excitement he suppressed when he felt stirrings of desire for her. As soon as he recalled these things, it was as if a dead flower in the desert received the spring rains. His mind unfolded in layers, bringing back image after image from the past, and with them the emotions he had wanted to extinguish. He was badly dehydrated, and soon his tear ducts had nothing more to offer.

Gautama rolled his head back and stared at the jungle. It gave back nothing. It was neither a friendly haven nor a dangerous wilderness. The flowers weren't smiling, the air was not luxuriously moist and enveloping. The blank face of Nature was all he saw, and a surge of horror ran through Gautama. He wanted to vomit, but with all his will he forced the sweet rice and water to stay down. Weak as he was, he could dimly hear his thoughts, and they told him he had to survive. Karma hadn't died, and neither had he.

The light began to fade. Gautama knew it was close to noon, so he must be fainting. His head grew light; a cold sweat beaded his chest. It was a relief to lose consciousness, so he allowed himself to sink into the sensation of falling and falling. Scarlet parrots scolded loudly overhead; he lay so still that a couple of curious monkeys began to advance down the tree trunk with caution. Gautama wasn't aware of this. His mind was captured by the face of Ganaka, which he saw clearly. It wore an expression he couldn't read. Grief? Contempt? Compassion? Blackness swallowed up whatever it was.

SUJATA'S HUT WAS FLIMSY, its mud walls cracked. There was almost no protection from the weather, which meant that spring could enter as it pleased. Gautama lay in bed, weak and feverish, for some weeks before he noticed this. One morning a white sal blossom floated down from the trees, slid sideways on the breeze, and came in through a large crack in the wall. It landed on Gautama's face and rested there. The fragrance opened his eyes.

"Aren't you pretty?"

Sujata laughed and lifted the flower to her nose. "Thank you, noble sir." She pinned it behind her ear. The girl took her nursing duties lightly, hiding any worries she might have from her patient.

"Nothing seems pretty to me," Gautama said. He had taken to speaking his mind.

"I don't believe you," said Sujata.

They were alone together every day. The hut had been abandoned after her grandmother died, and she had begged her family to let the stranger recover there. Her family didn't want to set eyes on his skin-covered skeleton anyway, so Sujata got what she wanted without objection.

Gautama lifted himself up on his elbows. It was the most effort he had expended since arriving there. "I want to go outside."

"I won't stop you," said Sujata with mock indifference.

Gautama gave a wry smile. "Since when did you become so cruel?" He fell back onto his pillow. She was right; he wasn't strong enough to be helped into the sunlight yet. "Are you still marking the days?"

Sujata glanced at a piece of bark nailed to one wall; it had twenty *X*'s scratched into it. "There, see?"

"You must have left out quite a few. Has it been a month, maybe three months?"

Not wanting him to know that he had been ill for five weeks, Sujata defended herself. "I'd have no fiancé if you stayed three months. It's bad enough already." She began to feed him a mixture of boiled rice and lentils. She wasn't complaining. Her good-hearted husband-to-be didn't mind waiting a while longer; they had been engaged since she was eleven.

"Will you go home when you're well?" she asked.

Gautama turned his face away, avoiding the next bite of food. "I'm sorry," Sujata said. "You've taken vows."

He gave her a serious look. "Would you respect a man who would keep a vow even if he died?"

"You mean you?" She shook her head. "No."

Gautama didn't mind that he was as passive and dependent as a baby. All he basically knew how to do was be still. There wasn't a scrap of enlightenment left. The gods had had their joke. Now he was just another starving wretch who had been found, addled and lost, wandering in the forest.

Because his healing was so slow, time slowed down with it. He'd idle an hour watching a sunbeam move across the floor in the morning. Specks of dust floated hazily in it, and a holy verse came to mind. "Worlds come and go like dust motes in a beam of sunlight shining through a hole in the roof." He used to think those words were beautiful; now they were flat. He got stronger every day, but inside he never lost his horror. Nature's blank face continued to stare back at him wherever he looked. His eyes would move from the sores on his skin to the sun shining through the open window, then to Sujata's face and the sal blossom in her ear. They were all the same dull nothing.

"Starting tonight, I'm going to feed myself," Gautama announced. "And tomorrow I'm going outside, even if you have to carry me."

Sujata smiled. "You've gotten too fat. I'll drop you."

Because he couldn't stop himself from speaking his mind, Gautama said, "Do you know how beautiful you are?"

"Oh!" Sujata had picked up a broom to sweep the packed-mud floor. Her hair was roughly tied back; she was too poor to own any makeup, and she rouged her cheeks with berry stain when she knew her fiancé was coming. "Why do you talk like that? You said you took a vow." She looked embarrassed and displeased.

"My vow must be very powerful. I can see that you're beautiful, but I don't care."

Now Sujata looked more displeased. Turning her back, she swept the floor with a vengeance, throwing up clouds of dust. For half an hour they had nothing to say to each other. But then two monkeys fighting in the yard made Sujata laugh, and when she adjusted Gautama's bedclothes, her eyes regarded him mildly, without a hint of resentment.

After that, as promised, he fed himself and was taken on wobbly legs out into the yard. He wasn't a limp doll anymore, so he could be sat in a wicker chair instead of being propped against a tree. Sujata was surprised that he didn't care where he was put, in sun or shade. One day she came out to find that he'd stepped on some foraging red ants, and now a hundred of them, fierce biters, were climbing up his leg. Gautama didn't wince; he didn't even look down at them.

Brushing the attackers off, and with them the blood from their bites, she said, "What are you doing to yourself? I didn't pull you out of the woods so you'd care about nothing. Find something, and do it quick." She turned away and began to cry.

"I'd obey you if I could," said Gautama. "I owe you everything."

His voice sounded humble and sincere, but inside he was as detached from her distress as from everything else. Sujata sensed this, no doubt. Otherwise how to explain the fact that he woke up the next day to find the hut empty? She left pots of food but nothing else. The door was locked, the floor still damp from being washed.

Gautama took this all in and waited. He wondered, as an impartial spectator might wonder watching a stranger, if his mind would grieve or feel abandoned. When nothing happened, he went outside to watch the clouds, something he did every day.

Every day that he grew stronger, he felt more removed from that fiercely certain monk who had been willing to die for God. Gautama wasn't a zealot anymore, but there was nothing to put in its place. He took his eyes off a camel-humped cloud and looked at his hands. They had fleshed out again, and so had his wasted arms and legs. He tried to remember how old he was. Thirty-five seemed right. Young enough to take up honest labor or return to the monk's life, or even go home and become the good prince again.

It was time to choose one, since he couldn't remain alone in Sujata's hut. Choosing seemed impossible, though. He was a blank. At best he was a vaporous, drifting cloud, like the ones he stared at. After a while, Gautama decided to imitate a cloud by going nowhere in particular. He cleaned the hut of any sign that he had ever stayed there, shut the door behind him, and walked away.

When his sandals contacted the familiar packed dirt of the road, his gait settled into a mechanical tread. Soon he passed other travelers, but they didn't look his way. Maybe he'd lost his presence too, or perhaps it was just his half-starved appearance. Gautama's eyes saw the sights of the jungle—birds, animals, the light streaming in bright bars through the still leaf canopy—and he had the impression that every sensation was passing through him. *I am water,* he thought. *I am air.*

This wasn't unpleasant. If he was going to spend the rest of his life as a blank, feeling transparent wasn't the worst thing. He walked a bit farther, and he had another thought. *I am not suffering.* When had he stopped suffering? He didn't know, because his body had been in pain for those weeks, which distracted him. Physical pain wasn't the same as suffering, he realized that. Suffering happens to a person, and he was fairly sure he had turned into something new, a nonperson.

He stared at the sunset, its red-gold streaks breaking through tall white clouds. Over the jungle canopy he saw the crest of a tall tree and headed for it. The ground around the tree was soft and springy, free of fungus. He looked up and saw that this was a pipal or fig tree. The sky darkened quickly; soon it was barely possible to see sapphire patches between the black silhouettes of the foliage. Gautama sat down to meditate.

He wondered if a nonperson needed to meditate, and at first the answer seemed to be no. When he closed his eyes he didn't sink into a cool, safe silence. Instead, it was like being in a lightless cave where there was no difference between having his eyes open or shut. But since he had nothing to do and nowhere to go, he decided that meditation was as good as anything else. He caught sight of the waning moon, which was three-quarters full. Vaguely Gautama thought it would be nice to be the moon. And then he was.

It didn't happen immediately. He sat, and the waning moon turned into a sliver, then a hairline of luminescence in the sky, before it waxed again. He caught a glimpse of it only once a night; otherwise he had his eyes closed. Nothing was changing inside him. Only by the moon did Gautama realize when seven weeks had passed.

"I'm here. You can open your eyes now."

Gautama was past having delusions, so the voice must be real. He opened his eyes. A yogi with long locks and a beard had found him and was sitting with crossed legs under the tree. The moonlight was bright enough to reveal the face of the doomed monk Ganaka.

"You don't have to disguise yourself," said Gautama. "I was expecting to see you, Mara."

"Really?" The form of Ganaka smiled. "I didn't want to shock you. I am, as you know, basically kind."

"Kind enough to show me an image of grief? I am past grieving," Gautama said.

"Then take this image as a greeting from Ganaka instead. I know him well," said Mara. "He is in my care now."

"Then he must be in a place of torment. But I am beyond horror too. So tell me quickly why you've come, with as few lies as you can."

"I'm here to teach you. Remember, that was my offer when you were young," Mara said. "But you misjudged me, as everyone does. Now you must be wiser."

"You think it's wiser to have a demon for a teacher?" As they bantered, Gautama felt nothing toward Mara, neither fear nor dislike. Even wondering why the demon had sought him was a faint impulse on the edge of his mind.

"You still misjudge me," Mara said in a cajoling voice. "I know the secrets of the universe. No knowledge can be kept from me since my role is to see into the crevices of every soul. I will share all that I know with you."

"No."

"I didn't hear that. You've craved knowledge ever since I met you. I saw it in your eyes. Why turn your back on me now? I'm greater than these yogis you've wasted your time with," the demon said.

"The one who wanted to know everything no longer exists," said Gautama. "I have nothing left to ask."

"Stubbornness doesn't become you, my friend. I'm disappointed." Mara's tone of voice was smooth and assured, but he was sitting close enough that Gautama felt the demon's body tremble with suppressed rage. Mara said, "I thought you were above other souls. But if you insist on being common, let me satisfy what you really want."

These words were greeted with peals of laughter. Through the trees came three beautiful women carrying oil lamps; incense swirled around them. As Gautama watched, a pool of water appeared in the forest. The women began to disrobe, casting glances at him and giggling softly.

"My three daughters," said Mara. "They never fail to charm, so why pretend? You want them."

The women had silky pale skin and full breasts. Gautama looked on while they bathed themselves, using every suggestive gesture they could find; their hands were delicate, and the way they touched themselves only faintly hinted at lewdness.

"I told them you weren't coarse, but as you can see, they will adapt themselves to your every desire," said Mara.

"Yes, I see that," said Gautama. "The man who once had a wife no longer exists. I can accept your daughters as new wives. Tell them to approach."

Mara smiled with satisfaction. The three women emerged from the bathing pool and draped themselves with gossamer saris that showed their naked bodies in the moonlight. Mara made a gesture, and the first daughter knelt submissively before Gautama.

"What is your name, beautiful one?" Gautama asked.

"I am Tanha."

"Your name means 'desire.' I will take you for a wife, but unfortunately I have no desire for you. If you marry me, you will never feel desire or be desired ever again. Is that acceptable?"

Before his eyes the lovely face of Tanha turned into the face of a long-toothed demon, and with a howl she vanished from sight.

"Let me see your second daughter," said Gautama. Mara, looking displeased, waved his hand abruptly, and the second young woman knelt before them.

"What is your name, beautiful one?" asked Gautama.

"Raga."

"Your name means 'lust.' I was born a male, and therefore your appeal is well known to me. I will take you for a wife, but if we marry, you must respect my vows. Your heart of fire will be turned to ice, and you will never lust or be lusted after again. Is that acceptable?"

In an instant Raga was transformed into a ball of fire, which rushed at Gautama to sear his flesh. Instead, the fire passed through him and vanished.

"Show me your last daughter," Gautama said. "The first two won't have me."

Mara jumped to his feet in a rage. "You treat my gentle girls badly. They only want to serve you, and in return you cruelly abuse them."

"But your third daughter is so beautiful, I can't possibly mistreat her. Bring her to me. I'm sure we will be married," Gautama said gently. Mara regarded him with dark suspicion but made a small gesture. The third daughter knelt before them.

"Don't ask me my name," she said. "I am free of all desire and lust. I am as indifferent to you as you are to me. We are perfectly matched."

"You're very subtle," said Gautama. "But I already know your name. It's Arati, or 'aversion.' You want nothing because you hate everything. I will make you my wife, but only on the condition that you open yourself to love. Is that acceptable?"

Arati's face assumed a look of unspeakable disgust. In alarm Mara reached his arms out to hold on to her, but he was too late. In an instant she vanished like the others. The demon gave a howl that grew louder and fiercer until it filled the whole forest. He swelled in size, and the form of Ganaka dropped away. Mara began to grow his four horrible faces.

"I'm going to see you as you really are. Good," said Gautama.

"Arrogance!" Mara screamed. "You shall see me, all right, and the moment you do, you will die."

He began to make mysterious signs in the air that Gautama didn't understand, and like magic, the kingdom of the demons descended to earth. The forest floor crawled with poisonous snakelike demons, slithering over Gautama's lap, while batlike demons tried to bite his face. A phalanx of elephants crashed through the trees, trampling other demons of damned souls whose bodies were crushed underfoot. Because the demon world consists of the most disgusting and terrifying forms that the human mind can conceive of, there was no end to the waves of Mara's subjects that emerged in the moonlight.

Mara himself rode a massive bull elephant that held writhing souls between its jaws. At first he remained aloof, waiting for his army to annihilate Gautama by sucking it into a maelstrom of torment. But when he saw the calmness of Gautama's gaze, Mara became agitated.

"Resist me all you like. I will never depart from you, and neither will my subjects. This spectacle is what you will see for the rest of your life."

"I am not resisting. You are all welcome to stay," said Gautama. "You cannot attack what isn't here, and I am not here."

"Not here?" said Mara. "You're insane."

"Or perhaps I just lack a soul. Doesn't it take a soul to be damned?"

The calmness of Gautama's speech not only infuriated the demon king but caused his subjects to begin to fade away like shadow puppets on a screen or summer lightning inside a cloud.

"Prove it to yourself," said Gautama. "If you can find my soul, it's yours. I have stopped caring, myself."

Mara leaped from the elephant and crouched on the ground in front of Gautama. "Done!" he hissed. He had never experienced any creature, mortal or divine, without a soul, and now this fool had freely surrendered his. "You're mine, and I will claim you when it pleases me." Every other spectre had disappeared by now. Mara's four malignant faces lingered for a few more seconds before he too vanished.

Gautama doubted he would ever see him again. The existence of his soul, like everything else, held no interest. Total detachment is the one great healer of karma. Yet the whisper of desire softly said, "Do not kill me. Have pity. Let me know even your slightest wish."

He looked up and remembered the moon, which was perfectly full as it floated above the jungle canopy.

"Let me become the moon," Gautama replied. "I have nothing to wish for down here."

He had only wanted to have sway over his own destiny. It was the simplest of human wishes, yet it had been a source of fear and uncertainty his whole life. Everyone had told him, directly or indirectly, that it was impossible. Gautama felt a slight resistance even now, as if the gods would destroy him on the spot for usurping their power. Instead, he felt the last veil fall away from his mind, a sensation a hundred times more delicate than dropping a layer of gossamer. Then he became the moon and experienced what the moon experienced. It was impossible to put into words: a cool serenity that thrilled at its own existence. A concern for nothing but light itself. Gautama was aware of all these ingredients, yet the thing itself was ineffable.

The moon seemed to know that he had arrived, and he felt it bow down. *I have waited.* His gaze searched the sky, and these words seemed to come from everywhere, not just the moon but also the stars and the blackness between the stars. His heart began to swell.

I have waited too.

The sky bent down to envelop him. Now he understood why he had to become a nonperson. He had to be naked. Only in innocence does the mask fall away. *So this is it,* he thought. *The truth.* Gautama gave his heart permission to swell beyond the sky. He didn't know what lay beyond, or how far he could go. He had found his freedom, and in freedom everything is permitted.

17

The sun rose, and Gautama found himself sitting on the soft, springy ground under the pipal tree. He got to his feet and tried walking. It was a strange experience—as he passed through the forest, the forest seemed to pass through him. Its breath mingled with his; its trees and vines extended from his body. He could feel the wind blowing through the swaying canopy overhead.

Gautama knew that everything had changed permanently. From now on, living in the physical world would be like dreaming. He could make things appear and disappear as easily as a dreamer does. A castle made of gold or a circle of angels around his head, stars exploding into bursts of white light or a deer nestling in his lap to sleep—they all appeared instantly at the hint of a thought.

Now he could sit under the pipal tree, silent and unmoving, and never return to the world. His journey was complete. But he still had a choice. To leave or stay?

Everyone from his past had given up on him long ago. And if he suddenly reappeared, how would he explain what he had become? The priests would certainly call him a fraud. Great souls are safe only as long as they stay put in the scriptures.

Gautama's choice weighed heavily on him. Several mornings he felt that someone was thinking about him. Yashodhara. When her name came to him, Gautama saw her clearly. His wife was sitting alone in her room, mending a hem by the light of an open window. Gautama had seen her face many times during his wandering, but this was different. He was in the room with her, feeling her yearning, which was always for him. One person hadn't given up.

Gautama thought of other people and found them as well. Channa was saddling a roan warhorse in the stables, and Gautama sensed that he was now master there; old Bikram had died. Suddhodana was asleep, alone with the drapes drawn. He was trying to escape a bad dream about an old battle.

Gautama could be anywhere and everywhere he wanted. Just by thinking of people, he could touch their minds. Not everyone would listen. Not everyone would feel his touch, but for a moment their troubles would ease. Is that what a Buddha did? Without warning, he started weeping. He was no longer husband, lover, or friend. He was a new Buddha, untried, wobbly, three days out of the womb. But he had no doubt that Gautama no longer existed.

The new Buddha arose, adjusted his saffron robe, and began walking toward the road, the same as on a thousand other days. Once he reached the road, he found it completely empty, even though the time was early morning, when farmers' carts should have been trundling to market. The emptiness seemed even odder after hours had passed and still he hadn't met a single wagon or foot traveler.

Buddha could be completely alone in the world. Why not? It was his world to do with as he pleased. He was the one dreaming it. Some skittish parrots overhead burst into flight as Buddha laughed out loud. This was outrageous! If a king ruled the world, he would run wild. He would tear it to shreds in anger, toy with it, wrap his body in its sensual delights.

Instead, he possessed the world as Buddha, so none of those possibilities came true. His powers flowed from the other side of silence, where the mind can make anything happen. For a little while the new Buddha enjoyed himself, pulling the sun through the sky like a toy cart, swirling the winds around the poles, shedding rain on a parched desert. This private diversion didn't last long. Buddha's world should have people in it whom he could care for. He recalled what Canki had said about a Golden Age—an age without suffering, where abundance was normal and scarcity forgotten in the dim past.

At that moment his vision was shattered by a scream. He saw a woman running toward him, her sari torn to shreds, her arms bleeding. In her panic the woman was blind to Buddha's existence until she was nearly upon him. Then her eyes registered him standing there, still and calm.

With a cry she rushed to throw herself into his arms, overwhelmed with relief. When she was two steps away, he held his hand up in blessing. The woman stopped in her tracks. She quivered with terror, her breast heaving.

"No more fear," Buddha whispered. "Give it to me."

She dropped to the road as if her body had melted and began to weep.

"All," said Buddha. "Give it all to me."

The woman became very still; the crying had stopped. Buddha erased the images of terror from her mind. He saw a knife. Teeth like fangs. A necklace made of severed fingers. The images were nightmarish. With the slightest touch, he made them vanish. But one image wouldn't melt away—the body of her dead husband. He lay in the dust of the road, his throat slashed.

The woman was touching Buddha's feet now in supplication. Something inside her knew who he was. She gazed at him through her eyes and said, "Please."

Buddha stopped himself from consoling her. He lifted the woman's head and met her gaze. "It is done," he said. She shuddered and fainted. After a moment, as Buddha stood motionless, a man rounded the corner driving an ox cart. Her husband. Buddha gestured for him to approach, and he sped up. Seeing his wife on the ground, the husband jumped down in alarm.

"What happened?" he cried.

"It will be all right. Let's put her in the cart." The two of them gently laid her in the straw behind the driver's seat. The husband had some fresh water in a goatskin bag; he wanted to splash it on her to reassure himself that she was all right. Buddha stopped his hand. "Let her wake up on her own. She may be surprised to see you, but calm her with loving words. You understand?"

The farmer nodded. By imagining the farmer alive and well again, he had erased the whole attack. It wasn't difficult. He hadn't raised the husband from the dead. All he did was say no softly to himself. The event he refused to accept no longer existed. Buddha smiled at the husband, and when he had nothing more to say, the farmer thanked him and left.

Power over time and fate. Buddha mused on this as he walked. Does a Buddha reverse every harm? Even if he had that power, did he have the right to change karma on a whim?

In a short while he saw the first huts of a small village. As he approached, people came out wearing suspicious and fearful looks. Some carried pitchforks and rusty swords. They glared as Buddha passed, and in each mind he heard the same word: *Angulimala*. He soon realized that this was the name of someone they all feared. A killer. A madman. A monster.

Buddha continued to the local temple, whose tiled roof was the highest point in the village. In the shadowy cool of the inner sanctum he saw an old priest cleaning the altar of faded flowers and burnt incense ashes. He approached.

"Namaste."

The priest barely acknowledged him. Remote as this temple was, he maintained the air of a Brahmin. Instead of praying beside him, Buddha sat cross-legged before the altar and waited. The old priest threw a few fresh flowers onto the Shiva statue and turned to leave.

"Angulimala," Buddha said.

The priest got angry. "Don't say such a thing. This is a holy place."

Buddha said, "I think you forbid the name of Angulimala because you fear he might hear and invade your kingdom." The old priest squinted his eyes, wondering if he was being mocked. "I can help," Buddha added.

This offer was greeted with a harsh laugh. "How? Are you a warrior monk? It wouldn't matter. Angulimala has killed his share of warriors. He has powers. He exchanged his soul for them."

"What powers?"

"He can outrun a horse. He can hide without being seen and spring down on travelers from the tops of trees. Enough?"

"Perhaps, if any are true. I doubt that these powers have been observed if he kills everyone he meets and the few survivors are terrified," said Buddha.

The priest, who was bald and slightly hunched, relented slightly. "You're right about that, stranger. Come with me. I can feed you, and with a little food in your stomach you might stop deluding yourself that you can help." The old priest managed a tight smile; something deep inside had been touched by the stranger's offer. They retired to the temple kitchen, and when the stranger's bowl was filled with rice and lentils, the two sat outside in the shade to eat.

"As you know, *anguli* means fingers," said the priest. "To terrify everyone the more, this killer collects the fingers of his victims and wears them as a necklace around his throat. Very few know his real story, but I am one. The monster began life as the mild son of a Brahmin family with no money. At fourteen he was sent to school in a nearby village, with the hope that once he was educated he could perform rites at the temple and restore his family's fortunes.

"But the Brahmin who ran the school was of unbalanced mind. He accused the boy of sleeping with his wife and threw him out in disgrace." Buddha didn't detect much pity for suffering in the old priest's heart, but he genuinely felt sorry for the wronged boy.

"The scandal reached home before the boy did. When he crossed the threshold, his father beat him brutally and threw him out to fend for himself. The family's hopes for restoring their fortunes were dashed. It didn't matter that their son was innocent."

As the priest recounted the tale, Buddha could see every event in his mind. What lay ahead looked much darker. "There was nothing for him to live for but death," Buddha murmured.

"He was born cursed, and there's no hope for him," the old priest said severely.

"Did anyone try to give him hope?" asked Buddha. The priest scowled, but their meal was over. In gratitude, Buddha bowed his head. He didn't prostrate himself at the Brahmin's feet. This caused the old priest to keep a moody silence as he escorted his visitor to the gate.

"You're a fool to go after him. I can see that's what you have in mind," the Brahmin said. "But if you must, here's a charm to protect you." He held out some dried herbs bundled with a prayer scribbled on a leaf. Buddha accepted it.

"Tell me one thing," said Buddha. "Why does Angulimala kill so many people?"

"To save himself," the old priest replied. "The disgraced boy took to the woods. He began to live like an animal. He ate roots and insects and covered his body with hides. They say by chance he met a wandering fortune-teller, who told him the curse could be lifted only by collecting a thousand fingers and offering them as sacrifice to Shiva. That's why he wears his terrible necklace."

"Then I must help him," said Buddha. "Otherwise Angulimala will show up here one day to sacrifice his necklace on your altar."

The old priest shuddered visibly and then slammed the gate shut behind him.

THOUGHTS OF ANGULIMALA stayed in Buddha's mind that day and the next morning. Why was he drawn to the monster?

He walked deeper into the jungle to face the question. It was a blazing afternoon when Buddha found himself on a hidden trail through the jungle. There was a rustle, then before he could turn his head, a wild beast jumped down from the trees and crouched before him. The covering of matted hides made Angulimala look like a giant ferocious ape baring its fangs.

Buddha regarded the wild man's teeth, which had been crudely filed to a point, and his necklace of withered fingers. In his left hand he carried a long curved blade. "Namaste," said Buddha. Angulimala growled.

"I cannot save you unless you tell me how you are suffering," said Buddha. "An animal doesn't need saving."

The wild man showed no reaction. He could reach his prey in one leap, so he raised his knife and with a howl sprang toward Buddha. When he came to earth, however, his knife slashed at empty air. Buddha was standing, as before, two paces away. Angulimala looked bewildered.

"You do not have to ask for mercy or forgiveness," said Buddha. "Speak your real name, not the monster's that you have assumed."

The wild man took another leap at Buddha, and as before, when he landed his blade swished through the air. Buddha was standing two paces away.

"I can only stop a moment," Buddha said. "But if you want my help, come to me."

He turned his back on Angulimala and began slowly walking away. Behind him there was a scream of rage. One thing the old Brahmin had said was true: Angulimala possessed enough demonic energy that he could outrun a horse. He charged at Buddha, his knife stretched out in front like a spear. It should have taken only a few seconds to reach his prey, but Buddha remained a step ahead. Angulimala sped up, panting as he ran. His bare feet stirred up a cloud of dust, but he couldn't close the gap between himself and Buddha. This kept up for ten minutes, until the wild man fell to the ground, clutching at his cramped legs. Buddha turned around and regarded him.

"There's a small distance between you and me," he said mildly. "Shall I close it? I can."

He reached down and touched the killer's matted hair, and Angulimala began to weep. "Please tell me your real name," Buddha urged. There was a pause, and Angulimala shivered from head to toe. "Why?" he moaned. By this he meant, *Why should anyone help me? I am damned.*

"I will tell you, but I can't explain to an animal," said Buddha.

Angulimala clutched at himself, writhing on the ground. Buddha stood quietly, letting the demonic energy drain away. It would take more than a single seizure to purify the wild man, but this was a beginning. After he had thrashed in the dust for some minutes, a name came out. "Anigha," he said.

"Look at me, Anigha," Buddha said. "We are brothers."

The wild man was pacified from exhaustion, his body spent. He raised his head as Buddha bent over to bless him. "You were once a great saint," said Buddha. "Now you have become a great sinner. This was not a curse. The cycle of birth and rebirth has brought you full circle. The same thing happens to everyone. It has happened to me."

Each word he spoke caused a change in Anigha. His eyes looked far away; he seemed to remember something deep and profound. Tears rolled down his cheeks. "I am damned," he said aloud, his voice becoming more human.

"No, you share the same fate as everyone," said Buddha. "You wanted to find a way out of suffering. The only difference is that you asked for the life of a monster. You imagined that if you caused enormous suffering, you would be immune to it."

The weight of Anigha's crimes was crushing him—he groaned.

"It's horrible to bring hell on earth," said Budddha. "There was another purpose, though, that no one sees." Anigha stared in bafflement. "You hungered for the supreme truth many lifetimes ago.

The gods failed you; your vows as a monk led to nothing but deeper disappointment. So you swore that you would not be redeemed unless the greatest sinner received the same treatment."

Now Anigha grasped Buddha's feet and was sobbing loudly as his pain poured out. Buddha took his hands away and lifted him up. "If you are part of me, you need nothing else to be saved," he said.

Anigha said, "But I have killed."

"You fell into evil so that you could prove to yourself that there is a reality that evil cannot touch. Will you let me show it to you?"

Anigha listened quietly, then he looked down at his filthy body clothed in bloodied hides. They were unrecognizable now as part of him. He led Buddha to a stream and washed the dirt away. When he had washed off as much as he could, he came out of the water. "I will follow you anywhere," he said. "Angulimala is dead."

"You will always be with me. But for the moment you need to stay here," said Buddha. "Devote yourself to atonement. Leave food for the poor. Offer flowers and water at the temple gate for those who want to make sacrifice. Help lost travelers whom you once terrified. Whatever you do, don't show yourself. I will return for you very soon."

Anigha didn't find it easy to let Buddha go; he still half-believed that he was in a dream devised by a mischievous demon. After a while, though, his exhaustion made him nod off as the two sat under a tree talking. Buddha arose and left quietly. He gave no thought to where he was going next. But something had happened that he alone knew. He had altered the course of evil with a touch and a word.

He was still a new Buddha, four days out of the womb, but every moment was bringing him greater power and more wisdom to use it well.

18

The five monks had retreated to a forest glade near Benares after they parted from Gautama. Months passed. Now the glade was beautiful with overhanging trees in the riotous bloom of spring. They knew Gautama must be dead, although the subject was never raised. The five monks lived a secluded life, but their time of extreme austerity was over and done with.

Returning to a moderate life seemed sensible, but a faint gloom settled over their existence because every forest monk wanted to reach enlightenment. Gautama's failure spelled failure for them too. Therefore, when he walked into their camp one morning, the five monks were relieved for themselves as much as for him.

After they greeted him with exclamations and expressed their joy, the monks sat and waited for their brother to describe what had happened. It was as if someone had returned from the dead. They expected a miracle story. At the very least, he would describe the wonders of enlightenment. But Buddha only wanted to be with them quietly, his glance occasionally moving from one to the other.

"We mourned for you, Gautama," Kondana, the youngest, said.

"Because you knew that Gautama was no more," said Buddha. "And you were right."

This was something they understood since it's a matter of course that someone who reaches enlightenment has severed all connections to his former personality. But none of the five monks had actually met anyone who had gotten there.

"If you aren't Gautama, who are you?" Assaji asked.

"I keep Gautama's body, and you can call me by his name if you like," said Buddha, smiling. "You need some way to find me in the dark. But I am not this body or this name. I am not a person any longer as you know it."

"That tells me what you are not, but I still don't know what you are," said Assaji, pressing the point.

Instead of replying, Buddha closed his eyes and went into samadhi, something they had seen Gautama do a thousand times. Assaji was about to signal that they should follow suit when Gautama unexpectedly opened his eyes again. The monks were used to him being lost in silence for days.

"Do you want to meditate alone?" Assaji asked. "We can leave you."

"It's not that, dear friend," said Buddha. "I have talked with only a few people since I came to be awakened. One blessed me with knowledge of good and evil. But no one has asked me who I am until now. You have given me another blessing."

Assaji looked confused. "How is that?" he asked.

"When I closed my eyes, I saw my past lifetimes. Ten thousand of them, and I lived each one moment by moment."

The five monks were amazed. "In the blink of an eye?" Kondana exclaimed.

Buddha smiled. "Two blinks, if you like. We have all been told since childhood that the cycle of birth and rebirth has brought us back many times. But as I went back to those lifetimes, I found that all of them were equal. I am every life I've ever lived, and yet I am none of them, for I can be here or there whenever I want."

"Is this the knowledge that set you free?" said Assaji.

"Do you ask me that because you really want to know or because you feel worried and insecure?" asked Buddha.

Assaji looked uncomfortable. "Your feat seems superhuman," he said. "If it takes something like that to reach enlightenment, what hope do we have? We're just ordinary monks." The others murmured in agreement.

"I didn't return to discourage you or to awe you. You asked me who I am, and now I can tell you. I can also tell you who you are. You are not the separate self. You have a name that you answer to, but you have also answered to ten thousand other names. Which one is the real you? None of them. You identify with a set of memories. You know who your father and mother are. You set your sights on a goal that you cherish.

"But you have done exactly the same thing ten thousand times before. Therefore your memories, your parents, and your cherished goals are transient. They change as swiftly as mayflies, which are born and die in a single day."

The five monks were riveted by Buddha's talk, but more than that, his words drew them deep inside themselves. It was almost like going into samadhi with one's eyes open. They saw exactly what he had described. But Assaji was still worried.

"I would be wasting my life to try and unravel ten thousand past lives," he said. "And if you want me to renounce this lifetime as a phantom, haven't I already renounced it by becoming a monk?"

"You renounced only the outer trappings," said Buddha. "A saffron robe doesn't make you free of desire, and desire is what has kept you a prisoner."

"You already told us that on the mountain," Kondana said. "But in six years we never rid ourselves of desire. Our karma still follows us and makes us obey its commands."

"Which is why I have come for you instead of going first to my family," said Buddha. "What I urged you to do on the mountain was a mistake. I want to make amends."

"You owe us nothing," Assaji said quickly.

"I'm not speaking of a debt," said Buddha. "Debts end when karma ends. My mistake led you into a trap. I believed that I was in a war with desire. I despised the world and my own body, which craved all the delights of the world."

"Surely that's not a mistake," said Assaji. "Otherwise it would be pointless to take vows. The holy life must be different from the worldly life."

"What if there is no holy life?" asked Buddha. The five monks became extremely uncomfortable, and none answered. "You see," said Buddha, "even holiness has become food for your ego to feed on. You want to be different. You want to be safe. You want to have hope."

"Why is that wrong?" asked Assaji.

"Because these things are dreams that lull you," said Buddha.

"What would we see if we weren't dreaming?"

"Death."

The five monks felt a chill pass over them. It seemed pointless to deny what their brother said but hopeless to accept it. Buddha said, "You are all afraid of death, as I was, so you make up any story that will ease your fears, and after a while you believe the story, even though it came from your own mind." Without waiting for a reply, he reached down and picked up a handful of dust. "The answer to life and death is simple. It rests in the palm of my hand. Watch."

He threw the dust into the air; it remained suspended like a murky cloud for a second before the breeze carried it away.

"Consider what you just saw," said Buddha. "The dust holds its shape for a fleeting moment when I throw it into the air, as the body holds its shape for this brief lifetime. When the wind makes it disappear, where does the dust go? It returns to its source, the earth. In the future that same dust allows grass to grow, and it enters a deer who eats the grass. The animal dies and turns to dust. Now imagine that the dust comes to you and asks, 'Who am I?' What will you tell it? Dust is alive in a plant but dead as it lies in the road under our feet. It moves in an animal but is still when buried in the depths of the earth. Dust encompasses life and death at the same time. So if you answer 'Who am I?' with anything but a complete answer, you have made a mistake.

"I have come back to tell you that you can be whole, but only if you see yourself that way. There is no holy life. There is no war between good and evil. There is no sin and no redemption. None of these things matter to the real you. But they all matter hugely to the false you, the one who believes in the separate self. You have tried to take your separate self, with all its loneliness and anxiety and pride, to the door of enlightenment. But it will never go through, because it is a ghost."

As he spoke, Buddha knew that this sermon would be the first of hundreds. It surprised him that words were so necessary. He had hoped to heal the world with a touch or simply by existing in it. The universe had other plans.

"How can I see myself as whole," asked Kondana, "when everything I call 'me' is separate? I have only one body and one mind, those I was born with."

"Look at the forest," Buddha replied. "We walk through it every day and believe it to be the same forest. But not a single leaf is the same as yesterday. Every particle of soil, every plant and animal, is constantly changing. You cannot be enlightened as the separate person you see yourself to be because that person has already disappeared, along with everything else from yesterday."

The five monks were astonished to hear these words. They revered Gautama, but now his beliefs called for a revolution. If what he said was true, then nothing that they had been taught could be true at the same time. No holy life? No war between good and evil? None of them spoke for a long while. What was there to say to a man who claimed that they didn't even exist?

"I've brought agitation with me," said Buddha. "I didn't mean to." He said this sincerely, after due consideration. He hadn't realized that being awake would create such a disturbance to other people.

In the blink of an eye, as quickly as he had seen ten thousand previous lifetimes, he saw the human predicament. Everyone was asleep, totally unconscious about their true nature. Some slept fitfully, catching scattered glimpses of the truth. But they quickly fell asleep again. They were the fortunate ones. The bulk of human beings had no glimpse of reality. How could he tell them what he really wanted to say? *All of you are Buddha.*

"I realize that if I stay here I will only agitate you more," he said. "So help me. Together we must devise a Dharma that will not frighten people. Beginning with you, my frightened brothers." The five monks smiled at this, and they began to relax a little. Buddha pointed to the trees in bloom all around them. "The Dharma should be this beautiful, and just as effortless," he said. "If Nature is awake everywhere we look, then human beings deserve the same. Waking up shouldn't be a struggle."

"You struggled," said Assaji.

"Yes, and the more I did, the harder it was to wake up. I made my body and mind into an enemy. On that road lies only death and more death. As long as your body is your enemy, you are tied to it, and the body has no choice but to die. Death will never be defeated until it becomes unreal."

Years later Assaji would remember that a rainstorm began to pass through the forest as Buddha spoke. Lightning punctuated his words and lit up his face, which wasn't the fiercely zealous face of Gautama but something unearthly and serene. They heard the patter of raindrops on the forest canopy, which increased to a steady drumming, yet no rain fell on the five monks, not even a stray drop sizzling in the campfire. In this way Nature was telling them that Buddha was more than a man who had become enlightened. They followed him devotedly after that night.

FOR THE FIRST TIME in six years Buddha's feet touched the road to Kapilavastu. He traveled with the five monks, who gradually lost their anxiety but not their awe. They ate and slept beside their master. They bathed with him in the river, but he no longer meditated or said prayers. One at a time he took each of his brothers aside and gave them private instructions. They were overjoyed to be told that they were very close to enlightenment and would achieve it very soon.

There was one monk who never spoke up. His name was Vappa, and he seemed the most insecure about Gautama coming back to life. When he was taken aside and told that he would be enlightened, Vappa greeted the news with doubt. "If what you tell me is true, I would feel something, and I don't," he said.

"When you dig a well, there is no sign of water until you reach it, only rocks and dirt to move out of the way. You have removed enough; soon the pure water will flow," said Buddha. But instead of being reassured, Vappa threw himself on the ground, weeping and grasping Buddha's feet.

"It will never happen," he moaned. "Don't fill me with false hope."

"I'm not offering hope," said Buddha. "Your karma brought you to me, along with the other four. I can see that you will soon be awake."

"Then why do I have so many impure thoughts?" asked Vappa, who was prickly and prone to outbursts of rage, so much so that the other monks were intimidated by him.

"Don't trust your thoughts," said Buddha. "You can't think yourself awake."

"I have stolen food when I was famished, and there were times when I stole away from my brothers and went to women," said Vappa.

"Don't trust your actions. They belong to the body," said Buddha. "Your body can't wake you up."

Vappa remained miserable, his expression hardening the more Buddha spoke. "I should go away from here. You say there is no war between good and evil, but I feel it inside. I feel how good you are, and it only makes me feel worse."

Vappa's anguish was so genuine that Buddha felt a twinge of temptation. He could reach out and take Vappa's guilt from his shoulders with a touch of the hand. But making Vappa happy wasn't the same as setting him free, and Buddha knew he couldn't touch every person on earth. He said, "I can see that you are at war inside, Vappa. You must believe me when I say that you'll never win."

Vappa hung his head lower. "I know that. So I must go?"

"No, you misunderstand me," Buddha said gently. "No one has ever won the war. Good opposes evil the way the summer sun opposes winter cold, the way light opposes darkness. They are built into the eternal scheme of Nature."

"But you won. You are good; I feel it," said Vappa.

"What you feel is the being I have inside, just as you have it," said Buddha. "I did not conquer evil or embrace good. I detached myself from both."

"How?"

"It wasn't difficult. Once I admitted to myself that I would never become completely good or free from sin, something changed inside. I was no longer distracted by the war; my attention could go somewhere else. It went beyond my body, and I saw who I really am. I am not a warrior. I am not a prisoner of desire. Those things come and go. I asked myself: Who is watching the war? Who do I return to when pain is over, or when pleasure is over? Who is content simply to be? You too have felt the peace of simply being. Wake up to that, and you will join me in being free."

This lesson had an immense effect on Vappa, who made it his mission for the rest of his life to seek out the most miserable and hopeless people in society. He was convinced that Buddha had revealed a truth that every person could recognize: suffering is a fixed part of life. Fleeing from pain and running toward pleasure would never change that fact. Yet most people spent their whole lives avoiding pain and pursuing pleasure. To them, this was only natural, but in reality they were becoming deeply involved in a war they could never win.

As the gates of Kapilavastu drew close, Buddha prepared the way. He sent his presence ahead, and he could feel a growing excitement in Yashodhara. She ordered her servants to throw away the somber saris of a widow; she brought out old portraits of Siddhartha to show their son, Rahula, who might be frightened to see the return of a father he knew only in the cradle. Every day Yashodhara performed the same ritual. She would gather Rahula by her side and sit in the gazebo by the lotus pond, the place where Suddhodana's pleasure pavilion used to stand. The old structure had been torn down and the courtesans given honest places as serving women. Siddhartha had never visited them. It was one way he could show his fidelity to Yashodhara. Now she waited there to show her fidelity to him.

Buddha knew that feeling his presence was not enough, though. His wife was still young; for that matter, Siddhartha would be only thirty-five. There was time for more children. Buddha's presence couldn't reach this part of Yashodhara's nature. How could he change her mind without crushing her? The bliss of wedded life was what she lived for.

His mind was preoccupied when the five monks began to stir with agitation. Buddha looked up the road where they were pointing. A horse lathered with sweat and streaming with blood was running toward them in a panicked gallop. The five monks scattered to get out of the way. It was a powerful black stallion. None of them dared to pull Buddha from harm's way; he stood his ground, and as the animal got near, it reared, slashing out with its iron-shod front feet. For a second the huge animal balanced in midair, thrashing. Then its hooves came to earth without hitting their target. The stallion trembled with pain and terror, but it didn't rear again and slowly began to calm down.

"What happened?" asked Assaji, pressing the cloth of his robe to the horse's worst wound. "Where did this come from?"

"Only one thing is possible," said Buddha. "War. We'll be in the thick of it soon enough."

They hadn't gone another mile before his prediction came true; the din of battle could be faintly heard in the distance. "I am the cause of this," said Buddha. The five monks protested, but Buddha said no more. The group had their hands full keeping the wounded stallion from bolting when he caught the scent of death. More than once Buddha had to pause and look the animal directly in the eye. "The only way to convince him that he doesn't need to be afraid is to show him that I am not. Animals are wiser than us in that regard. If they don't feel peace, they aren't fooled by peaceful words."

The monks knew that Buddha did not make casual remarks. His every utterance was dedicated to teaching them the truth. Very soon the noise of battle grew loud enough that they could hear steel striking against steel and the anguished cries of dying soldiers. Buddha stopped and listened. "Words of peace fooled my father. Devadatta has tricked him into war." Then he pointed away from the conflict. "Home first." An hour later they saw the towers of the gates to the capital city. The road widened, and the last hundred yards were paved with cobblestones.

"Who's there?" a sentry cried.

"One you called Siddhartha," said Buddha.

"I can't let anyone in who isn't a citizen, and I don't know that name," said the sentry, peering through a slot above them. He was young, almost a boy. The real soldiers were all away to do the king's killing.

"Send for Princess Yashodhara's maid. She will recognize me," said Buddha. The sentry's face vanished from the top of the gate. They waited, then the great wooden gates opened just wide enough to admit them and the stallion. Buddha saw where his wife was. Having heard the name Siddhartha, she sent her maid scurrying to the gates while she hurriedly examined herself in the mirror and wrapped herself in a sari threaded with gold.

She was panting and sweating slightly when she seated herself in the gazebo. Rahula was taking a nap, and Yashodhara almost woke him up, but she didn't want him to see her weep uncontrollably, so she came alone. The wind was light, but whenever it turned slightly she could faintly catch the sounds of war, which increased her anxiety.

"My dear."

She had been so distracted that he was there before she heard him. With a cry, Yashodhara jumped to her feet, ran to Buddha, and threw her arms around him. She was sensitive to his slightest response, and her heart swelled when she felt his arms hold her without hesitation. This came as such an enormous relief that she began to sob. A husband would have said, "There's no cause for that. I'm home now. It's all right." Yashodhara's husband said none of those things.

Buddha let go of her, and for an instant Yashodhara felt completely abandoned. She wanted to clutch at him, but he raised a finger in a small gesture, and her arms fell to her sides. "You are my beloved wife. It's your right to embrace me," said Buddha. "No one shall ever do that again. Not even you."

Yashodhara trembled. She had spent years blocking out of her mind any image of Siddhartha as a monk. Even at that moment she kept her eyes fixed on his face, refusing to see his saffron robes. His features began swimming before her, but she wasn't fainting—no black curtain descending over her eyes, no cold sweat and chill moving up toward her head. Instead, Yashodhara felt warm, and the warmth began in her heart. It radiated outward. What was happening to her? The world disappeared from sight, not in blackness but in the glow of a white light that had no source. She caught one last glimpse of the sun, but it was pale compared to the light that now filled up her whole being. Now she was certain that the light came from this man who used to be her husband.

"This is your time, Yashodhara. Surrender and be free."

19

Buddha didn't spend the night in Kapilavastu but took the five monks and headed for the battlefield. It was near sunset when they arrived at a hilltop overlooking the fighting. In the waning light neither side was leading a charge. Elephants and horses had been pulled back from the front. All that remained of the din of war was the clash of swords. Foot soldiers fought in bands with the enemy, raising dust around them.

Buddha sat down on the ridge. From above, every soldier was like a frantic puppet flailing away. Some puppets ran around, bumping into other puppets. They bounced off each other, then one would fall and not get up again. Many puppets littered the field, some writhing a little, others very still.

"Are we going down there?" Kondana asked nervously. "What place is it for monks?"

"We have no other choice," said Buddha. "War is no different from what happens every day. It's another way that men have found to suffer."

"But life isn't always a war," Kondana pointed out.

"Not openly," said Buddha. "But if men weren't so afraid of dying, they would fight every day, and in their hearts their dearest wish would be to see every enemy destroyed." By now the light had faded, ending the skirmishes on the field. The last thing one could see were the scavengers who crept onto the scene to loot dead bodies. The wind carried sweet birdcalls up the hill, mixed with moans of wounded soldiers.

"Master, what you're saying is very dark. It makes the situation hopeless," said Kondana.

"Hope never ended a war."

That was Buddha's last word for the night. He folded his robes around him and lay on the ground. The five monks had learned that he had no concern for where he slept or who was nearby. But they had gotten into the habit of seeing after his comforts to the small extent he would allow. They fetched a gourd of water to place by his side and some food brought from the capital. They built a fire and together lay down apart from him out of respect.

Buddha usually urged them to sleep nearby, but they might have been worried to see that he needed no sleep anymore. He rested his body, but his mind remained awake all the time. Now he sent a blessing to Yashodhara and visited his six-year-old son, Rahula, who could hardly stay in bed with the excitement of once more having a father. The boy had been raised to believe secretly that Siddhartha was still alive, so he wasn't as wonder-struck as the courtiers who set eyes on Buddha. Buddha repeatedly told them that he hadn't come home to assume the throne, but many kept hoping he would do so.

When the sun rose and all the monks were awake, Buddha pointed to the scene down below, where clusters of soldiers stirred around their campfires. Some ate hurriedly, but most were tending to their horses, sharpening their swords, and repairing ripped leather armor.

"How many will die?" asked Assaji soberly.

"All of them, if not today then one day," said Buddha curtly. The monks had never heard a heartless remark from their master, and this astonished them. His voice softened. "I told you that the first fact of the world is suffering. We can end suffering, but not by speaking of God." Buddha's arm swept across the entire battlefield. "Which of these fighters doesn't believe that God is on his side?"

"But God relieves suffering too," said Assaji.

"Never promise such a thing," said Buddha, shaking his head. "All this religious talk has nothing to do with us. I will tell you how to consider any person you meet. Look on them as being like a man whose house has caught on fire. Would such a man cry, 'I'm not leaving until someone tells me why God made this happen'? No. He runs out of a burning house as fast as he can. The same is true of suffering. We must show people how to run away from it as fast as they can. It's no use spending years discussing whether someone is cursed or loved by the gods."

The closest fighting was no more than a quarter mile away, and they reached it in a few minutes. One horseman had chased another away from the center of battle. He had gotten close enough to thrust a spear into his enemy's mount, which had stumbled and thrown its rider. Now both soldiers were on their feet fighting hand-to-hand; they both were experienced enough to use a dagger in one hand and a sword in the other.

As they walked closer, the monks attracted no attention—the two soldiers were blind to everything but their struggle. Even so, the five monks were shaken at the sight of violence. Buddha stopped for a moment to let them regain their nerve.

"When I was a warrior," he said, "I learned that victory could never be achieved without weapons. We have no weapons, but we will prevail anyway."

Without a word he walked directly up to the two fighters and without hesitation strode into the space between them.

"Get away, stranger," one soldier shouted. "If you don't move, you'll be hurt."

"Is that possible?" said Buddha. "Try."

The two enemies stared at him in disbelief. "You must be insane," said one. "Run away, monk. If I have to, I'll slice you through with my blade."

"That would be interesting to see," Buddha said. His calmness was so unnerving that the two soldiers lowered their weapons, losing the edge of their fighting rage. From the sidelines Assaji shouted, "If you touch him, you are hurting a holy man. That's a sin."

Buddha turned and gave him a sharp look. "None of that," he rebuked. He shifted his attention back to the two soldiers. "You both do your duty to the gods, but that hasn't saved you from a lifetime of killing and fear. Why stop now? If you are so reckless with fate that you risk meeting your dead enemies in hell, I won't stop you. I invite you to run me through with your blade. I will even forgive you in advance."

By the time he spoke the last word, the two fighters were hanging their heads. Buddha reached out and lightly touched the daggers and swords, which dropped to the ground. "Shame has made you lose your taste for killing," he said. "Go home and find a better way to live."

"I can't," said one fighter. "If I run away from battle, the king will take away my house; there will be no food for my family."

"I promise you that won't happen," said Buddha. "Your king is going to disband his whole army today."

The two soldiers were amazed and wanted to ask more questions, but Buddha signaled to the five monks and walked on. When they looked over their shoulders, the fighters were gone.

"I've shown you the first way peace can prevail," said Buddha. "Some people can be reached by speaking to their conscience. Those are the ones who already know that they want to find an end to suffering. Through conscience, guilt, and shame, they will recognize their wrong when it is told to them."

"How many people are like that?" asked Assaji.

"Not enough."

Next Buddha led them to where the fighting was more concentrated: clusters of soldiers clashed in a whirling chaos of steel, horses, and shouts. For a moment Buddha stood apart. "What do you see?" he asked.

"Bloodshed and carnage. Something I wouldn't look upon willingly," said Assaji.

"Look a little deeper," said Buddha. "These are people who cannot listen to conscience, not because they are bad but because they are too caught up in action. You cannot preach to someone who is fighting for life and breath, not just in war but in the ordinary struggle of existence."

Buddha approached the fray, and a wildly flailing sword missed his head by inches. The monks cried out, but Buddha reached out and caught the blade in midair. He seized it from the swordsman, who turned his head with eyes that began to bulge out. Buddha was holding the sharp edges of the blade tight in his fist. The opposing swordsman saw his chance and lunged at his enemy. Buddha reached out and grabbed the second sword by the blade, wrenching it from the soldier's hand.

The soldiers were stunned with disbelief. "Who are you?" one cried as they fell to their knees.

"I am what you need at this moment," said Buddha.

He dropped the weapons and walked deeper into the combat. As he got nearer, the fighting calmed. Fighters held their weapons frozen in midair like statues. Buddha seemed to cut an open swath in the battlefield as he passed. The five monks rushed after him in his wake.

"What's happening?" asked Assaji breathlessly.

"What do you suppose?" said Buddha. "This is a miracle."

Buddha proceeded through the entire army. "I am showing you another way to prevail," he said. "Sometimes you must show yourself as you really are. People who are lost in the struggle of existence have become prisoners of illusion. Just remember one thing: you are made of light, and when it is fitting, you may have to prove it."

Assaji remained baffled by the awe that Buddha was creating among the soldiers, some of whom actually held their hands over their eyes to shield them. To Assaji, however, Buddha looked completely normal. "Why don't I see the miracle?" he asked.

"Because you are even more distracted than these soldiers," said Buddha with a smile. "You keep thinking I'm here to get you killed."

At that, Assaji suddenly found himself relaxing; he had been as tense as a tightened wire. He exhaled deeply, and then he saw that Buddha was surrounded by an aura of brilliant white light. The army beheld a being of light moving through their midst, and the sight brought them to their knees.

"Master, forgive me. I see now that you can save multitudes," said Assaji in awe.

"This isn't salvation," said Buddha. "Just a glimpse of reality. Everyone is deeply asleep. It will take more than one glimpse to wake them up."

Vappa, who had been listening close by, said, "No one will ever see me this way."

"Why not?" said Buddha. "I do already."

He remained silent as they made their way through the heart of battle. On the fringes one could still hear the clash of war, but as far as the eye could see, every soldier had laid down his weapons. It took half an hour to cross the entire field. The tents of the generals came into view. Buddha pointed to the highest tent pole, which flew a brilliant red and yellow ensign. "My father." The older generals shivered when they saw the return of the prince from the dead; all the officers bowed low, then they followed in Buddha's wake as he approached the royal tent.

Buddha parted the tent flap and went inside. In the dim, hot interior, the old king lay on a cot. He had fallen asleep while putting on his armor. He was groaning and turning over restlessly, his arms thrashing. Buddha made a gesture, and Assaji came inside.

"I want you to see everything," Buddha said. "But keep in a corner for now. We don't want to overwhelm him."

Assaji backed away into the shadows. Then Buddha approached the cot and touched his father on the shoulder. Suddhodana didn't start but woke up slowly, rubbing his eyes. It took a moment for his mind to grasp what he was seeing, and three words escaped his mouth separated by long pauses. "Who? No. You!" The old king began to weep.

"Don't be afraid, father." Buddha embraced the old man, and they stood together like that, while to Assaji's surprise Buddha himself was silently weeping. Suddhodana recovered his speech in broken expressions. Where did Siddhartha come from? Who had been beheaded? But more frequently he recriminated himself for being such a fool.

A surge of anger hardened the old king and brought a sudden burst of energy. "Devadatta will pay for this." he said crisply. "I have to fight. This is no place for you. Have some men escort you back to the palace." Suddhodana reached for the chest plate and helmet he was putting on before he fell asleep. He averted his eyes from his son. "I know you are a monk now, Siddhartha, but unless we win this battle, your father will be a beggar." Suddhodana had never reconciled himself to his son's choice, and now his only thought was that the kingdom needed a defender. Instead of stopping him, Buddha stood aside and let the old king armor himself, pick up his sword, and rush from the tent.

"You're going to let him fight?" asked Assaji, disbelieving.

"He's a warrior; his nature is conflict," said Buddha.

"But two seconds ago he was weeping over you. And you were weeping too," said Assaji awkwardly.

"That was love," said Buddha. "Love sometimes weeps; don't be ashamed of it. With some people, an appeal to love prevails."

"Love didn't stop him from running back to fight," said Assaji.

Buddha opened the tent flap. They saw the generals trailing after Suddhodana, who was shouting exhortations the way he used to when he was young. Some of his staff tried to calm him down, but he ferociously threw them off. After a moment the officers mounted their horses or jumped into chariots. Buddha watched them rush off toward the left flank, where some fighting was still raging.

"What if he's killed?" asked Assaji anxiously. "Aren't you here to save your father?"

"This is the moment of faith, when nothing seems to work," said Buddha, beginning to walk after the departing fighters. "Don't preach faith the way it's usually preached, to keep people quiet and forbid them to think on their own. That kind of faith is blind, and being blind, it is useless. Call on faith only when the mind has given up."

"But sometimes it's right to give up," Assaji protested.

"No, dear friend, that's not true. Never forget that all this is a dream." Buddha passed his gaze over the dead bodies fallen on either side, the carrion birds picking at their remains, the fleeing horses without a rider. "Winning and losing are the same thing. Both are nothing."

Buddha quickened his pace. Assaji summoned the other monks to catch up. He said, "This is a profound day for us, master. We will never forget it."

"Every day is like this," Buddha replied. "You'll see."

Now they arrived at the thick of the fray where Suddhodana, against the earnest entreaties of his officers, was standing in his stirrups and screaming. "Come face me, coward! I am one old man, but you won't walk away alive."

From the opposing ranks came a stir, then a single horseman rode out into the space between the two armies. It was Devadatta, fully armored with upraised sword. "I would gladly kill you, old fool," he shouted. "But half your army follows me already. Surrender or watch your men be killed before sunset."

"Who is he?" asked Assaji.

"I could give you many answers. My cousin. A lost soul. A man trapped in a nightmare," said Buddha. "But the truth is that he is an aspect of me."

Raising his voice, Buddha called, "Devadatta!"

His cousin looked his way, but instead of registering surprise he laughed harshly. "Come to see your last hope die?" he cried. "Tell your father to lay down his arms or I'll take the throne by force."

Since convincing Suddhodana that his son was dead, Devadatta had spent his time well. He raised dissent among some garrisons of the king's army, offering them more fighting and gold once Suddhodana was deposed. He plotted with a neighboring king, Bimbisara, to invade the country so that Devadatta would have overwhelming numbers on his side.

"Stop, cousin, for your own sake," Buddha said, coming nearer. "This is a mistake."

"Only for your family," said Devadatta bitterly. "You've held me like a prisoner all my life."

"Revenge isn't yours," said Buddha. "Surrender, and I promise you freedom from your pain."

Devadatta became enraged. "Surrender to you?" he screamed. "You weak, pious fraud!" He swung his sword in a circle overhead and kicked his horse with his spurs to make it charge. On the other side Suddhodana had lost the will to fight. Without warning, he felt his body drained of energy, and he slumped in the saddle like the old man he was.

Prepared to die, Suddhodana closed his eyes and prayed. He had done that only in the Shiva temple before a battle. But he worried about his soul, so he asked Maya to forgive him for letting her die. He thanked the gods for allowing him to live long enough to see his lost son once again. And finally, since he was what he was, the king prayed fervently that Devadatta would die by violence and go directly to hell. When he opened his eyes again, Suddhodana thought that his last prayer had come true because Devadatta was not hard upon him with his sword. Instead, the traitor was rolling in the dust, and his mount had bolted. Confusion broke out in the ranks.

The next instant made matters clear. A lone soldier had run up at the last moment and cut the cinch to Devadatta's saddle, unhorsing him. That soldier was standing over him now, ripping off his helmet. It was Channa, who shouted at Suddhodana, "Get out of here! I can't kill a whole army for one old fool."

Suddhodana backed up until he was safe among the ranks of his men. He watched as Devadatta leaped to his feet. The two fighters circled each other, swords held forward.

"So you still pick fights you can't lose," Channa snarled. "Not today. Today, nobody becomes king without going through me."

Devadatta lunged with his weapon, hoping for a clean kill with his first strike. Channa stepped aside quickly, and his enemy rushed by, almost losing his balance. With an arrogant smile, Channa waved for Devadatta to come at him again.

"Why waste time?" he taunted. "This low-caste scum was always the one who would kill you. I'll rub a little of my blood in your wounds to make sure you get to hell."

Devadatta had gained some control over his rage and backed off warily. All this time the five monks stared at Buddha, waiting for him to intervene. "Master, all day you've shown us the things we can do," whispered Assaji. "Why do you stand back now?"

"It only seems that I'm standing back."

The authority in Buddha's voice silenced Assaji. Devadatta and Channa continued circling each other, making tentative jabs to see if they could catch the other off guard.

"Their whole lives have come to this moment," said Buddha. "Yet in an instant a life can be thrown away. Watch how easy it is." He bent over and picked up a round pebble. With a deft toss he threw it, and the pebble landed behind Devadatta's right heel. He took his next step backward and slipped on it, stumbling to one knee. Channa's eyes flashed toward the spectators. He had been so intent on attacking Devadatta that he hadn't even noticed Buddha among the crowd. His face flushed deep red, but in the same instant he couldn't stop himself from leaping on his enemy and pressing his sword to Devadatta's throat. No one would ever know if he intended to give Devadatta a moment's final mercy because Suddhodana's voice filled the air. "No! Hold your hand."

Channa hesitated; he knew if he disobeyed that he would be executed. His mind was confused, having to absorb the fact of Siddhartha's return at the very moment that he was revenging Siddhartha's death. Suddhodana came forward.

"You are forbidden to kill him," he said with command. "Devadatta is still a prince."

Channa let go of Devadatta's head and pulled his blade away. He gave a curt bow of obedience. This was the moment his enemy had waited for. Devadatta raised his sword and stabbed Channa in the back. The blade pierced Channa's aorta, and he crumpled to the ground. Devadatta got to his feet, panting and dripping with sweat. Within seconds, Suddhodana's men had captured him and hauled him away. The enemy ranks stirred with confusion, then the trumpets sounded and they beat a retreat. Suddhodana gave orders to let them go; without Devadatta to lead them, Bimbisara's men would sneak back home, and the rebels from Suddhodana's army had no choice but to follow them into banishment.

The only ones who remained on the field were Buddha and the five monks, who were in shock. "Wasn't that your friend?" asked Kondana. "You caused him to be killed."

Buddha replied, "Every single life is woven into the web of karma, which has no beginning or end. Until you accept that every life is woven into every other, you will never know who you really are."

"So Channa must surrender to death today?" asked Kondana.

"Death is not the point," said Buddha. "As long as you are caught in karma's web, death comes with birth. The two are inseparable. Find the part of you that is unborn; then you will be free of birth and death together."

As he taught them, Buddha was heading back to the royal tent. Devadatta was tied to a stake, and a hooded man began to whip him. By his side was a broad scimitar lying on the ground. Buddha looked away and walked into the tent. Suddhodana stood over the cot where Channa lay, barely breathing.

"I sent orders for a physician," Suddhodana said mournfully. "But it should have been for a priest."

Buddha knelt beside the cot. "What can I do for you, dear Channa?"

His words seemed to make the dying man revive. He opened his eyes slightly, the lids fluttering. Instead of looking at Buddha, Channa pinned Suddhodana with a bitter glance. "Your pride has killed me," he muttered. His words were clotted, and a trickle of blood appeared on his lips.

"Look at me, not at him," said Buddha gently.

"I can't. I've sinned against you."

"Why do you talk of sin? Do you think you're going to die?" asked Buddha. His voice was so calm and tender that Channa stared at him. "I've come to show you the one who was never born and therefore cannot die."

Buddha closed Channa's eyes. No one in the tent ever found out what he made Channa see, but the vision created a smile of deep bliss on Channa's face. He gave a muffled, ecstatic cry, then his head fell back on the pillow. His stillness would have been mistaken for death except for the slight rise and fall of his chest.

"How can he survive such a wound?" asked Assaji.

"That's the one advantage of dreaming," said Buddha. "You can't be killed unless you want to be. Let him decide. It's no one's dream but Channa's. He will do what he will do."

Buddha gathered Suddhodana, who was so overwhelmed by the day's events that he was on the verge of collapse, and the others and led them all outside. The old man allowed himself to be half carried on Buddha's shoulder, but he stiffened with rage when he beheld Devadatta, who had been whipped so severely that he was unconscious. The king was about to order that the traitor be revived so that he could witness his own execution.

Then he noticed something. Everyone present was bowing on one knee to Buddha or prostrating themselves on the ground.

"Why is this?" Suddhodana asked.

"Let me show you," said Buddha. "In your heart you want to kill Devadatta, even after he is helpless and defeated." The old king hung his head slightly but didn't deny it. Buddha said, "One who kills a killer takes on his karma, and so the wheel of suffering never stops. Let it stop here, today, for you." His father trembled, nodding almost imperceptibly. "I will show you how to make this a kingdom of peace," said Buddha.

No one saw him do anything unusual, but it was as if the clouds passed away from the face of the sun. The mood of war lifted; the atmosphere became calm and pure.

As they looked around, the Sakyan soldiers seemed not to recognize where they were. Many stared at their weapons as if they had never seen these strange implements.

Buddha leaned closer to Assaji. "I begin this new age so that you can continue it forever. Remember that."

Devadatta was cut loose and his unconscious body carried away. He woke up that night in his bed at the palace. His room was sealed and guarded for three days while he contemplated what had happened to him. At first he simply felt hollow and numb. Being dedicated to evil had supplied him with a ferocious energy that he couldn't summon back. On the night of the third day, he tried the handle and found the door to his room open. Cautiously, Devadatta looked up and down the corridor, which was empty. Noises came from the great hall, and after considering whether to run, he felt an impulse to go toward the sound. His whipping at the stake had been so severe that it befuddled his memory, and Devadatta wasn't even sure how the battle had ended or who was king.

No one saw him lingering at the entrance of the hall. There was a great celebration under way. The entire court sat at table while servants rushed back and forth with platters of meat and saffron rice, ripe mangoes and honeyed berries. Suddhodana presided at the head. To one side at a lower table the five monks were eating rice and lentils with Buddha. The room was filled with a quiet joy that the palace had not seen in years.

Devadatta paused, examining the festivities, then turned and left.

"Did you see that?" asked Assaji, who was on Buddha's right hand.

"Yes."

"He was your sworn enemy, and now you're letting him leave?"

"Devadatta is the one person in the world who could never leave me," said Buddha. "That's his blessing, but he saw it as a curse. He's tied to me by a rope he can never let go of."

"Then he'll be back?" asked Assaji, not relishing the thought.

"What choice does he have?" said Buddha. "When you're obsessed with hatred for someone, it's inevitable that you will return one day as his disciple."

"Master, I just hope he's better when he comes back," Assaji said doubtfully.

"He will still be arrogant and proud," said Buddha. "But it won't matter. The fire of passion burns out eventually. Then you dig through the ashes and discover a gem. You pick it up; you look at it with disbelief. The gem was inside you all the time. It is yours to keep forever. It is *buddha*."

Epilogue

For a storyteller, it would be ideal if Buddha's life came to a spectacular end. We're holding our breath for it. First came the fairy-tale beginning as a handsome prince, then a second act with a wandering monk who goes through all manner of trials and suffering, reaching a brilliant climax when enlightenment is achieved in a single night under the bodhi tree. Where did this stunning life finally wind up?

Squarely back on earth, as it turns out. Buddha lived quietly for another forty-five years, traveling throughout northern India as a renowned teacher before dying at the ripe old age of eighty. The cause of death was eating a bad piece of pork, an embarrassingly humble and mundane way to depart.

To satisfy our dramatic longings, we have to turn to the incidental characters in the tale. The ones who were intimates of Siddhartha enjoyed a warm reunion with him. His wife, Yashodhara, and son, Rahula, became devotees of Buddha, which seems fitting enough. They were revered to the end of their days. Other characters had a more curious fate. The ever-widening circle of monks around Buddha, known as the *Sangha*, came to include two misfits, his archenemy, Devadatta, and the rough-hewn warrior Channa. According to tradition, Devadatta remained proud and resentful; even as a disciple he caused trouble. In one famous episode Devadatta tries to kill Buddha by starting a rockslide; in another he gets an elephant drunk on liquor and sends it on a rampage against the Compassionate One. (Buddha deflects the danger in both cases.) As often happens, the villain of the piece is too much fun to let go, so there are other stories of political intrigue with a neighboring prince named Ajatashatru and more mundane tales of Devadatta objecting to the rules Buddha laid down for his monks. A storyteller has a hard time making much drama out of ashram politics.

Following the rules didn't sit well with Channa, either. Having given up his role as brave charioteer, Channa chafed at being reduced to the status of a holy monk. His chief sin was pride. He never let anyone forget that he had been Siddhartha's best friend. He treated Buddha with too much familiarity, causing distress among the other devotees. At a certain point Channa's misbehavior became too much for even Buddha's tolerance. The head disciple, Ananda, who historically was Buddha's cousin, was sent to reprimand him, and from there the road divides. In one version Channa sullenly takes his scolding and reforms. In the other, he sinks into despair and commits suicide.

But we would be wrong to be disappointed in our hero. Enlightenment was just the beginning of Buddha's spiritual ascent, which was spectacular by any measure. Buddhism caused an earthquake in the spiritual life of India, crushing the privileges of the Brahmin caste and raising even the despised untouchables to spiritual dignity.

Buddha blew through the temples like a strong wind and with the simplicity of genius reduced the human predicament to one key issue: suffering. If suffering is a constant in every life, he said, then until there's an end to suffering, enlightenment is pointless. Equally pointless is talk of God or the gods, heaven and hell, sin, redemption, the soul, and all the rest. This was reform of the severest kind, and a lot didn't stick. People wanted God. Buddha refused to speak on the subject of whether God even existed. He adamantly denied that he himself was divine. People wanted the comfort of rituals and ceremonies. Buddha shunned ceremony. He wanted each individual to look inside and find liberation through a personal journey that began in the physical world and ended in Nirvana, a state of pure, eternal consciousness. Nirvana is present in everyone, he taught, but Nirvana is like pure water lying deep beneath the earth. Reaching it requires concentration, devotion, and diligent work.

It's no wonder that Buddha's call to awakening proved so enticing and so difficult. The Middle Way, which gained its name because it was neither too harsh nor too easy, proved very appealing, but the journey to Nirvana is solitary and contains little in the way of entertaining scenery. Yet there was no arguing against the teaching. Everything Buddha preached grows logically from the First Noble Truth, which also happens to be the first thing Buddha said to the five monks after he became enlightened: life contains suffering. The next three teachings sound more like modern psychotherapy than conventional religion:

FIRST NOBLE TRUTH: Life contains suffering.

SECOND NOBLE TRUTH: Suffering has a cause, and the cause can be known.

THIRD NOBLE TRUTH: Suffering can be brought to an end.

FOURTH NOBLE TRUTH: The path to end suffering has eight parts.

Now we've gone beyond the role of the storyteller, since these four simple statements created an explosion of theology that spread throughout Asia and the rest of the world. Thanks to Buddha's decades of teaching, a cadre of disciples totally committed to the Buddhist path crossed the Himalayas and journeyed everywhere it was possible for sandals to tread. The list of cultures that these ascetic wanderers revolutionized is staggering: Tibet, Nepal, China, Japan, Korea, Sri Lanka, Thailand, Cambodia, Burma, Vietnam, and far into Malaysia and Indonesia. In many cases a handful of Buddhist missionaries actually created a new culture. Any outside observer can only stand back in awe.

Why did people accept this new teaching so readily? Because the First Noble Truth was undeniable. People knew that they were suffering, and instead of showing a way out, their old religions gave them surrogates, in the form of dogma, prayers, rituals, and the like. At its simplest, Buddhism walked into the village square and said, "Here are eight things that will open the way to peace instead of pain." The Eightfold Path asks for each person to change how the mind works, plucking out what is wrong, inefficient, and superstitious, then exchanging those outworn habits for increasing clarity. In other words, the waking-up process, which Buddha experienced in one night, is laid out as a lifelong program:

- Right view or perspective
- Right intention
- Right speech
- Right action
- Right livelihood
- Right effort
- Right mindfulness
- Right concentration

Some of these steps sound natural. We all want to believe that our actions and words are virtuous. We don't want to go wrong in our effort and intentions. Other parts of the path need special guidance. What is right mindfulness? Right concentration? These aspects have their roots in the meditation practices of Yoga, which Buddha also reformed and brought within reach of ordinary people.

As a storyteller, I didn't feel it was my place to spread Buddhism. That's best left to the modern equivalents of the wandering missionaries who first preached Buddhism. It would be unseemly for me to step on their toes. But I'd like to speak to you, the reader, who might be coming to Buddha from the cold. I came to Buddha that way, and I asked the obvious question: What can this teaching do for me? Is there something that will open my eyes and make me more awake, right this minute?

Personally, I found three things. They are known as the three Dharma seals, or to put it in plain English, three basic facts about Being. They spoke to me far more than the Middle Way because of their universality, which extends far beyond the boundaries of religion.

1. Dukkha

Life is unsatisfactory. Pleasure in the physical world is transient. Pain inevitably follows. Therefore, nothing we experience can be deeply satisfying. There is no resting place in change.

2. Anicca

Nothing is permanent. All experience is swept away in flux. Cause and effect is endless and confusing. Therefore one can never find clarity or permanence.

3. Anatta

The separate self is unreliable and ultimately unreal. We apply words like *soul* and *personality* to something that is fleeting and ghostly. Our attempts to make the self real never end but also never succeed. Therefore, we cling for reassurance to an illusion.

• • •

READING THIS, CAN anyone escape being shaken to the core? Buddha wasn't just a kindly teacher who wanted people to find peace. He was a radical surgeon who examined them and said, "No wonder you feel sick. All this unreal stuff has filled you up, and now we have to get rid of it." Naturally, a lot of listeners ran back to conventional religion, and just as many ran back into materialism, which promises that body, mind, and the physical world are absolutely real.

Why should we accept Buddha's word that they aren't? That, I think, is the crucial question. There's not much challenge in accepting that one's life contains suffering, and only a small challenge in accepting that flux and change create dissatisfaction. Both facts seem psychologically self-evident. But to accept that the entire world, and everyone in it, is an illusion? That's an enormous challenge, and it requires a complete shift in consciousness to meet it.

The word *illusion* has a host of meanings, and some are very enticing. The illusion, for example, that when you fall in love it will last forever. The illusion that you will never die. The illusion that ignorance is bliss. Buddha saw the danger hidden in these enticements. He rarely spoke harshly, but I can imagine him bursting all these bubbles: love ends, everyone dies, ignorance is folly. But if he had stopped there, Buddha would have wound up a tiresome moralist.

His definition of illusion was so absolute it almost freezes the blood. Whatever can be seen, heard, or touched is unreal. Whatever you cling to as permanent is unreal. Whatever the mind can think of is unreal. Does that leave anything free from the withering grip of illusion?

No.

Yet once we get over our shock, Buddha declares that with a shift in consciousness, reality reveals itself. Not as a thing. Not as a sensation. Not even as a wisp of thought. Reality is purely itself. It is the ground of existence, the source from which everything else is projected. In the most basic terms, Buddhism exchanges a world of infinite projections for the single state of Being. A freedom so complete it doesn't have to think of freedom or say its name.

Which brings me to the subversive reason I decided to write a novel on the life of Buddha. By telling his story from the inside (early on I intended to call the book *I, Buddha*), I could trace every step that led Siddhartha to stop believing in the world. His tale isn't really that of a romantic prince, suffering monk, or triumphant saint. It's a universal soul journey that begins asleep and ends awake. Siddhartha woke up to the truth, which sounds inspiring, but in this case the truth demolished his entire self. It overturned every belief, purified every sense, and brought total clarity to the mind's confusion. In sum, this book has been a kind of seduction, coaxing the reader step by step toward a vision that none of us was brought up to see. Through the eyes of Buddha, the root of suffering is illusion, and the only way out of illusion is to stop believing in the separate self and the world that supports the separate self. No spiritual message has ever been so radical. None remains so terribly urgent.

The Art of Non-Doing

A Practical Guide to Buddhism

After being inspired by Buddha's life, the most important thing is not to let him slip through your fingers. This can easily happen. First of all, because he didn't want anyone to hold on to him. Buddha was like a supernova exploding in the sky, spreading light in all directions. Before the explosion you could locate him in time and space. He was a person like any other, however brilliant and charismatic. But after the explosion known as enlightenment, he turned into something else, something very impersonal. Call it pure spirit, essence, or transcendent wisdom. By any name, he was no longer a person, which makes for special difficulties. How do you follow a teacher who is everywhere at once?

I can imagine sitting down with a reader and being asked that question, which would lead to quite a few more.

How am I supposed to follow someone who constantly insisted that he was no longer a person and didn't have a self?

Ideally, you follow him by losing your own self. Which seems impossible, since it's your self that's fascinated by him. It's your self that's suffering and wants to be rid of suffering. The primary message of Buddhism is that this self cannot accomplish anything real. It must find a way to disappear, just as Buddha did.

The self reaches its goal by not being the self? It sounds like a paradox.

Yes, but Buddhists found three ways to live the wisdom their teacher left behind. The first way was social, forming groups of disciples into a Sangha, like the group of monks and nuns that Buddha gathered in his lifetime. The Sangha exists to establish a spiritual lifestyle. People remind themselves of the teaching and keep the Buddhist vision alive. They meditate together and create an atmosphere of peace.

The second way to follow Buddha is ethical, centered on the value of compassion. Buddha was known as The Compassionate One, a being who loved all of humanity without judgment. Buddhist ethics bring the same attitude into everyday life. A Buddhist practices being kind and seeing others without judgment, but in addition displays love and reverence for life itself. Buddhist morality is peaceful, accepting, and joyous.

The third way to follow Buddha is mystical. You take to heart the message of non-self. You do everything possible to break the bonds of attachment that keep you trapped in the illusion that you are a separate self. Here your aim is to tiptoe out of the material world even as your body remains in it. Ordinary people are doing things all day, but in your heart you've turned your attention to non-doing, as the Buddhists call it. Non-doing isn't passivity but a state of openness to all possibilities.

If I practice non-doing, what would I actually do? It still seems like a paradox.

The third way confronts Buddha's most enigmatic side. How can you shed the separate self when it's the only thing you've known? The process sounds frightening, for one thing, because there's no guarantee. Once you accomplish "ego death," as it's often called, what will be left? You might wind up enlightened, but you also might wind up a blank, a passive non-self with no interests or desires. People find the Buddhist path rigorous because you are asked to re-examine everything you think will get you ahead in life—money, possessions, status, accomplishments—and see them as a source of suffering. For example, having money doesn't directly cause suffering, but it ties you to the illusion by hiding from sight the fact that there's another way to live that's actually real. Money, like possessions and status, creates a treadmill that brings one desire after another.

So enlightenment is the same as having no desires?

You have to understand "no desires" in a positive sense, as fulfillment. At the moment a musician is performing, there's a state of no-desire because he feels fulfilled. At the moment you're eating a wonderful meal, hunger is fulfilled. Buddha taught that there is a state, known as Nirvana, where desire is irrelevant. Everything desire is trying to achieve exists in Nirvana already. You don't have to pursue one desire after another in a futile quest to end suffering. Instead, you go right to the source of Being, which is neither full nor empty. It just is.

Do you still want to live after that?

Nirvana is no longer about life and death, which are opposites. Buddha wanted to free people from all opposites. If you are following his teachings the second way, through morality and ethics, then being good, truthful, nonviolent, and compassionate is important. You don't want to practice the opposite behavior. But if you follow Buddha the third way, the mystical way of non-doing, duality is the very thing you try to dissolve. You go beyond good and evil, which is scary to many people.

What is the non-self?

It's who you are when there are no personal attachments. This sounds mystical, but we shouldn't be distracted by semantics. The non-self is natural; it's rooted in everyday experience. When you wake up in the morning there's a moment before your mind gets filled with all the things you have to do today. In that moment you exist without a self. You don't think about your name or your bank account; you don't even think about your spouse and children. You just are. Enlightenment extends that state and deepens it. You aren't burdened by having to remember who you are, ever again.

When I wake up in the morning I remember who I am almost immediately. How does that change?

By gradually shifting your allegiance. Consider how you relate to your body. You mostly forget about it. Heartbeat, metabolism, body temperature, electrolyte balance—literally dozens of processes go on automatically, and your nervous system coordinates them perfectly without interference from the conscious mind. Buddha suggests that you can let go of many things that you're certain you must control. Instead of devoting so much effort and struggle to thinking, planning, running after pleasure, and avoiding pain, you can surrender and put those functions on automatic, also. This is accomplished gradually by a practice called mindfulness.

You mean, I simply stop thinking?

You stop investing yourself in thinking, because Buddha teaches that you haven't been in control of your mind anyway. The mind is a series of fleeting, impermanent events, and trying to ground yourself in impermanence is an illusion. Time is exactly the same, a sequence of fleeting events that has no solid basis. Once you hear this teaching, you put it into practice through mindfulness. Whenever you are tempted by the illusion, you remind yourself that it's not real. In a way, a better term might be *re-mindfulness.*

The process of shifting your consciousness takes time. This is an evolution, not a revolution. We're all pulled in by the temptation to choose between A and B. Duality makes us believe that making good decisions and avoiding bad ones is all-important. Buddha disagrees—he says that getting out of duality is all-important, and you'll never escape as long as you keep burying yourself deeper into the game of "A-or-B?" Reality isn't A or B. It's both and it's neither. Mindfulness keeps you aware of that fact.

How am I to understand "both and neither"?

You can't, not with the mind. The mind is basically a machine that processes the world only in terms of "I want this" and "I don't want that." Buddha taught that you can step outside the machinery and simply watch it working. You witness the whole fantastic jumble of desires, fears, wishes, and memories that is the mind. When you gain practice doing that in meditation, things change. You begin to be aware of yourself in a simpler way, without so much mental jumble. In time your allegiance shifts, and the space between thoughts—the silent gap—dominates instead of thoughts.

Is that Nirvana?

No, it's just a sign that you are successfully practicing mindfulness. The silent gap between thoughts goes by too fast for anyone to live there. You have to give the gap a chance to expand, and at the same time silence deepens. It may sound strange, but your mind can be silent the whole time it's also thinking. Ordinarily, silence and thought are considered opposites, but when you go beyond opposites, they merge. You identify with the timeless source of thought rather than the thoughts emerging from it.

What advantage does this bring? Assuming I take the time and effort to achieve such a state.

One can speak of the advantages in glowing terms that sound very alluring. You gain peace; you no longer suffer. Death no longer holds any fear. You stand unshakably on your own Being. In reality the gains are highly individual and proceed at their own pace. Everyone is in a different state of unreality that's highly personal. I may be obsessive, while the person next to me may be anxious and the person next to him depressed. In meditation these knots of discord and conflict begin to unravel of their own accord. Yet there's always an evolutionary unfolding. In your own way you walk the path to peace, non-suffering, fearlessness, and everything else Buddha exemplified.

From the outside this third way of following Buddha looks mystical, but over time it becomes as natural as breathing. Buddhism survives today and thrives all around the world because it is so open-ended. You don't have to obey a set of rules or worship God or the gods. You don't even have to be spiritual. All you have to do is look into yourself and yearn to become clear, to wake up and be complete. Buddhism counts on the fact that everyone possesses at least a bit of these motivations. Mindfulness and meditation form the basis of Buddhist practice—although every sect and teacher has a particular slant on them. Za-zen, the style of Buddhist meditation practiced in Japan, isn't the same as Vipasana meditation in South Asia. In the end, however, Buddhism is a do-it-yourself project, and that's the secret of its appeal in the modern world. Don't we all ultimately concentrate on personal suffering and what our individual fate will be? Buddha asked for nothing else as a starting point, and yet he promised that the end point would be eternity.

Acknowledgments

First and foremost I must thank a friend whose imagination sparked this project, film director Shekhar Kapur. We spent long, fascinating sessions together trying to imagine Buddha's life. Without his contributions, the best parts of this book would never have appeared.

Thanks to Gideon Weil, my editor, who made invaluable suggestions every step of the way and intervened at just the right moments.

As always, my family and everyone at the Chopra Center provided their support and love. I am deeply grateful and hope that this book makes you proud.

DEEPAK CHOPRA is the founder of The Chopra Center for Wellbeing. He has been a bestselling author for decades, and his writings have sold millions of copies.

Visit the author online at www.chopra.com.

'Buddha was as mortal as you and I, yet he attained enlightenment and was raised to the rank of an immortal. The miracle is that he got there following a heart as human as yours and mine, and just as vulnerable.'

—from the Authorís Note

Bestselling author Deepak Chopra brings the Buddha back to life in this gripping novel of the young prince who abandoned his inheritance to discover his true calling. This iconic journey changed the world forever, and the truths revealed continue to influence every corner of the globe today.

A young man in line for the throne is trapped in his fatherís kingdom and yearns for the outside world. Betrayed by those closest to him, Siddhartha abandons his palace and princely title. Alone and face-to-face with his demons, he becomes a wandering monk and embarks on a spiritual fast that carries him to the brink of death. Ultimately recognizing his inability to conquer his body and mind by sheer will, Siddhartha transcends his physical pain and achieves enlightenment.

Although we recognize Buddha today as an icon of peace and serenity, his life story was a tumultuous and spellbinding affair filled with love and passion, murder and loss, struggle and surrender. From the rocky terrain of the material world to the summit of the spiritual one, Buddha captivated and inspires-ultimately leading us closer to understanding the true nature of life and our selves.